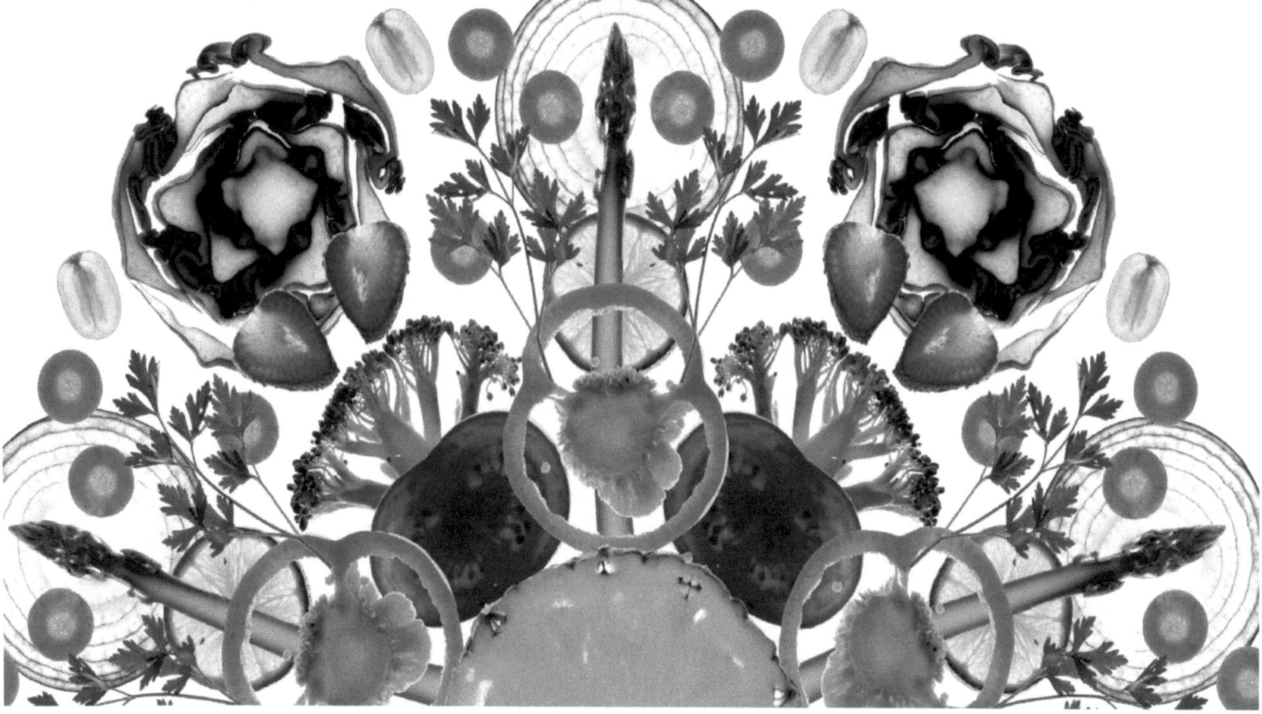

The BEST of BROCK

The Best of Brock

A Collection of Recipes, Fun Facts, and Nutrition Information Celebrating Our Many Years of Cooking

Additional copies of this book can be ordered by sending $25.00 and $5.00 shipping to:

Brock and Company, Inc.
257 Great Valley Parkway
Malvern, PA 19355

Edited by Claudie Brock
Copy-editing by Eric Rappaport
Cover Design by Dennis Goldsborough
Published by Brock and Company, Inc.
Book Packaging by S2 Press, Bethesda, MD

ISBN Number: 978-1493787173
Library of Congress Control Number: 2014942683

© 2015 Brock and Company, Inc.

Printed in the USA
by CreateSpace

Visit us on the web at www.brockco.com
Email Claudie Brock at cjbrock@brockco.com

Dedication

We dedicate this cookbook to all our Associates present and past, who with their talent and enthusiasm have helped and continue to make Brock and Company, Inc., a premier Food Service Operation.

—Andrew, Lynmar, and Claudie Brock, Brock and Company, Inc.

Preface

Brock and Company, Inc. celebrates its success since 1927 with continuing innovations. It is exciting adjusting to taste and habits with continuing changes in style.

Lynmar Brock Sr. in 1927 determined to offer factory workers a boxed lunch containing a ham sandwich, salad, slice of spiced lunch meat, slice of American cheese, sweet pickles, dessert, a cup of cream cabbage, spiced cake with lemon icing, and an apple, all for 25 cents. The depression of the 1930's was a demanding time for the country, but Brock's Box Lunches continued to expand offering even more at a greater value.

The War years were a time of expansion of manufacturing. The company moved into a new and larger plant on December 6, 1941 and was well prepared to service the increased demands of a country at war. The company soon further expanded into corporate food service operation where on site chefs made it possible to increase the freshness and variety of food offered.

In the following years, Brock operated restaurants that combined freshness and variety with ever-changing menu selections. More recently, adding food service for private and independent schools has provided an increased ability to serve fresh, local, and healthful foods to not only students, but to an increasingly broad range of corporations and enterprises.

Today the food offerings at each corporate and school location are prepared on site. This allows Brock to support and serve a wide range of foods to satisfy individual desires, needs and demands. The company now operates throughout the eastern United States along with a Rocky Mountain division.

Brock and Company carries on with the same foresight and imagination of Lynmar Brock, Sr.

This cookbook is but a reflection of the variety of offerings possible. We hope you will find the recipes delicious and nutritious and wish to learn more about how we can provide quality and value to your corporate or school food service systems.

Change is wonderful. Change is exciting. Remember the past embrace the future.

—Lynmar Brock, Jr., President of Brock and Company, Inc., 1962–2007

Introduction

"The doctor of the future will give no medicine, but will interest his patients in the care of the human body, in diet, and in the cause and prevention of disease." This is a quote from the famous brilliant inventor Thomas Edison, who had more than a thousand patents to his name.

In this cookbook we not only have a collection of delicious recipes provided by our associates, but we also include information and recommendations for a healthy life style, with plenty of exercise, fresh air, and healthy eating.

We start with the premise that everyone knows that smoking has been proven very detrimental to good health. So, that if you are smoking, it would be wise to look into some smoke secession programs. Many of these programs are available through your health insurance provider.

Many studies have shown the great benefit of regular cardio-type exercises for at least 150 minutes a week, including a good amount of stretching before starting. Studies have also shown that exercising in the morning burns more fat cells than doing it in the afternoon because during sleep time fat cells accumulate. Doing it in the morning seems to be more beneficial, if you are trying to lose weight. Exercise also helps to improve the brain cognitive function, because it produces more synapses in the brain.

Being overweight is a problem in our time because many people are unaware of the amount of sugar they consume. Sugar turns into fat cells. Our ancestors consumed an average of 5 pounds of sugar, per year. Today it is said that on average we consume 10 times that much.

The information in this cookbook provides nutrition facts, for one serving only, indicating the number of calories, total fats, saturated fats, cholesterol, sodium, carbohydrates, proteins, vitamin A, and calcium content.

The information in this cookbook is for educational purpose only and not to be construed as medical advice. Consult a medical practitioner before making any major life style changes.

Acknowledgements

We thank the many people who have contributed to the success of this cookbook such as those who submitted the delicious recipes and those who made sure that the recipes were correct. In particular we thank Debbie O'Donovan for her many hours of research, and typing; Alison Niles for her typesetting and art direction; Tracey Woomer for her advice; Eric Rappaport, Sharon DeFelices, Carl Scharle and Lynmar Brock for their proofing; Dennis Goldsborough for the design of the covers; Shasha Juliard for his photography and above all many heartfelt thanks go to Paul Pruitt for his many efforts to make this cookbook a reality!

Book Packager's Note

This cookbooks was put together with recipes submitted by the chefs and employees of Brock and Company, Inc., which is a food service company. With 17 of the chef submitted recipes, the yields are more characteristic of restaurant or food service setting than home cooking. In order to attempt to preserve the use of these recipes for the home, ingredient amounts were also calculated for a smaller yield, usually at a quarter or a fifth of the original recipe amounts, and these amounts were placed in parenthesis next to the original amounts. These recipes can be identified by having two yields, one for a "food service" and one for a "home version." No attempt were made with the food service yield recipes to use different scaling factors for different categories of ingredients, as technically should be done.

Table of Contents

Dedication	iii
Preface	iv
Introduction	vi
Acknowledgements	vii
Healthy Living	**1**
5 Ways to Turn off Your Hunger Switch	2
Chocolate	4
Healthy Snacks	5
Stress Management	7
The Benefits of Yoga	8
More Suggestions for Healthy Living	9
Ergonomics	10
Eye Exercises to Reduce Eye Strain	11
Notes	12
Beef	**13**
Braised Short Ribs	14
Broiled Flank Steak Chimichurri Sauce	15
Cajun Beef and Root Vegetable Stew	16
Cajun Meatloaf with Sweet Pepper Sauce	17
German Beef Roulades over Spaetzle	18
German Braised Veal Shanks	19

Homemade Meatballs for Spaghetti	20
Marinated and Grilled Buffalo Flank Steak with Lime Chipotle Sauce	21
Meatloaf	22
New Mexican Burger	22
Russian Cutlets	23
Spare Ribs in Wine Sauce	24
Stuffed Flank Steak	25
Teriyaki Burger	26
Texas Style BBQ Brisket	26
Wiener-Bean Casserole	27
Notes	28

Breakfast and Breads — 29

Bread Pudding	30
Butternut Squash Bread Pudding with Leeks and Parmesan	31
Cheese-Garlic Biscuits	32
Chocolate Brioche Bread Pudding	32
Crème Brûlée French Toast	33
Crunchy French Toast with Banana and Strawberry	34
Currant Scones	35
Golden Baked French Toast	36
Guatemalan Banana Bread	36
Open Faced Broiled Egg, Spinach and Tomato Sandwich	37
Pizza Dough	38
Puffy Maine Pancakes	39
Quick and Easy Eggs Benedict	40

Roasted Vegetable Pizza	41
Scones	42
Scrambled Egg Beggar's Purses	43
Sweet Milk Griddle Cakes	44
Syrniki Cottage Cheese Pancakes	45
Notes	46

Chicken 47

Adobo Seasoned Baked Chicken Wings	48
Anjyab Sandale	49
Baltimore Chicken	50
Cheese Encrusted Chicken	51
Chicken and Broccoli Casserole	52
Chicken and Stuffing	53
Chicken Mole Verde	54
Chicken Sicilian	55
Chicken Tingas	56
Chinamerica Chicken Pineapple Feast	57
Grilled Chicken Kabobs with Greek Style Barley Salad	58
Grilled Chicken Penne Alfredo	59
Latin Combo—Sky, Sea and Land	60
Rotisserie Style Chicken	61
Tortellini with Chicken, Basil and Tomato	61
Notes	62

Desserts and Sweets 63

Apple Cream Pie	64
Apple Crumb Cake	65
Apple Fritters	66
Apple Oat Bars	67
Apple Pie Bars Home Version	68
Apple Strudel	69
Banana Granola Cookies	70
Bavarian Apple Torte	71
Cedar Planked Apples with Walnut Praline Stuffing	72
Cheesecake Supreme	73
Cherry or Cranberry Pie	74
Cherry-O Cream Cheese Pie	74
Chocolate Chip Cheeseball	75
Coconut Mango Rice Pudding	75
Cream Cheese Flan	76
Dirt	77
Donut Bread Pudding with Chocolate	78
Fresh Berry Trifle	79
Gluten Free Banana-Oatmeal Chocolate Chip Cookies	80
Jell-O Pie	81
Lemon Basil Smoothie	81
Mexican Flan	82
Mini Peanut Butter Cup Cheese Cakes	83
Oatmeal Raisin Spice Cookies	84
Peanut Butter Bars	85

Poppy Seed Cake	86
Pound Cake	86
Russian Cheese Wheels	87
Sand Dessert	88
Shoo-Fly Pie	89
Strawberry Topping	90
Sweet and Spicy Pecans	90
Swiss Apple Pie	91
Tiramisu	92
Tookies	93
Warm Nutty Caramel Brownies	94

Dips and Sauces — 95

Artichoke Crab Spread	96
Buffalo Shrimp Dip	96
Celeste's Best BBQ Sauce	97
Cranberry Salsa	97
Hot Artichoke Heart Dip	98
Maple Chipotle BBQ Sauce	99
Nacho Bake	100
Peach Salsa	100
Pepperoni Dip	101
Pizza Dip	101
Pizza Sauce	102
Southwest American Indian Salsa Salad	102
Spinach Dip	103

Spring Pea Dip	103
Vidalia Onion Relish	104

Family Heirlooms — 105

Carrot Cake	106
Cream Cheese Pie	107
Granny Sullivan's Pineapple Upside Down Cake	108
Green and Red Peppers with Crabmeat	109
Hungarian Beef Paprika	110
Mary's Easter Bread	111
Mary's Zucchini Bread	112
Mom's Meatloaf	113
Mom's Peach Cobbler	114
Pork Adobo	115
Ratatouille	116

Pasta — 117

20-Minute Tuna Casserole	118
Cheaty Ziti	119
Easy Add-In Macaroni and Cheese	120
Fettuccine Carbonara	121
Orecchiette with Mixed Greens and Goat Cheese	122
Pasta Primavera	123
Philly Mac and Cheese Steak	124
Skillet Lasagna	125
Notes	126

Pork — 127

- Apple Butter Pork Loin — 128
- Apricot Pork Chops — 129
- Heaven on a Bun — 129
- Home-Style Asian Burger — 130
- Pork Roast with Ginger Peach Glaze — 131
- Pork Stew — 132
- Roast Pork Tenderloin with Balsamic Reduction, Fall Fruit Compote — 133
- Root Beer-Glazed Ham — 134
- South Carolina Style Pulled Pork Sandwich — 135
- Southwest Roasted Pork Loin — 136

Salads — 137

- Apple Spinach Salad — 138
- Baby Blue Salad — 139
- Baby Mixed Greens with Apple Pear, Pecans and Feta — 140
- Barley and Mushroom Salad — 141
- Broccoli Slaw Salad — 142
- Brown Rice Salad with Citrus-Basil Vinaigrette — 143
- California Mango Chicken Salad — 144
- Carolina Cabbage — 145
- Celyodka pod Shuboy—Herring Under a "Fur Coat" — 146
- Couscous Salad — 147
- Crabmeat Salad — 147
- Cucumber Salad — 148
- Dan's Country Style Coleslaw — 148

Deconstructed Chicken Ratatouille Salad	149
French Green Lentil Salad	150
Georgian Style Bean Salad	151
Kielbasa and Lentil Salad with Warm Mustard Fennel Dressing	152
Panzanella (Bread Salad)	153
Quinoa Salad	154
Red Bliss Potato Salad	155
Sesame Snow Pea Salad	156
Seven-Layer Salad	157
Spinach Pasta Salad	157
Turkey Barley Mandarin Salad	158
Vegetarian Pasta Salad	159
Warm Potato Salad with Honey Dressing	159
Notes	160

Seafood — 161

Bay Scallops and Bulgur Wheat with Fresh Mint	162
Braised Sea Bass and Fennel with Saffron and Harissa	163
Caramelized Salmon with Citrus Salsa	164
Crab Cakes with Peach Salsa	165
Fresh Tuna Tacos	166
Lemon Shrimp Bean Thread Vermicelli	167
Maryland Crab Cake Salad	168
Maryland Jumbo Lump Crab Imperial	169
Salmon Reuben	170
Scallops and Shrimp Sambuca	171

Seafood Gumbo	172
Seared Scallops with Parmesan Risotto	173
Shrimp and Grits	174
Shrimp and Feta Cheese Pasta	175
Teriyaki Grilled Salmon	176

Soups and Stews — 177

Asopao De Marisco (Seafood Stew)	178
Black Bean Chili	179
Butternut Squash Soup	180
Cheddar Asparagus and Crab Chowder	181
Chilled Cucumber Soup with Lobster, Mint and Lobster Brioche Sandwich	182
Cold Strawberry Soup	183
Crab and Corn Chowder	184
Cream of Crab Soup	185
Dovga	186
Green Borscht	187
Italian Wedding Soup	188
Jambalaya	189
Lemongrass-Scented Noodle Soup with Shrimp	190
Maryland Crab Soup	191
Peanut and Chestnut Soup	192
Pulled Pork Green Chili	193
Russian Okroshka Soup	194
Sopa De Caracol (Conch Soup)	195
Thai Sweet Corn Soup	196

Vegetarian Chili	197
Notes	198

Veggies and Sides — 199

Armenian "Musaca"	200
Asparagus and Hollandaise Sauce	201
Baked Beans	202
Basil Roasted Vegetable Couscous Salad	203
Black Bean Cakes with Tomato and Jack Cheese	204
Bulgur Risotto with Spring Peas and Asparagus	205
Bulgur Stuffed Tomato Au Gratin	206
Creamed Cabbage	207
Dinsztelt Wilted Greens	208
Dolma (Stuffed Grape Leaves)	209
Home Style Baked Beans	210
Hummus	211
Olive Balls	212
Potato Salad	213
Red Quinoa	214
Roasted Parsnips	215
Russian Golubtsi—Stuffed Cabbage Rolls	216
Russian Mushrooms	217
Spaetzle Noodles Bergkase	218
Spicy Asian Lettuce Wraps	219
Sweet Potato Salad	220
Unstuffed Cabbage	221

Healthy Living

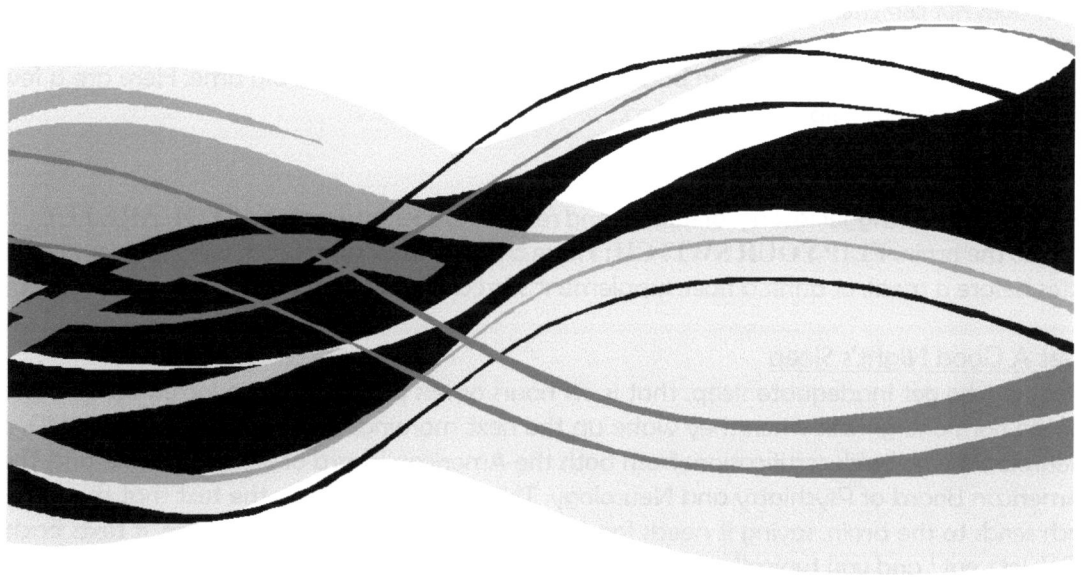

Brock's Best

Brock's Best

5 Ways to Turn Off Your Hunger Switch

"It's the single most exciting breakthrough in weight management in the last 10-plus years, and yet, no one is talking about it," says Doug Kalman, PhD F.A.C.N. What he is talking about is research reveals that it is your brain which is Command Central for weight management, and not your stomach.

The breakthrough came when researchers finally discovered that the brain uses a type of messaging system very similar to "texting" to determine what to eat, and when you are hungry and when you are not.

"This understanding now allows people to take a simple approach to weight management that does not ask them to change their life style," says Kalman. "It is something that everyone can do." When used in tandem with smart eating and exercise, bolstering your personal will power with a brain that is also on board can boost weight loss goals big time. Here are a few simple strategies to help you get started.

Fill Up With Fiber And Water
Fiber and water trigger feelings of fullness and reduce hunger by sending a "**YOU ARE FULL!**" text to the brain. **FLIP YOUR SWITCH:** Have a cup of clear soup broth with veggies 15 minutes before a meal, or drink a fiber supplement stirred into a glass of water for similar effect.

Get A Good Night's Sleep
People who get inadequate sleep, that is, six hours or less per night, have increased amounts of the hormone ghrelin when they wake up the next morning, says Christopher Nolte, MD, a neurologist who holds certifications from both the American Board of Sleep Medicine and The American Board of Psychiatry and Neurology. Think of the ghrelin as the text that the stomach sends to the brain, saying it needs food. "When the brain gets the message, it texts back, 'OK, let's eat,' and you typically go looking for carbs," says Nolte. "The reality is that you don't need to eat carbs right then, despite what your brain is telling you." **FLIP YOUR SWITCH:** "Allow yourself seven hours or more sleep," says Nolte. And when you get some carb cravings, have water or a cup of brewed tea, and fiber instead.

Healthy Living

Punch Up Your Polyphenols
Green and red teas, along with other polyphenol-rich foods and supplements (most notably those with high levels of two types of polyphenols-anthocyanins and stilbenes) have been shown to be very good at turning off the hunger switch. Stilbenes are found in grapes, blueberries, and cranberries. The best-known stilbene is the anti-aging compound resveratrol, mostly found in red grapes and red wine. Anthocyanins are present in popular superfruits such as acai berries, blueberries, and red grapes and are also found in red wine. In a study published in Molecular Nutrition and Food Research from the US Department of Agriculture found that purified berry anthocyanins normalized the fat levels in mice that were fed a high-fat diet. Scientists attribute this effect to the ability of anthocyanins to assist cell burning energy, inducing satiety and, ultimately, turning off the hunger switch. **FLIP YOUR SWITCH:** Increase you intake of green teas, red teas, and berries, or, take 200 mg of resveratrol in supplement form daily.

Don't Buy These Bad Boys
Some ingredients turn on your hunger switch, so it pays to read labels. Some of the worst offenders: high-fructose corn syrup (HFCS) and palmitic acid (the main fat in palm oil, palm kernel oil, and saturated fat in beef). These troublemakers stop the hormones leptin and insulin, two of the brain most important "hunger messengers," from reaching Command Central. When leptin and insulin, are blocked from the brain, the brain cells tell you to keep on eating, which can mean making the difference between having a few chips and eating half the bag. In fact, in a study published in The Journal of Clinical Investigation, researchers from UT Southwestern Medical Center in Dallas found that palmitic acid's ability to block leptin and insulin was so great that it that it may be the root cause of both obesity and Type 2 diabetes. **FLIP YOUR SWITCH:** Choose whole, fresh unadulterated foods. Shop the perimeter of your supermarket, where the least processed foods are found. Reduce your intake of beef and/or opt for "grass-fed" beef, which contains less of the problematic saturated fat.

Power Your Protein
While increasing your consumption of protein can satiate your appetite, two of protein's building blocks, namely the amino acids tyrosine and 5-hydroxytryptophan (5-HTP), have been identified as the most crucial to relay messages to the brain. Simply stated, tyrosine and 5-HTP work as neuromessengers, speeding up messages to the brain that turn off the desire for food. That means with tyrosine and 5-HTP, whether in food or supplements, craving ends faster

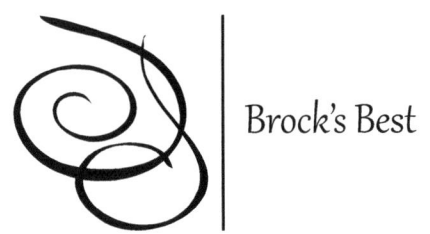

Brock's Best

and fewer calories are consumed. FLIP YOUR SWITCH: Take 150–250 mg of tyrosine and 100–200 mg of 5-HTP daily. In addition, protein will turn off your hunger switch to a greater extent than carbohydrates or fat, so replacing some carbs with protein may help to reduce your overall caloric intake. Eat a minimum of 20 grams of protein at each main meal.

– http://www.gnclivewell.com.au/blog-details.asp?id=284

Chocolate

Chocolate and its main ingredient, cocoa, appear to reduce risk factors for heart disease. Flavanols in cocoa beans have antioxidant effects that reduce cell damage implicated in heart disease. Flavanols also help lower blood pressure and improve vascular function. Dark chocolate contains more flavanols than does milk chocolate. One caveat: The evidence for the healthy benefits of flavanol-rich chocolate comes mostly from short-term and uncontrolled studies. More research will be needed to confirm chocolate's role in heart health.

In the meantime, if you want to add chocolate to your diet, do so in moderation. Why? Most commercial chocolate has ingredients that add fat, sugar, and calories, and too much can contribute to weight gain, a risk factor for high blood pressure, heart disease, and diabetes.

Choose dark chocolate with cocoa content of 65 percent or higher. Limit yourself to no more than 3 ounces (85 grams) a day, which is the amount shown in studies to be helpful. Because this amount may provide up to 450 calories, you may want to cut calories in other areas or step up the exercise to compensate.

—Content from the Mayo Clinic

Healthy Snacks

Healthy Living

They say when you work out, your muscles are torn down, and built back up. The body's natural healing process restores your muscles to a stronger state than they were before. Healthy protein snacks can help this recovery process.

10 High-Protein Power Snacks
Numerous studies, including one published in the Journal of the American Medical Association have shown that skipping high-protein foods may lead to overeating and is often one of the biggest causes of excess weight gain. As any devoted exerciser knows, protein is essential for the growth and repair of muscle and organs, especially after a hard workout. Fill up on powerful proteins with these tasty options.

High-Protein Snack: Eggs
One large egg contains 6 grams of protein and only 70 calories. If you're concerned about cholesterol, many egg substitutes on the market offer lower-cholesterol alternatives that still pack a protein punch. One of the best ways to eat eggs is hard-boiled. Keep a bowl of them in your fridge for an instant, healthy snack or an addition to a larger meal.

High-Protein Snack: Nuts
Whether you go for almonds, cashews, walnuts, pistachios, or any of the other varieties, whole, raw nuts are a healthy high-protein snack. If you're concerned about calories, limit your nut intake to a handful or two, and remember that although nuts are high in fat, it's healthy monounsaturated fat, which doesn't clog arteries and is an essential part of a healthy diet. Plus, nuts are high in fiber, and keep you feeling full longer.

High-Protein Snack: Greek Yogurt
This yogurt's power comes from its protein. Greek yogurt contains 15–20 grams of protein in a 6 ounce serving versus 9 grams in regular yogurt.

High-Protein Snack: Turkey
When you're going for lean protein, nothing beats low-calorie turkey. Three ounces of turkey provides 25 grams of protein for only 140 calories.

Brock's Best

High-Protein Snack: Protein Shakes
Simply combine whey protein with nonfat milk, frozen fruit, all-natural nut butter, or whatever other healthful ingredients sound good to you, and you have a healthy meal replacement or snack.

High-Protein Snack: Cottage Cheese
Cottage cheese is an excellent protein source with a half-cup of low-fat cottage cheese providing 14 grams of protein for only 81 calories. Paired with fruit or plain, it makes a terrific snack when you want to stay full between meals.

High-Protein Snack: Lentils
Lentils pack a powerful punch of protein, fiber, and minerals while containing comparatively few calories and almost no fat. A cup of cooked lentils offers 22 grams of protein, about 300 calories, and less than 1 gram of fat.

High-Protein Snack: Tofu
Tofu or soy bean curd is another excellent high-protein meal base and source of healthy fats and nutrients. Because it absorbs flavors so well and can be cut into cubes, strips, or chunks, it can be prepared in a variety of ways.

High-Protein Snack : Nut Butter
Almond, cashew, peanut, and other nut butters are high-protein foods with about 2 tablespoon. It provides 7 grams of protein. Although nut butter contains fat, it can be part of a healthy diet when eaten in small amounts. Just remember not to slather it on crackers; spread it on carrot or celery sticks for healthy snacking instead.

High-Protein Snack : Pumpkin Seeds
Pumpkins are full of fiber, vitamins, and body-boosting carotenoids, but it turns out tiny pumpkin seeds might pack even more of a nutritional punch. With 8 grams of protein in just one ounce, pumpkin seeds or pepitas are also very rich in minerals, including potassium, manganese, and iron. Just take heed: Pumpkin seeds are calorie-dense, so do your healthy snacking in moderation.

—Source: everydayhealth.com

Healthy Living
Stress Management

Stress can be good because it helps to increase productivity, creativity, and can provide the spark needed to get things done. But when stress becomes too great and unmanageable for too long it can be harmful to both productivity and health. Stress management is a do it yourself project: you can learn the tools, but you have to use them as circumstances change, then you have to re-evaluate, and learn new ones. Your emotional and physical response and your personal effectiveness depends on the meaning you give to the stressful experience. Stress affects you emotionally, physically, and biologically with the release of the fight and flight hormones.

Here are some suggestions:

Take a breather from stress:
1. Stay in a comfortable position
2. Close your eyes
3. Deeply relax all muscles and keep them relaxed
4. Breathe through the nose, and be aware of your breathing in and breathing out.
5. Repeat a word silently that feels good to yourself and keep doing this for 20 minutes
6. Stay sitting with eyes open for a few minutes

Yoga is another activity for a sound mind and body. Medicine can cure disease but Yoga can prevent them.

 Brock's Best

The Benefits of Yoga

Any physical exercise can be an enhancement to good health. Whether you are involved in cardio physical exercises or other forms of exercises such as Tai chi, shiatsu massage, Yoga practice as an additional regimen is great because it encourages stretching, breathing, and meditation.

Yoga means "union" in Sanskrit, the language of ancient India, where Yoga originated from. Meaning the union between the mind, the body, and the spirit, it has been practiced for thousands of years.

The discipline involves the practice of physical poses or postures, mixed with breathing exercises, and mediation. It makes you aware of your body alignment and pattern of movements. It makes the body more flexible and helps one to relax from the stress caused by today's pressures.

It is a good idea to take classes from a knowledgeable teacher to learn the different positions and poses in order to avoid any injuries.

More Suggestions For Healthy Living

Tricks to Improve Brain Power
Practice mentally what you need to do: rehearsing the activity uses most of the same brain connections, which are switched on during the real thing.

Scientist experts believe that the brain is most active right after you wake up or before you go to sleep, so use these times to think about solutions and be creative.

So that you don't lose things as easily, focus your attention to try to remember where you put them. Pay attention to the time of the day, the weather, the day's headline news, or what you are wearing at the moment. You can also create a funny picture with the object, so that will come to mind when you are trying to recall where you put it.

Researchers are now saying that you need to continue to be actually active as you age, try learning a new skill, a new language, how to play a musical instrument or learn to be involved in a new type of activity such as putting together puzzles. The Center of Disease Control and Prevention recommends that all adults get a minimum of 150 minutes per week of moderate aerobic activity, such as a brisk walk. Sedentary living, not high cholesterol is the single biggest factor in heart attack deaths, and perhaps mental decline as we age as well.

Foods for Healthy Living
Eat foods that are rich in brain boosting beta-carotene. Omega 3s boosts your heart health, and can be found in salmon, walnuts, soy, and flaxseed. Good heart health boosts brain power. Fiber: 21–38 grams a day helps the digestive tract and controls cholesterol levels. Legumes which are low in fat food like the peas and beans family are excellent sources of proteins, fiber, and flavor, and also excellent served as a side dish.

Quotes
"Approach love and cooking with reckless abandon!" Dalai Lama
"Enthusiasm is contagious. Be a carrier."

 Brock's Best

Ergonomics

This is your friendly Ergonomics Checklist. Aim to check off all of these ergonomics best practices as they apply at work or at home.

- When you sit at your workstation, keep your feet flat on the floor. The seat edge should not press against the back of your knees or your lower legs.

- When you type, your elbows should remain comfortably at your sides, each elbow at right angles, and your forearms parallel to the floor.

- Your monitor should be at eye level, in front of you, and at a distance so you read your screen without leaning forward or backward.

- Place your work material within easy reach.

- Position your keyboard so that keystrokes can be performed with your wrists, hands, knuckles, and fingers in a relaxed, natural, and neutral position.

- Type gently.

- Position your armrests so they do not interfere with your movement.

- Maintain good posture—no slouching.

- When possible, vary your work activities to break from repetitive motions and static work positions.

Eye Exercises to Reduce Eye Strain

Because we are so often typing and staring at the computer screen, these activities can create eye fatigue and eyestrain. To help reduce this, you can practice these easy exercises:

1. Blink your eyes a couple of times.

2. Open your eyes and look up, then close them and look down.

3. Open your eyes and look left, then shut them. Open them again and look left.

4. Open your eyes and look down, then shut them. Open your eye lids halfway and look down.

5. Open your eyes and look right, then shut them and look right.

6. Do the "rock around the clock," by blinking your eyes twice. Open them again and look right, up top, left, and then down.

 Brock's Best

Notes

Beef

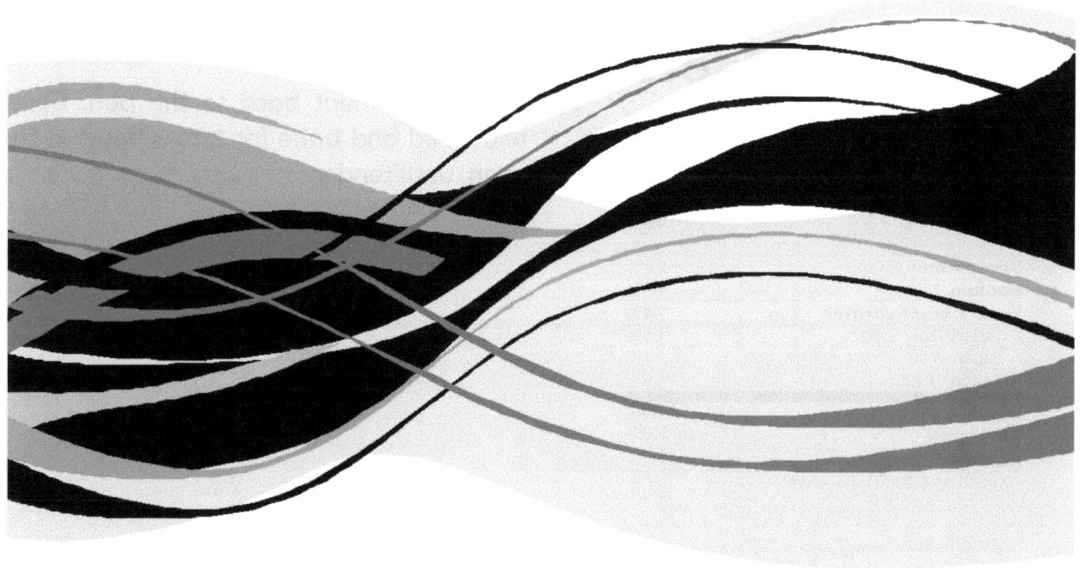

Brock's Best

Brock's Best

Braised Short Ribs

4 pounds boneless beef short ribs
4 tablespoons olive oil
Kosher salt
Freshly ground black pepper
1 large Spanish onion, chopped
4 ribs of celery, chopped
4 carrots, chopped
6 cloves fresh garlic
3 cups red wine
1 tomato, crushed
¼ bunch thyme
3 bay leaves

Preheat your oven to 350° F. Season the short ribs with olive oil, salt, and pepper. On the stovetop and in a preheated heavy oven-safe pan, heat the olive oil and brown the short ribs on all sides, about 5 minutes per side. Remove the meat from the pan and reserve any remaining stock.

Sauté the onion, celery, carrots, and garlic in the pan that was used for the meat. Add a little more oil if necessary. Cook until tender. Deglaze the pan with the red wine. Add the tomatoes, thyme, 2 cups of the reserved stock, and bay leaves.

Return the meat back to the pan. Cover with a lid and bake for 2 to 3 hours in the oven, until tender.

Yield: 4 to 6 servings
Scott Triola

Nutrition Facts

Serving Size 570 g

Amount Per Serving

Calories 835	Calories from Fat 273
	% Daily Value*
Total Fat 30.3g	47%
Saturated Fat 9.2g	46%
Trans Fat 0.0g	
Cholesterol 296mg	99%
Sodium 257mg	11%
Total Carbohydrates 12.9g	4%
Dietary Fiber 2.9g	11%
Sugars 4.5g	
Protein 101.6g	
Vitamin A 138%	Vitamin C 19%
Calcium 8%	Iron 366%

Nutrition Grade B-
* Based on a 2000 calorie diet

> Did you know that in some cases pepper has been used to stop bleeding? Dr. Robert Lee of Beth Medical Center recommends that you wash the affected area first with water and soap and then sprinkle pepper and apply gentle pressure. It will not sting since pepper is analgesic, antibacterial, and has antiseptic properties.

Beef

Broiled Flank Steak Chimichurri Sauce

12 pounds (2 pounds) flank steak
Kosher salt
Freshly ground black pepper

Chimichurri Sauce
1 cup (5 tablespoons) packed Italian parsley leaves
2 cloves garlic (⅓ teaspoon), peeled and smashed
½ cup (4 teaspoons) olive oil
2 tablespoons (1 teaspoon) red wine vinegar
¼ cup (2 teaspoons) packed fresh cilantro leaves
1 small shallot, quartered (¼ teaspoon)
1 teaspoon (1 pinch) red pepper flakes

Preheat your broiler. Trim any fat from the flank steaks, and then score them several times diagonally across the grain on both sides. You will use these scores later to cut the steak into strips. Season both sides of them with salt and black pepper.

Broil the steaks for 3 to 4 minutes per side until they reach your desired doneness. Remove from heat and allow the meat to rest.

Thinly slice the steaks along the scores into strips. Arrange the meat on a serving platter. Pour Chimichurri sauce (recipe follows) over steaks and serve.

Chimichurri Sauce
In a food processor, place parsley, smashed cloves of garlic, olive oil, red wine vinegar, cilantro, shallot, and red pepper flakes. Process until they form a well-combined sauce.

Transfer the sauce to a bowl, cover securely with plastic wrap, and store at room temperature.

Yield: 24 servings-food service version
(4 servings-home version)
Jose Belteton

Nutrition Facts

Serving Size 461 g

Amount Per Serving	
Calories 898	Calories from Fat 354
	% Daily Value*
Total Fat 39.4g	61%
Saturated Fat 15.9g	79%
Trans Fat 0.0g	
Cholesterol 249mg	83%
Sodium 267mg	11%
Total Carbohydrates 0.8g	0%
Protein 126.4g	
Vitamin A 3%	Vitamin C 4%
Calcium 7%	Iron 47%

Nutrition Grade B-
* Based on a 2000 calorie diet

Brock's Best

Cajun Beef and Root Vegetable Stew

Yield: 80 servings-food service version
(8 servings-home version)

Chuck Wilde

2 to 2 ½ pound (1 cup) flour
32 ounces (6 tablespoons) vegetable oil
20 pounds (2 pounds) beef bottom rounds, cubed
Salt and freshly ground pepper
2 ½ pound (1 cup) carrots, diced
2 ½ pound (1 cup) turnips, diced
5 (½) yellow onions
1 bunch (½ cup) celery, chopped
2 teaspoons (¼ teaspoon) cayenne pepper
10 cups (1 cup) dry red wine
10 (1 leaf) bay leaves
1 cup (2 tablespoons) hot sauce
8 teaspoons (1 teaspoon) Cajun seasoning
2 bags (¼ cup) pearl onions
5 pounds (½ pound/1 potato) Yukon potatoes
5 tablespoons (1 ½ teaspoon) chopped garlic
10 teaspoons (1 teaspoon) dried thyme

Preheat your oven to 300° F. To prepare the roux thickener in advance, mix flour and oil. Bake for 45 minutes to a thick, dry mud consistency.

Next, toss the raw cubed beef in a tad more of oil, then add a pinch of salt and pepper. Brown the beef in the oven for 20 to 30 minutes. Remove the meat and reserve the stock.

Place the browned meat into a heavy-duty stockpot. Add enough stock to cover the meat. Bring to a boil, then decrease to medium-low heat and simmer for 45 minutes. Add the carrots and turnips, and continue cooking for 20 minutes. Add the chopped onions, celery, and cayenne pepper. Also add the wine, bay leaves, hot sauce, and Cajun seasoning. Cook for 20 minutes more. Next, add the pearl onions, potatoes, garlic, and thyme. Season with more salt, and pepper. Return to a boil, then decrease the heat to medium-low. Cover and simmer for another 30 minutes, or until the meat is tender.

Take some of the liquid out of the pot, and mix all the roux in it, whip until smooth. Add this back to the meat and vegetables. This should thicken everything up nicely.

Remove the bay leaves. Adjust the seasoning if needed and serve over noodles, rice, or even grits.

Nutrition Facts

Serving Size 227 g

Amount Per Serving	
Calories 453	Calories from Fat 237
	% Daily Value*
Total Fat 26.3g	40%
Saturated Fat 8.0g	40%
Trans Fat 0.0g	
Cholesterol 120mg	40%
Sodium 189mg	8%
Total Carbohydrates 10.7g	4%
Dietary Fiber 1.6g	6%
Sugars 2.2g	
Protein 36.4g	
Vitamin A 3%	Vitamin C 24%
Calcium 3%	Iron 28%
Nutrition Grade C-	

* Based on a 2000 calorie diet

Beef

Cajun Meatloaf With Sweet Pepper Sauce

1 cup finely chopped sweet red peppers
½ cup finely chopped sweet green peppers
½ cup finely chopped onions
½ teaspoon salt
1 cup breadcrumbs
1 pound ground beef
½ cup ketchup
2 eggs
1 teaspoon Cajun seasoning or
1 teaspoon hot pepper sauce

Sauce
1 tablespoon oil
1 cup diced sweet red peppers
1 cup diced sweet green peppers
½ cup finely chopped onions
¼ cup water
Salt
¼ cup cider vinegar
¼ cup brown sugar
1 teaspoon spicy mustard

Yield: 8 servings
Patrick McHale

Preheat your oven to 325° F. Combine all the meatloaf ingredients (everything apart from the sauce ingredients) into a bowl then pat into the prepared loaf pan.

Bake for 1 hour. Top each serving with sauce (recipe follows) and serve.

Sauce
Heat the oil in a large skillet over medium heat. Add the red and green peppers, onion, and water. Season with salt. Cook, stirring occasionally over medium heat until tender. Stir in the cider vinegar, brown sugar, and spicy mustard. Cook over medium-high heat until most of the liquid has evaporated and the sauce thickens, about 8 minutes.

Nutrition Facts
Serving Size 174 g

Amount Per Serving	
Calories 240	Calories from Fat 65
	% Daily Value*
Total Fat 7.2g	**11%**
Saturated Fat 2.1g	**10%**
Trans Fat 0.0g	
Cholesterol 92mg	**31%**
Sodium 510mg	**21%**
Total Carbohydrates 21.6g	**7%**
Dietary Fiber 1.7g	**7%**
Sugars 10.8g	
Protein 21.1g	
Vitamin A 20%	Vitamin C 79%
Calcium 4%	Iron 66%

Nutrition Grade A
* Based on a 2000 calorie diet

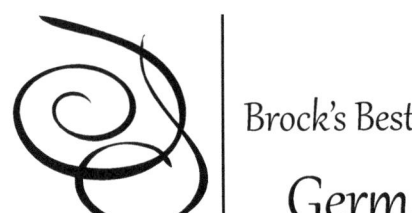

Brock's Best

German Beef Roulades over Spaetzle

Beef Roulades
½ cup finely diced onion
1 tablespoon minced garlic
3 pounds beef top round, thinly sliced
4 whole dill pickles, julienned
½ cup red wine
1 cup beef stock

Spaetzle
6 eggs
Salt and freshly ground black pepper
3 cups flour
4 tablespoons butter

Beef Roulades
Preheat your oven to 350° F. Sauté the onions and garlic until golden brown. Cut the beef into workable sizes, about 5 by 5-inches. Place 3 to 4 pieces of pickle in each piece of beef, and then top with the sautéed onions and garlic. Roll up and pin closed with a toothpick. Repeat with the rest of the beef. In a large pan on high heat with a little oil, sear the roulades until golden brown. Finish cooking the beef in the oven for 8 to 10 minutes.

Pour off the excess grease from the pan, and then add the wine. On a stovetop, reduce the wine, add beef stock, and reduce some more until the gravy is a thin syrup. Serve the beef over the spaetzle (recipe follows) with the gravy.

Spaetzle
In a large stockpot, bring about 8 cups (2 quarts) of water to a boil with a pinch of salt. Beat the eggs with a pinch of pepper and a pinch more of salt. Add flour to make a thin dough. Thin with milk if needed. Set a perforated pan with small holes (like a colander) over the boiling water. Pour the dough into the pan and – using a scraper – force it though the holes to form little dumplings.

Boil until all the dumplings are floating, and then drain. Add the butter to the pot and sauté the dumplings until golden brown. Further season with salt and pepper.

Nutrition Facts
Serving Size 773 g

Amount Per Serving

Calories 878	Calories from Fat 312
	% Daily Value*
Total Fat 34.7g	**53%**
Saturated Fat 14.6g	**73%**
Cholesterol 377mg	**126%**
Sodium 945mg	**39%**
Total Carbohydrates 50.9g	**17%**
Dietary Fiber 2.5g	**10%**
Sugars 1.6g	
Protein 81.3g	
Vitamin A 11%	Vitamin C 4%
Calcium 7%	Iron 57%

Nutrition Grade C
* Based on a 2000 calorie diet

Yield: 6 servings
Derek Chimel

Beef

German Braised Veal Shanks

Yield: 4 servings
Eric Rappaport

½ cup flour
Salt and freshly ground black pepper
4 (3-inch-thick cut) veal shanks with bone
¼ cup olive oil
¼ cup butter
2 cups diced onions
1 cups diced carrots
1 cup diced celery
6 cloves garlic, minced
2 bay leaves
3 tablespoons chopped fresh dill
1 cup Trollinger or Black Hamburg wine
2 cups good quality veal or chicken stock
1 teaspoon caraway seeds
1 teaspoon fresh thyme
2 cups peeled, seeded, and diced tomatoes
2 teaspoons grated rind from a lemon
2 teaspoons grated rind from an orange
2 cloves garlic, minced
2 tablespoons fresh minced chives

Season the flour with salt and pepper. Dredge the veal shanks in the flour and seasoning mixture, and tap off any excess. Heat a large heavy bottom skillet or Dutch oven, over medium-high heat, and then add oil and butter. Sear the shanks on all sides. Add more oil and butter if needed. Remove the browned veal shanks and set aside.

Keep the skillet/Dutch oven on the stovetop, and add the onions, celery, carrots, garlic, bay leaves, and dill and cook until softened. Season with salt and pepper. Raise the heat to high, add wine, and deglaze the pan.

Return the shanks to the pan. Add stock, caraway seeds, thyme, and tomatoes. Reduce the heat to low, cover, and cook for about 1 ½ hours, or until meat is tender. Baste the meat a few times during cooking. Remove the cover; continue to simmer for 10 minutes to reduce the sauce a bit.

For the topping, combine the grated rind of the lemon and orange, the garlic, and the chives. Mix well and hold for service.

To serve, place the veal shank on a plate and top with basting sauce. Sprinkle with the grated rind mixture. Serve with Spaetzle Noodles Bergkase (page 218) and Dinsztelt Wild Greens (page 208).

Nutrition Facts

Serving Size 591 g

Amount Per Serving

Calories 697 — Calories from Fat 303

% Daily Value*

Total Fat 33.7g — 52%
Saturated Fat 11.5g — 58%
Trans Fat 0.0g
Cholesterol 283mg — 94%
Sodium 705mg — 29%
Total Carbohydrates 28.1g — 9%
Dietary Fiber 4.6g — 19%
Sugars 6.6g
Protein 69.3g

Vitamin A 107% • Vitamin C 47%
Calcium 17% • Iron 36%

Nutrition Grade B+
* Based on a 2000 calorie diet

Brock's Best

Brock's Best

Homemade Meatballs for Spaghetti

Sauce
2 (10 ¾ ounce) cans condensed tomato soup, undiluted or 2 cans tomato, chopped
2 ¾ cup water
1 (12 ounce) can tomato paste
1 (4 ½ ounce) jar sliced mushrooms, undrained
1 onion, chopped
3 tablespoons Worcestershire sauce
3 tablespoons chili powder
1 teaspoon salt
½ teaspoon cayenne pepper
2 cloves garlic, minced
Pinch of freshly ground pepper

Meatballs
2 pounds ground beef
2 eggs, beaten
¼ cup chopped onions
1 teaspoon garlic salt
½ teaspoon pepper

Make the sauce (recipe follows). After simmering the sauce for about 1 ½ hours, make the meatballs (recipe follows). Add the meatballs to the sauce and simmer together for another hour.

Serve over spaghetti, prepared during the last 15 minutes that the meatballs and sauce are simmering. In addition to the spaghetti, this dish can be served with fresh salad and garlic breadsticks.

Sauce
In a large Dutch oven or kettle, combine the first eleven ingredients (all the ingredients up to but not including the ground beef). Simmer uncovered for 2 hours, stirring occasionally.

Meatballs
In a bowl combine the beef, eggs, onions, garlic salt, and pepper. Shape into meatballs. Brown them in a skillet.

Yield: 6 servings
Maria Reed

Nutrition Facts

Serving Size 380 g

Amount Per Serving	
Calories 447	Calories from Fat 112
	% Daily Value*
Total Fat 12.5g	19%
Saturated Fat 4.3g	22%
Trans Fat 0.0g	
Cholesterol 190mg	63%
Sodium 1245mg	52%
Total Carbohydrates 31.7g	11%
Dietary Fiber 5.7g	23%
Sugars 18.5g	
Protein 53.2g	

Vitamin A 50%	•	Vitamin C 54%	
Calcium 6%	•	Iron 182%	

Nutrition Grade A
* Based on a 2000 calorie diet

Beef

Marinated and Grilled Buffalo Flank Steak with Lime Chipotle Sauce

Steak and Marinade
1 tablespoon minced chipotle peppers in adobo
½ tablespoon minced garlic
1 ½ tablespoon minced cilantro
2 ounces olive oil
3 ounces red wine
2 ounces soy sauce
1 ½ pound flank steak, cleaned of fat and silverskin

Sauce
½ cup honey
2 tablespoons minced chipotle pepper in adobo
3 tablespoons balsamic vinegar
2 tablespoons Dijon mustard
½ cup freshly squeezed lime juice
1 ½ tablespoon minced garlic
1 teaspoon ground cumin
½ teaspoon ground allspice
½ cup minced cilantro
Salt and freshly ground pepper

In a small bowl, combine the marinade ingredients. Add the flank steak and turn to coat well. Refrigerate for 1 hour or overnight.

In a food processor, combine the sauce ingredients and process briefly to blend. Season with salt and pepper. Transfer this sauce to a saucepot and simmer, and then hold warm over low heat.

Remove the steak from the marinade, pat dry, and grill to desired doneness. Let rest before slicing.

At service, drizzle sauce over meat.

Yield: 3 servings
Joshua Stayrook

Nutrition Facts
Serving Size 342 g

Amount Per Serving	
Calories 626	Calories from Fat 251
	% Daily Value*
Total Fat 27.9g	43%
Saturated Fat 7.8g	39%
Trans Fat 0.0g	
Cholesterol 94mg	31%
Sodium 1479mg	62%
Total Carbohydrates 41.6g	14%
Dietary Fiber 1.2g	5%
Sugars 36.9g	
Protein 49.6g	
Vitamin A 9% •	Vitamin C 12%
Calcium 6% •	Iron 25%

Nutrition Grade C-
* Based on a 2000 calorie diet

Brock's Best

Meatloaf

2 pounds ground beef
1 can Ro-Tel Hot Tomatoes
1 egg
1 cup breadcrumbs
2 spring onions
½ teaspoon pepper
½ teaspoon salt
1 small can of mushrooms
½ cup ketchup

Preheat your oven to 350° F. Combine all the ingredients aside from the ketchup, and mix gently to combine. Shape into a round mold and bake for about 1 hour. Drain any grease. Top with ketchup, and cook for 15 minutes longer. Cut and serve.

Nutrition Facts
Serving Size 314 g

Amount Per Serving	
Calories 478	Calories from Fat 121
	% Daily Value*
Total Fat 13.4g	21%
Saturated Fat 4.8g	24%
Trans Fat 0.0g	
Cholesterol 195mg	65%
Sodium 979mg	41%
Total Carbohydrates 25.5g	8%
Dietary Fiber 2.1g	8%
Sugars 8.2g	
Protein 60.6g	
Vitamin A 11%	Vitamin C 12%
Calcium 6%	Iron 199%

Nutrition Grade B+
* Based on a 2000 calorie diet

Yield: 4 to 6 servings
Marie Marsh

New Mexican Burger

6 beef burger patties
3 cup Ortega refried beans
1 cup chopped Buenos green chilies
¾ cup yellow onion
6 large (12-inch) tortillas
16 ounces cheddar cheese
1 cup sour cream

Cook the beef burger patties on a grill until their internal temperature reaches 165° F. Heat the refried beans in a saucepan, (or on the grill) also to a temperature of 165°F. Grill the chopped chilies and onions for 3 to 4 minutes. Warm a flour tortilla.

Load a warm, soft tortilla with a beef patty, refried beans, chilies, onions, cheddar cheese, and sour cream. Wrap with aluminum foil and serve with french fries.

Nutrition Facts
Serving Size 427 g

Amount Per Serving	
Calories 907	Calories from Fat 531
	% Daily Value*
Total Fat 59.0g	91%
Saturated Fat 30.7g	153%
Trans Fat 0.8g	
Cholesterol 201mg	67%
Sodium 1309mg	55%
Total Carbohydrates 38.9g	13%
Dietary Fiber 8.5g	34%
Sugars 2.8g	
Protein 54.0g	
Vitamin A 20%	Vitamin C 36%
Calcium 67%	Iron 32%

Nutrition Grade C+
* Based on a 2000 calorie diet

Yield: 6 servings
Patrick Baca

Bef

Russian Cutlets

1 pound ground beef
1 pound ground pork
1 pound ground chicken
2 eggs
2 ½ cup Italian seasoning breadcrumbs
¼ cup water
3 large white onions
1 bunch cilantro
1 tablespoon mayonnaise
1 teaspoon salt
1 teaspoon pepper
3 tablespoons of vegetable oil for frying

In a large bowl, combine all the meats, eggs, ½ cup of the breadcrumbs, and the water. Set aside temporarily.

In a food processor, finely chop the onions and cilantro until almost the consistency of purée. Combine the purée in the large bowl with the meat mixture and thoroughly stir. Finally, add the mayonnaise, salt, and pepper.

Put the remaining 2 cups of breadcrumbs onto a large plate. Heat a large skillet with some vegetable oil. Using a tablespoon, scoop 2 spoonfuls of the meat mixture into your hands and shape with your palms into flat ovals.

Coat the forms with breadcrumbs from the plate and fry in a skillet until golden brown on both sides.

Yield: 20 servings
Veta Mesh

Nutrition Facts

Serving Size 118 g

Amount Per Serving

Calories 197 — Calories from Fat 54

% Daily Value*

Total Fat 6.0g	9%
Saturated Fat 1.7g	8%
Trans Fat 0.0g	
Cholesterol 74mg	25%
Sodium 276mg	12%
Total Carbohydrates 12.3g	4%
Dietary Fiber 1.3g	5%
Sugars 1.9g	
Protein 22.0g	

Vitamin A 7%	•	Vitamin C 8%
Calcium 4%	•	Iron 31%

Nutrition Grade A-

* Based on a 2000 calorie diet

Brock's Best

Spare Ribs in Wine Sauce

Yield: 3 servings
Jie Astri

1 ⅓ pound spare ribs
3 tablespoons Shaoxing wine plus 3 more tablespoons for final sauce
2 slices ginger
1 spring onion
2 teaspoons coarse salt
2 ½ tablespoon fish sauce
1 teaspoon sugar
1 teaspoon vinegar

Cut the spare ribs into two or three big portions – small enough to put inside a large saucepan. Parboil them in about 4 cups (1 quart) boiling water for 7 minutes. Remove, rinse, and wash, then set aside.

Boil the Shaoxing wine, ginger, spring onion, coarse salt, fish sauce, sugar, and vinegar in another large saucepan. Add the spare ribs and bring to boil, then simmer over low heat for about 40 minutes. Test the tenderness of the meat by pricking it with a chopstick. Remove the meat and cut it into small pieces, then and dish into a big bowl.

Discard the ginger and spring onion, and then remove excess fats from sauce. Add 3 tablespoons of wine and bring to a boil. Pour this wine sauce over the spare ribs. Cool and soak for at least 2 hours in the refrigerator, covered (it tastes best after 6 hours). When ready, serve hot or cold.

Nutrition Facts

Serving Size 572 g

Amount Per Serving

Calories 539	Calories from Fat 374
	% Daily Value*
Total Fat 41.5g	64%
Saturated Fat 16.2g	81%
Trans Fat 0.0g	
Cholesterol 144mg	48%
Sodium 3043mg	127%
Total Carbohydrates 3.7g	1%
Sugars 2.1g	
Protein 31.6g	

Vitamin A 1%	•	Vitamin C 2%
Calcium 2%	•	Iron 2%

Nutrition Grade F
* Based on a 2000 calorie diet

Stuffed Flank Steak

Beef

Yield: 4 to 6 servings
Chris LaFrance

1 ½ pound flank steak
1 bottle Italian or balsamic dressing
2 packages frozen spinach, thawed
¼ cup chopped fresh parsley
¼ cup grated Asiago cheese
2 fresh jalapeño peppers, diced
1 clove garlic, minced
Coarse ground pepper and sea salt
1 teaspoon olive oil
1 ball of kitchen twine

Butterfly the flank steak (cut into it edgewise until you have almost cut through it, and then flatten it out like a butterfly) and marinate it in Italian dressing for 4 hours.

Thaw the spinach and squeeze out as much water as possible. In a bowl, combine spinach, parsley, Asiago cheese, jalapeños, garlic, pepper, and salt.

Remove the flank steak from its marinade, lay it flat, and top with the spinach mixture. Roll the steak up over the mixture, pressing firmly and tying with kitchen twine. Rub with oil and more salt and pepper.

Broil the steak until brown, 10 minutes for medium rare, or longer if desired. Let it rest for 10 minutes, and then slice into ¾-inch rounds.

This recipe may also be cooked on an outdoor grill.

Note: be sure to allow your rolled stuffed steak to rest before slicing.

Nutrition Facts

Serving Size 423 g

Amount Per Serving

Calories 774	Calories from Fat 490
	% Daily Value*
Total Fat 54.4g	**84%**
Saturated Fat 11.7g	**59%**
Trans Fat 0.0g	
Cholesterol 85mg	**28%**
Sodium 1891mg	**79%**
Total Carbohydrates 24.1g	**8%**
Dietary Fiber 2.8g	**11%**
Sugars 15.1g	
Protein 44.1g	
Vitamin A 223% •	Vitamin C 62%
Calcium 22% •	Iron 33%

Nutrition Grade B
* Based on a 2000 calorie diet

Brock's Best

Teriyaki Burger

Yield: 4 to 6 servings
Cherwon Hawkins

5 (3 ounce) frozen burger patties
5 tablespoons of Teriyaki
2 onions, sliced
2 tbsp Sesame oil
5 Kaiser rolls
1 cup bean sprouts
5 tbsp duck sauce

Grill the frozen burger patties. Sprinkle them with Teriyaki sauce while cooking. Also sauté 2 full onion slices for each burger.

Spread the sesame oil on the Kaiser rolls and toast on your grill. When each burger reaches the safely cooked internal temperature of 165° F, remove from the grill and place on the toasted Kaisers. Top with the sautéed onion and raw bean sprouts. Serve with duck sauce for dipping.

Nutrition Facts
Serving Size 212 g

Amount Per Serving	
Calories 460	Calories from Fat 198
	% Daily Value*
Total Fat 22.0g	34%
Saturated Fat 8.0g	40%
Trans Fat 0.0g	
Cholesterol 71mg	24%
Sodium 513mg	21%
Total Carbohydrates 37.3g	12%
Dietary Fiber 2.2g	9%
Sugars 5.0g	
Protein 26.5g	
Vitamin A 0%	Vitamin C 20%
Calcium 7%	Iron 23%

Nutrition Grade B-
* Based on a 2000 calorie diet

Texas Style BBQ Brisket

5 pounds beef brisket, with a ¼ inch thick layer of fat
Salt and fresh ground black pepper
1 tablespoon sugar
2 tablespoons chili powder
1 teaspoon ground cumin
1 gallon Texas BBQ sauce
1 (6 ounce) can chipotle peppers
2 tsp cayenne pepper
6 oz garlic, minced

Prepare the meat by coating with salt, ground pepper, sugar, chili powder, and ground cumin. Place the brisket in the refrigerator for 8 hours to marinate.

Cook at 350° F, for 2 to 4 hours for an internal temperature of 165° F. Let set on the counter for 10 minutes. Slice into 2 pieces, across the grain.

Combine the Texas BBQ Sauce, chipotle peppers, cayenne pepper, and minced garlic. Heat the sauce to 165° F and pour over the meat. Serve.

Yield: 10 to 12 servings
Joseph T. Presler

Nutrition Facts
Serving Size 277 g

Amount Per Serving	
Calories 467	Calories from Fat 132
	% Daily Value*
Total Fat 14.6g	23%
Saturated Fat 5.4g	27%
Cholesterol 203mg	68%
Sodium 867mg	36%
Total Carbohydrates 10.0g	3%
Dietary Fiber 1.4g	6%
Sugars 2.5g	
Protein 70.6g	
Vitamin A 16%	Vitamin C 80%
Calcium 5%	Iron 243%

Nutrition Grade A-
* Based on a 2000 calorie diet

Beef

Wiener-Bean Casserole

1 pound ground beef
1 package of hot dogs
16 ounce can of pork and beans
1 envelope of dry onion soup mix
⅓ cup ketchup
¼ cup water
2 tablespoons brown sugar
1 tablespoon prepared yellow mustard

Preheat your oven to 350° F. Brown the ground beef in a skillet until no longer pink. Slice the hot dogs into bite-sized pieces. Add all of the remaining ingredients into the skillet with the ground beef. Stir thoroughly. Pour everything into a casserole dish.

Bake uncovered for 1 hour. Stir, then cover, and bake an additional 30 to 45 minutes.

Nutrition Facts

Serving Size 345 g

Amount Per Serving

Calories 692 — Calories from Fat 379

	% Daily Value*
Total Fat 42.2g	65%
Saturated Fat 16.9g	85%
Trans Fat 0.0g	
Cholesterol 165mg	55%
Sodium 2405mg	100%
Total Carbohydrates 32.5g	11%
Dietary Fiber 5.7g	23%
Sugars 13.3g	
Protein 47.3g	

Vitamin A 3% • Vitamin C 5%
Calcium 5% • Iron 115%

Nutrition Grade C
* Based on a 2000 calorie diet

Yield: 4 to 6 servings
Cheryl Teske

 Brock's Best

Notes

Breakfast And Breads

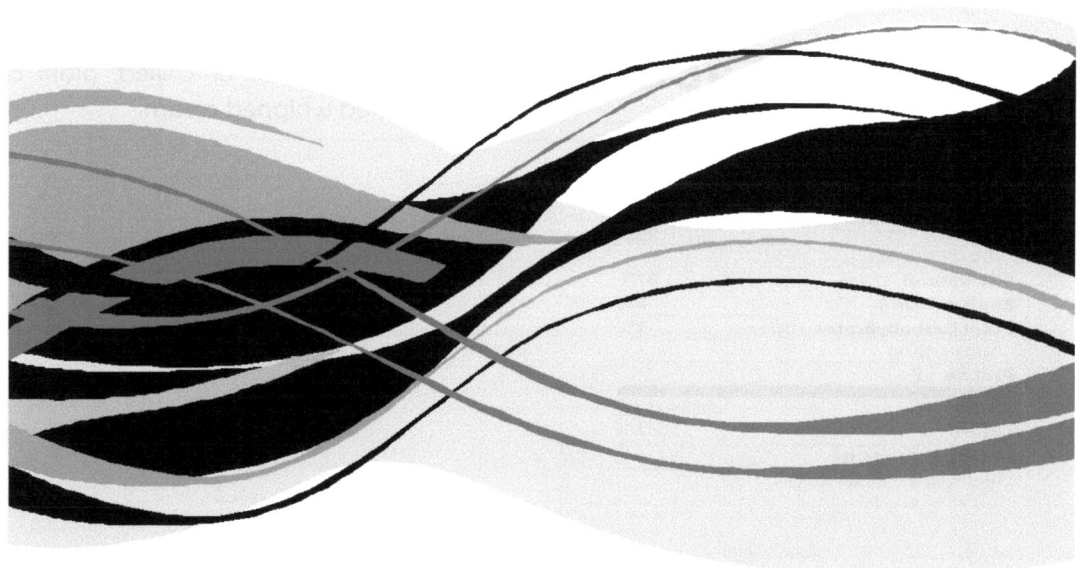

Brock's Best

Brock's Best

Bread Pudding

4 cups day old white, or crustless French bread cubes
½ cup seedless raisins
3 tablespoons butter, melted
8 eggs
1 teaspoon cinnamon
½ teaspoon nutmeg
½ teaspoon salt
⅔ cup sugar
3 cups half and half
1 ½ teaspoon vanilla
Sweetened whip cream

Preheat your oven to 350° F. Arrange the bread cubes and raisins in a buttered 1 ½-quart or casserole dish, and drizzle with butter.

Combine the eggs, cinnamon, nutmeg, and salt. Beat slightly. Dissolve the sugar in the half and half and add to the eggs in fine stream, stirring constantly. Stir in the vanilla.

Pour this mixture over the bread cubes and bake for 55 to 60 minutes, until a knife inserted into the center comes out clean.

Serve slightly warmed or chilled, plain or with sweetened whipped cream.

Yield: 14 to 16 servings
Barry Pinkowicz

Nutrition Facts

Serving Size 98 g

Amount Per Serving	
Calories 191	Calories from Fat 94
	% Daily Value*
Total Fat 10.4g	16%
Saturated Fat 5.7g	29%
Trans Fat 0.0g	
Cholesterol 111mg	37%
Sodium 203mg	8%
Total Carbohydrates 20.0g	7%
Sugars 12.3g	
Protein 5.6g	
Vitamin A 7% • Vitamin C 1%	
Calcium 7% • Iron 5%	
Nutrition Grade D+	

* Based on a 2000 calorie diet

Breakfast & Breads

Butternut Squash Bread Pudding with Leeks and Parmesan

3 cups diced in ½-inch cubes, butternut squash
Canola cooking spray
¼ teaspoon salt plus more for cooking leeks
1 tablespoon maple syrup
½ cup (1 stick) butter
3 leeks, washed well and chopped—white and light green parts only
3 cloves garlic, minced
Freshly ground pepper
6 eggs
2 cups heavy cream
1 cup milk
3 cups trimmed and stale bread cubes, from a brioche bread
1 cup shredded Gruyère
1 cup shredded Parmesan cheese or Grana Padano

Preheat your oven to 400° F. Spray a cookie sheet and the squash with cooking spray. Season the squash with ¼ teaspoon of salt and roast in the oven for 15 minutes. Drizzle maple syrup on the squash and continue to roast for 5 minutes more. Take out of oven to cool (do not turn the oven off).

Melt the butter in sauté pan over medium heat. Add the leeks and garlic. Season with pepper and additional salt. Cover the pan and cook at a lower heat (about 10 minutes).

In a large bowl beat the eggs, then add the roasted squash, the leek mixture, the cream, milk, bread, and one-half of the cheese.

Let the mixture sit for 10 minutes, spray a 9 by 12-inch glass baking dish and pour in the contents of the bowl. Top with the remaining cheese.

Decrease the oven heat to 350° F. Bake for 45 minutes, or until bubbling and golden brown.

Yield: 10 to 12 servings
Christine Trapaga

Nutrition Facts
Serving Size 183 g

Amount Per Serving

Calories 311	Calories from Fat 214
	% Daily Value*
Total Fat 23.8g	37%
Saturated Fat 13.5g	68%
Trans Fat 0.0g	
Cholesterol 162mg	54%
Sodium 224mg	9%
Total Carbohydrates 18.4g	6%
Dietary Fiber 1.3g	5%
Sugars 4.5g	
Protein 8.0g	
Vitamin A 114% • Vitamin C 20%	
Calcium 14% • Iron 8%	

Nutrition Grade B-
* Based on a 2000 calorie diet

 Brock's Best

Cheese-Garlic Biscuits

2 cups Bisquick Heart Smart mix
⅔ cup fat-free skim milk
½ cup shredded reduced fat cheddar cheese
½ teaspoon garlic powder
Butter flavored cooking spray, if desired

Preheat your oven to 450° F. Combine the Bisquick mix, milk, cheese, and garlic powder to make a soft dough. Beat vigorously 30 seconds. Drop the dough by 10 to 12 spoonfuls onto an ungreased cookie sheet.

Bake for 8 to 10 minutes, until golden brown. Spray the warm biscuits with cooking spray before removing them from the cookie sheet. Serve warm.

Yield: 10 to 12 servings
Teresa Flebbe

Nutrition Facts
Serving Size 43 g

Amount Per Serving	
Calories 100	Calories from Fat 23
	% Daily Value*
Total Fat 2.5g	4%
Saturated Fat 0.6g	3%
Cholesterol 4mg	1%
Sodium 234mg	10%
Total Carbohydrates 16.2g	5%
Dietary Fiber 0.6g	2%
Sugars 2.5g	
Protein 3.7g	
Vitamin A 2%	Vitamin C 0%
Calcium 18%	Iron 5%

Nutrition Grade C-
* Based on a 2000 calorie diet

Yield: 12 servings
Eric Bunton

Chocolate Brioche Bread Pudding

4 cups heavy cream
1 ½ cup granulated sugar
1 tbsp vanilla
4 egg yolks
3 chocolate muffin
1 brioche loaf

Preheat your oven to 325° F. Boil the cream, sugar, and vanilla together in a saucepan. In a bowl, pour the boiled cream mix slowly into the egg yolks to bring them up to heat. Pour the mixture back into the saucepan and let sit for 3 to 4 minutes. Strain out any egg white strands, using a strainer, and drain the custard into a bowl. Let cool.

Dice the chocolate muffins and brioche (with crust removed). Place in a pan and pour the custard on top. Bake for 25 minutes, or until firm. Cool and serve.

Nutrition Facts
Serving Size 130 g

Amount Per Serving	
Calories 466	Calories from Fat 314
	% Daily Value*
Total Fat 34.9g	54%
Saturated Fat 19.7g	99%
Trans Fat 0.0g	
Cholesterol 187mg	62%
Sodium 80mg	3%
Total Carbohydrates 36.5g	12%
Sugars 29.5g	
Protein 3.6g	
Vitamin A 25%	Vitamin C 1%
Calcium 6%	Iron 3%

Nutrition Grade F
* Based on a 2000 calorie diet

Breakfast & Breads

Breakfast & Breads

Crème Brûlée French Toast

½ cup unsalted butter
1 cup firmly packed dark brown sugar
2 tablespoons light corn syrup
6 (1-inch) day old challah slices
5 large eggs
1 ½ cup half and half cream
1 teaspoon vanilla extract
1 teaspoon orange liqueur
¼ teaspoon salt

Combine the butter, brown sugar, and corn syrup in a heavy saucepan. Cook the contents over medium heat until melted and smooth. Pour into a 13 by 9-inch baking pan.

Trim the crust of challah and discard the crust. Arrange the crustless bread slices in one layer in the baking pan. Whisk together the eggs, half and half, vanilla, orange liqueur, and salt in large mixing bowl. Pour over the bread. Cover, and refrigerate for 8 hours, or overnight.

Preheat your oven to 350° F and bring the bread mixture to room temperature. Bake uncovered, in the middle of the oven for 35 to 45 minutes, until the French Toast slices are puffed and the edges are pale golden.

Yield: 8 to 10 servings
Jon Kaplan

Nutrition Facts

Serving Size 139 g

Amount Per Serving	
Calories 433	Calories from Fat 224
	% Daily Value*
Total Fat 24.9g	38%
Saturated Fat 13.4g	67%
Cholesterol 235mg	78%
Sodium 392mg	16%
Total Carbohydrates 42.6g	14%
Dietary Fiber 0.8g	3%
Sugars 21.4g	
Protein 9.1g	
Vitamin A 16% •	Vitamin C 0%
Calcium 5% •	Iron 11%

Nutrition Grade F
* Based on a 2000 calorie diet

Brock's Best

Crunchy French Toast With Banana and Strawberry

2 cups liquid eggs (or 12 eggs, whisked)
2 cups skim milk
1 teaspoon pure vanilla or almond extract
1 teaspoon cinnamon
¼ cup sugar
1 box corn flakes, crushed lightly
1 loaf Texas toast
¼ cup oil
2 bananas, sliced
2 cups (1 pint) sliced strawberries
Confectioner's (powdered) sugar, if desired

Mix eggs, milk, vanilla, cinnamon, and sugar together and set aside. Lightly crush the cereal in its bag, and then pour into a bowl. Take a slice of bread and dip into the egg mixture, wetting both sides, then dip both sides into the bowl of crushed cereal. Set aside on a sheet tray. Do this process until all the bread is coated.

Heat your grill or skillet until it is hot. Pour a little oil, about 1 teaspoon, on the grill or pan and place a slice of the coated bread on top. Grill for 2 to 3 minutes on each side. Add more oil as needed to grill the rest of the loaf.

Slice the toast in half and serve topped with sliced bananas and strawberries. Sprinkle with confectioner's sugar, if desired.

Nutrition Facts
Serving Size 212 g

Amount Per Serving	
Calories 343	Calories from Fat 89
	% Daily Value*
Total Fat 9.9g	15%
Saturated Fat 2.0g	10%
Trans Fat 0.0g	
Cholesterol 165mg	55%
Sodium 454mg	19%
Total Carbohydrates 53.3g	18%
Dietary Fiber 4.7g	19%
Sugars 15.1g	
Protein 11.8g	
Vitamin A 16% •	Vitamin C 44%
Calcium 10% •	Iron 57%

Nutrition Grade A-
* Based on a 2000 calorie diet

Yield: 12 servings
Laura Walther

Breakfast & Breads

Currant Scones

2 cups flour
1 tablespoon baking powder
4 tablespoons sugar
½ teaspoon salt
½ cup unsalted butter, cut into pea-size pieces
1 cup currants or your favorite fruit
1 large egg
1 cup heavy cream
2 tablespoons sanding sugar (optional)
2 tablespoons melted butter (optional)
Confectioner's (powdered) sugar (optional)

Preheat your oven to 350° F. Mix the flour, baking powder, sugar, and salt in a bowl. Take cold cut up butter and work it into the flour mixture until it resembles crumbly meal. Add the currants and lightly work through dough.

Mix together the egg and heavy cream in another bowl, and then add to the dry ingredients. Mix all together, but do not over-mix.

Knead the dough until it comes together. Again note: do not over-knead; it will become tough.

Next, turn dough onto floured cutting board, or other surface. Roll the dough to ½ inch thick. Using a cookie-cutter 2 to 2 ½ inches round, or any shape you like, cut and place on a sheet pan. Do not butter the pan or use any spray at this point.

Once on cookie sheet, sprinkle with sanding sugar and/or once they are done brush tops with melted butter. Bake for about 25 minutes, until golden brown. You can also sprinkle the scones with powdered sugar after they have cooled.

Nutrition Facts
Serving Size 76 g

Amount Per Serving

Calories 276	Calories from Fat 151
	% Daily Value*
Total Fat 16.7g	26%
Saturated Fat 10.2g	51%
Trans Fat 0.0g	
Cholesterol 66mg	22%
Sodium 212mg	9%
Total Carbohydrates 28.9g	10%
Dietary Fiber 1.2g	5%
Sugars 8.2g	
Protein 3.7g	
Vitamin A 11%	Vitamin C 8%
Calcium 9%	Iron 8%

Nutrition Grade C+
* Based on a 2000 calorie diet

Yield: 10 to 12 servings
Theodore Geller

Brock's Best

Golden Baked French Toast

Yield: 8 servings
Donna Dunn

8 to 10 slices bread, cubed
8 ounces cream cheese, softened
1 teaspoon cinnamon
1 teaspoon nutmeg
1 teaspoon orange extract
1 cup milk
10 eggs
Brown sugar
Maple syrup

Layer the bread in the bottom of a greased 13 by 9-inch baking pan. Set aside. Combine cream cheese, cinnamon, nutmeg, orange extract, milk, and eggs in a blender. Blend well. Pour evenly over bread. You can turn over the bread to cover both sides. Cover with aluminum foil and refrigerate overnight.

Preheat your oven to 350° F. Uncover and bake about 35 minutes until golden brown. Sprinkle with brown sugar. Drizzle with maple syrup before serving.

Guatemalan Banana Bread

3 cups flour
2 teaspoons baking powder
½ teaspoon salt
4 cups bananas, mashed
½ cup coconut milk
½ teaspoon vanilla
½ cup melted butter
½ cup raisins (optional)
½ cup cashews (optional)

Preheat your oven to 350° F. In a large bowl, combine the flour, baking powder and salt. Stir in the bananas, coconut milk, vanilla and butter. Fold in the raisins and cashews, if desired. Pour into a greased 5 by 9-inch loaf pan. Bake for 1 hour and 15 minutes, or until a knife inserted in the center comes out clean.

Yield: 8 or more servings
Jose Belteton

Breakfast & Breads

Open Faced Broiled Egg, Spinach, and Tomato Sandwich

1 whole wheat English muffin, split, toasted
2 slices ripe tomato
8 ounces spinach, cooked
2 hard-boiled eggs, sliced
2 tablespoons mayonnaise
2 shredded basil leaves, for garnish
Salt free seasoning, for garnish

Top the muffin halves with the tomato, spinach, and the sliced egg. Spoon on the mayonnaise and broil for 2 minutes, or until the mayonnaise is lightly browned.

Garnish with the basil leaves and salt-free seasoning.

Nutrition Facts

Serving Size 442 g

Amount Per Serving

Calories 432 — Calories from Fat 188

	% Daily Value*
Total Fat 20.9g	**32%**
Saturated Fat 4.5g	**23%**
Cholesterol 335mg	**112%**
Sodium 979mg	**41%**
Total Carbohydrates 43.8g	**15%**
Dietary Fiber 9.8g	**39%**
Sugars 9.6g	
Protein 23.9g	

Vitamin A 441%	•	Vitamin C 113%
Calcium 45%	•	Iron 55%

Nutrition Grade A
* Based on a 2000 calorie diet

Yield: 1 serving
Gilbert Burns

 Did you know that studies show spinach contains magnesium, which improves the body's response to stress?

Brock's Best

Pizza Dough

2 ¼ cups warm water
2 teaspoons plus a pinch dry yeast
1 teaspoon plus a pinch sugar
2 tablespoons plus 1 teaspoon olive oil
1 tablespoon kosher salt
8 cups high gluten flour

Combine the water, yeast, and sugar. Let sit until it becomes a foamy mix (2 minutes or more).

Add the oil and salt. Mix well. Gradually add flour to the mixture. Mix with a dough hook for 8 minutes until the dough pulls away from the mixing bowl. (It may be necessary to add more flour during mixing.)

Cut the dough two equal sized balls. Rub with olive oil and refrigerate until ready to use.

Can be combined with the Pizza Sauce in the Dips and Sauces section (page 102)!

Yield: 2 twenty-two ounce dough balls which yield 2 pizzas of eight slices
Tony Paterno

Nutrition Facts

Serving Size 72 g

Amount Per Serving	
Calories 273	Calories from Fat 77
	% Daily Value*
Total Fat 8.5g	13%
Saturated Fat 2.3g	12%
Cholesterol 0mg	0%
Sodium 1746mg	73%
Total Carbohydrates 42.8g	14%
Dietary Fiber 1.8g	7%
Sugars 1.2g	
Protein 7.6g	
Vitamin A 0%	Vitamin C 0%
Calcium 0%	Iron 2%
Nutrition Grade D+	

* Based on a 2000 calorie diet

Breakfast & Breads

Puffy Maine Pancakes

Yield: 3 pancakes
Jody Charles

2 large eggs, lightly beaten
½ cup all-purpose flour
½ cup milk
Pinch of salt
Pinch of freshly grated nutmeg
3 tablespoons unsalted butter
Confectioner's (powdered) sugar, for garnish

Preheat your oven to 425° F. Put the eggs, flour, milk, salt, and grated nutmeg in a bowl, and whisk until combined. The batter may still be slightly lumpy. Making the batter a day ahead, and chilling overnight, improves the quality.

For each pancake, melt 1 tablespoon of butter in a 4-inch crepe pan or ovenproof skillet over medium-high heat. Using a ladle, pour one-third of the batter into the very hot pan. Transfer the pan or skillet immediately into the oven.

Bake until the pancake is golden brown and very puffy, about 10 minutes.

Dust with confectioner's sugar. Serve immediately.

Nutrition Facts

Serving Size 110 g

Amount Per Serving
Calories 247 — Calories from Fat 143

	% Daily Value*
Total Fat 15.9g	24%
Saturated Fat 8.9g	44%
Cholesterol 158mg	53%
Sodium 198mg	8%
Total Carbohydrates 18.5g	6%
Dietary Fiber 0.6g	2%
Sugars 2.5g	
Protein 7.8g	

Vitamin A 11% • Vitamin C 0%
Calcium 7% • Iron 9%

Nutrition Grade B-
* Based on a 2000 calorie diet

Brock's Best

Quick and Easy Eggs Benedict

8 slices Canadian bacon
1 teaspoon white vinegar
8 eggs
4 English muffins, split and toasted

Cream Sauce
1 cup butter
6 egg yolks
1 tablespoon heavy cream
Pinch of ground cayenne pepper
½ teaspoon salt
3 ½ tablespoon freshly squeezed lemon juice

In a skillet over medium-high heat, fry the Canadian bacon on each side until evenly browned.

Fill a large saucepan with about 3 inches of water and bring to a simmer. Pour in the vinegar. Carefully break four of the eggs into the water, and cook for 2 to 3 minutes, until the whites are set but the yolks are still soft. Remove the eggs with a slotted spoon.

For each serving, place one split English muffin onto a serving plate. Top each half with 1 slice of Canadian bacon and 1 poached egg.

Drizzle with the cream sauce (recipe follows), and serve at once.

Cream Sauce
Melt the butter until bubbly in a small pan or in the microwave. Remove from heat before the butter browns.

In a blender or large food processor, blend the egg yolks, heavy cream, cayenne pepper, and salt until smooth. Add half of the hot butter in a thin, steady stream, slow enough so that it blends in at least as fast as you are pouring it in. Blend in the lemon juice using the same method, then the remaining butter.

Nutrition Facts
Serving Size 303 g

Amount Per Serving

Calories 849	Calories from Fat 612
	% Daily Value*
Total Fat 68.0g	105%
Saturated Fat 37.0g	185%
Trans Fat 0.0g	
Cholesterol 798mg	266%
Sodium 1803mg	75%
Total Carbohydrates 28.2g	9%
Dietary Fiber 2.1g	8%
Sugars 3.2g	
Protein 32.6g	

Vitamin A 46%	•	Vitamin C 12%
Calcium 19%	•	Iron 28%

Nutrition Grade C-
* Based on a 2000 calorie diet

Yield: 4 servings
Debbie O'Donovan

Breakfast & Breads

Roasted Vegetable Pizza

1 green pepper, sliced thin
1 red onion, sliced thin
1 cup grape tomatoes
1 large Portobello mushroom cap, sliced thin
Olive oil
Salt and freshly ground black pepper
2 (7-inch) frozen pizza shells
1 cup grated Parmesan cheese
2 cups shredded mozzarella cheese

Preheat your oven to 400° F. Place the green pepper, onion, grape tomatoes and mushroom cap on a sheet pan and drizzle with the olive oil. Season the vegetable and mushrooms with salt and pepper. Roast until soft and the tomatoes "pop."

Thaw 2 (7-inch) pizza shells. Stretch out the dough to 8 ½ to 9 inches in diameter. Sprinkle half of the Parmesan cheese on each shell. Evenly spread the roasted vegetables and mozzarella cheese on top of the Parmesan.

Increase the heat to 425° F and bake for 12 to 16 minutes, until the crust and cheeses are good and brown.

Remove from the oven. Cut to make four to six pieces and serve.

Yield: 2 personal pizzas of four slices each
Norman Griese

Nutrition Facts

Serving Size 245 g

Amount Per Serving

Calories 587	Calories from Fat 176
	% Daily Value*
Total Fat 19.5g	**30%**
Saturated Fat 10.9g	**55%**
Trans Fat 0.0g	
Cholesterol 47mg	**16%**
Sodium 1182mg	**49%**
Total Carbohydrates 67.3g	**22%**
Dietary Fiber 1.9g	**8%**
Sugars 4.1g	
Protein 33.2g	
Vitamin A 18% •	Vitamin C 55%
Calcium 62% •	Iron 6%

Nutrition Grade C+
* Based on a 2000 calorie diet

Brock's Best

Scones

- 4 cups heavy cream (40%)
- 1 cup granulated sugar
- 1 tablespoon kosher salt
- 2 tablespoons vanilla extract
- 2 ½ tablespoon baking powder
- 7 cups all-purpose flour
- Egg wash
- Garnishes, as needed

Preheat your oven to 350° F. Put the heavy cream in a mixer and combine with the sugar, salt, vanilla, and baking powder. Whip until cream achieves medium-heavy peaks. Transfer the mix to a mixing bowl.

Add the flour into the bowl and incorporate by hand. Be very careful not to over-mix, as this will result in chewy scones. Remove the dough from mixing bowl and separate into two piles. Garnish with whatever is on hand and desirable (dried cranberries, chocolate, white chocolate, orange zest, etc.).

Mix the garnish in and form dough into wheels. Cut the wheels into eight pieces each. Place apart on a sheet pan and lightly coat with an egg wash.

Bake for 8 to 12 minutes, watching carefully and ensuring they are golden brown and completely cooked.

Nutrition Facts

Serving Size 137 g

Amount Per Serving	
Calories 471	Calories from Fat 207
	% Daily Value*
Total Fat 23.0g	35%
Saturated Fat 14.0g	70%
Cholesterol 92mg	31%
Sodium 468mg	20%
Total Carbohydrates 58.8g	20%
Dietary Fiber 1.6g	6%
Sugars 13.0g	
Protein 7.4g	
Vitamin A 18%	Vitamin C 1%
Calcium 15%	Iron 16%

Nutrition Grade D+

* Based on a 2000 calorie diet

Yield: 16 servings
Jeffrey Chamberlain

Breakfast & Breads

Scrambled Egg Beggar's Purses

Yield: 12 servings
Jen Foy

6 tablespoons butter or butter blend
2 dozen eggs, cracked, whipped to scramble
2 tablespoons mixed chopped herbs (parsley, thyme, dill)
¾ cup julienned sun-dried tomatoes
Salt and freshly ground black pepper
2 cups crumbled goat cheese or feta cheese
Butter flavored spray
1 box phyllo pastry
Baby spinach, for salad

Preheat your oven to 400° F. Melt the butter in a sauté pan and scramble the eggs with the herbs and sun-dried tomatoes. Season with salt and pepper. Transfer to a bowl and cool. Mix in the crumbled cheese.

Spray two large 6-muffin capacity muffin tins with butter spray. On a cutting board, lay out 1 sheet of phyllo, spray with butter spray, then lay another sheet on top. Spray again, add one more sheet and spray a final time. Cut into sixths.

Repeat the whole process to make a second layered sheet cut into sixths. Lightly press each piece into the 12 holes of the muffin tins. Fill each cup with the egg mixture, fold the pastry over the top, and spray to seal closed. Bake for 10 to 12 minutes, or until browned.

To serve, place a bed of baby spinach on a plate, and place a warm egg purse in the center.

Nutrition Facts

Serving Size 203 g

Amount Per Serving

Calories 529	Calories from Fat 312
	% Daily Value*
Total Fat 34.7g	53%
Saturated Fat 19.3g	96%
Trans Fat 0.0g	
Cholesterol 395mg	132%
Sodium 598mg	25%
Total Carbohydrates 24.3g	8%
Dietary Fiber 1.5g	6%
Sugars 3.4g	
Protein 30.0g	
Vitamin A 35% •	Vitamin C 3%
Calcium 51% •	Iron 23%

Nutrition Grade B-
* Based on a 2000 calorie diet

Brock's Best

Sweet Milk Griddle Cakes

2 cups flour
1 teaspoon salt
1 ½ teaspoon baking powder
2 tablespoons sugar
2 cups milk
1 egg
1 tablespoon butter

In a large bowl, mix and sift the flour, salt, baking powder, and sugar. Add the milk, egg, and butter. Mix well.

Drop by spoonfuls onto a lightly greased hot griddle. When puffed, full of bubbles, and cooked on the edges, turn and cook on the other side. Serve hot with syrup.

Nutrition Facts
Serving Size 83 g

Amount Per Serving
Calories 142 — Calories from Fat 26

	% Daily Value*
Total Fat 2.8g	4%
Saturated Fat 1.5g	8%
Cholesterol 23mg	8%
Sodium 271mg	11%
Total Carbohydrates 24.3g	8%
Dietary Fiber 0.7g	3%
Sugars 4.7g	
Protein 4.7g	

Vitamin A 1% • Vitamin C 0%
Calcium 10% • Iron 7%

Nutrition Grade B
* Based on a 2000 calorie diet

Yield: 10 pancakes
Renee Bloch

Did you know that to have a slimmer waist you should not skip breakfast? Eat a breakfast to get you started for the day with high fiber cereal, whole grain bread, or fruit, then bite into a pickle or lemon to curb your appetite. Brush your teeth. Post a list of things on the fridge of projects to do, and then tackle them and your cravings for food will diminish. Use a smaller plate and serve smaller portions!

Breakfast & Breads

Syrniki* Cottage Cheese Pancakes

1 cup cottage cheese
1 cup flour
1 ½ tablespoon sugar
1 egg beaten
2 to 3 tablespoons cooking oil
Toppings of choice

Mix the cottage cheese, flour, sugar, and egg in a bowl. Form small balls with the dough by rolling it in your hands. Then smash the balls so they form small, flat patties.

In a skillet or grill, heat oil over medium heat. Cook two patties at a time and fry on each side. When golden, remove and keep warm until all are prepared. Top with your favorite topping, e.g. sour cream, jelly/jam, or honey.

Nutrition Facts

Serving Size 38 g

Amount Per Serving

Calories 96	Calories from Fat 38

	% Daily Value*
Total Fat 4.2g	6%
Saturated Fat 0.9g	4%
Cholesterol 15mg	5%
Sodium 82mg	3%
Total Carbohydrates 10.2g	3%
Sugars 1.6g	
Protein 4.1g	

Vitamin A 1%	•	Vitamin C 0%	
Calcium 2%	•	Iron 3%	

Nutrition Grade B-
* Based on a 2000 calorie diet

Yield: 3 entrée portions or 12 side portions
[nutrition information is based on the side portions]
Bella Raykin

*SYRNIKI [sihr-NEE-kee]—Russian in origin, syrniki is a dish of fried cheese cakes that can be served sweet: sprinkled with confectioner's (powdered) sugar and sour cream, or savory: topped with sour cream and herbs such as dill.

Syrniki are made with a mixture of pot cheese or farmer's cheese, flour, and beaten eggs, which is formed into cakes before being sautéed on both sides until brown.

Brock's Best

 Brock's Best

Notes

Chicken

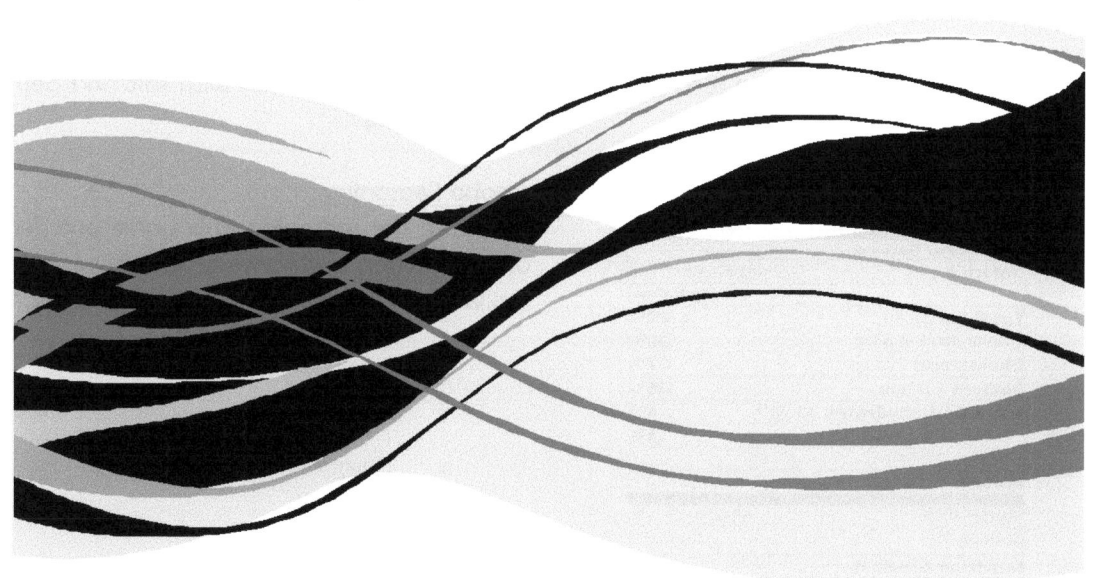

Brock's Best

Brock's Best

Adobo Seasoned Baked Chicken Wings

40 chicken wings, patted dry
2 tablespoons olive oil
2 tablespoons chopped fresh oregano, for sprinkling

Adobo Seasoning
Salt and freshly ground black pepper
2 teaspoons garlic powder
2 teaspoons onion powder
2 teaspoons ground turmeric

Glaze
½ cup mango nectar
¼ cup honey
¼ cup red hot sauce

Preheat your oven to 425° F. Toss the wings in a bowl with olive oil and adobo seasoning mix (recipe follows). Place the wings onto a large baking sheet in a single layer. Bake for 20 minutes, turn wings over, and bake for 20 minutes more.

Remove the wings. Brush with glaze (recipe follows) and bake for an 20 additional minutes. To serve, place cooked wings on a platter and sprinkle with oregano.

Glaze
Stir together mango nectar, honey, and hot sauce in a bowl. Season with salt and pepper. Set aside.

Adobo Seasoning
To make the seasoning, mix garlic powder, onion powder, and turmeric in a bowl. Season with additional salt and black pepper.

Yield: 8 five-wing servings
Craig B. Nurmi

Nutrition Facts
Serving Size 268 g

Amount Per Serving

Calories 513	Calories from Fat 185
	% Daily Value*
Total Fat 20.5g	32%
Saturated Fat 5.2g	26%
Cholesterol 202mg	67%
Sodium 1071mg	45%
Total Carbohydrates 13.2g	4%
Dietary Fiber 0.7g	3%
Sugars 11.4g	
Protein 66.0g	

Vitamin A 5%	•	Vitamin C 17%
Calcium 6%	•	Iron 20%

Nutrition Grade B-
* Based on a 2000 calorie diet

Chicken

Anjyab Sandale

2 pounds beef, stew meat pieces—
approximately 1-inch diced or
4 pieces chicken, on bone
4 to 5 potatoes
4 green peppers
4 red peppers
4 eggplants
5 white onions
1 bunch dill
2 bunch cilantro
1 bay leaf
Salt and freshly ground black pepper
Water

Cut the beef or chicken into ½-inch cubes. Boil the meat in a pot or kettle in a small amount of water. Peel and dice the potatoes. Keep in water to keep from turning brown. Remove the seeds from the green and red peppers, and cut them into strips the size of fettuccine.

Peel and halve the eggplant lengthwise and slice into ½-inch slices. Place the sliced eggplant in water seasoned with salt to remove the bitterness. Slice the white onions and chop the dill and cilantro.

Layer the ingredients in a large pot as follows: peppers, eggplant, potatoes, beef (or chicken), dill, cilantro, and the bay leaf. Season with salt and pepper.

Add a little water in the casserole, but only enough to come one-quarter of the way up the sides of the pot. Place on the stove and cook until the vegetables are done.

Yield: 4 to 6 servings
Suren Sarkisov

Nutrition Facts

Serving Size 1453 g

Amount Per Serving

Calories 1,004	Calories from Fat 175
	% Daily Value*
Total Fat 19.4g	30%
Saturated Fat 6.3g	32%
Cholesterol 276mg	92%
Sodium 265mg	11%
Total Carbohydrates 100.2g	33%
Dietary Fiber 32.1g	128%
Sugars 27.0g	
Protein 110.7g	

Vitamin A 37%	•	Vitamin C 431%
Calcium 20%	•	Iron 313%

Nutrition Grade A
* Based on a 2000 calorie diet

Brock's Best

Baltimore Chicken

1 tablespoon butter
5 ounce chicken breast
¼ cup all-purpose flour
2 ounces white wine
4 ounces chicken gravy
2 ounces heavy cream
Pinch of Old Bay seasoning
6 ounces angel hair pasta
3 ounces lump or jumbo lump crabmeat
2 ounces sliced (or ½ cup shredded) provolone cheese
Pinch of fresh parsley flakes, for garnish

Melt butter in a non-stick sauté pan. Tenderize the chicken breast, dust in flour, and place in the pan. Lightly brown on both sides.

Deglaze the pan with wine, add gravy, heavy cream, and the Old Bay seasoning. Let reduce by half and use as a sauce.

Cook the pasta according to package instructions and place on the center of the plate. Place chicken on top of pasta, and then top chicken with crab and provolone cheese. Smother in sauce. Garnish with chopped parsley and serve with a salad and garlic bread.

Yield: 1 serving
Joe Mathis

Nutrition Facts
Serving Size 731 g

Amount Per Serving

Calories 1,558	Calories from Fat 584
	% Daily Value*
Total Fat 64.9g	100%
Saturated Fat 32.4g	162%
Trans Fat 0.0g	
Cholesterol 480mg	160%
Sodium 1725mg	72%
Total Carbohydrates 127.8g	43%
Dietary Fiber 1.5g	6%
Sugars 1.8g	
Protein 103.4g	
Vitamin A 44%	Vitamin C 16%
Calcium 64%	Iron 62%

Nutrition Grade C-
* Based on a 2000 calorie diet

? Did you know that parsley gives great flavor and is nutritious in salads? Just 1 ounce provides 43% of the Recommended Dietary Allowance for Vitamin C and 18% and RDA for iron in men and 12% in women, plus 1 mg of beta carotene.

Chicken

Cheese Encrusted Chicken

½ cup flour
1 egg
¾ cup Asiago* or Parmesan cheese
¼ cup seasoned breadcrumbs
2 tablespoons water
4 chicken breasts, boneless, skinless
1 ½ teaspoon salt
1 ½ teaspoon freshly ground black pepper
¼ cup olive oil

Pour the flour onto a plate and set aside. Whisk the egg in shallow bowl, and set aside also. Place the cheese, breadcrumbs, and water in a food processor and blend lightly. Transfer this mixture to a bowl.

Liberally season the chicken with salt and pepper. Next, dredge the chicken pieces in the flour, then dip in the bowl with the egg, and finally coat with breadcrumb mixture.

Heat oil over medium-high heat. Sauté the chicken for 2 to 3 minutes, until golden brown.

*ASIAGO CHEESE [ah-SYAH-goh]—A semi-firm Italian cheese with a rich, nutty flavor.

Nutrition Facts

Serving Size 304 g

Amount Per Serving	
Calories 705	Calories from Fat 323
	% Daily Value*
Total Fat 35.8g	55%
Saturated Fat 9.7g	48%
Trans Fat 0.0g	
Cholesterol 257mg	86%
Sodium 1357mg	57%
Total Carbohydrates 17.5g	6%
Dietary Fiber 0.9g	4%
Protein 75.9g	
Vitamin A 6%	Vitamin C 0%
Calcium 22%	Iron 23%

Nutrition Grade C+
* Based on a 2000 calorie diet

Yield: 4 servings
Dawn Corder

Brock's Best

Chicken and Broccoli Casserole

3 tablespoons unsalted butter
3 tablespoons flour
3 cups chicken broth
1 shallot, minced
1 teaspoon salt
½ teaspoon freshly ground pepper
1 tablespoon freshly squeezed lemon juice
½ cup sour cream
2 cups grated Parmesan cheese
3 cups fresh or thawed previously frozen, broccoli florets
1 ½ pound boneless, skinless chicken breast—cooked and shredded
1 cup cracker crumbs (Ritz, or your favorite)

Preheat your oven to 325° F. In a saucepan, melt the butter and add the flour. Cook for 3 minutes. Add the broth and shallot, and bring the mixture to boil. Reduce to a simmer and stir until it thickens. Add the salt, pepper, and lemon juice. Remove from heat and stir in the sour cream and ¼ cup of the Parmesan.

Arrange the broccoli in a 2-quart gratin dish. Pour half the sauce over it. Arrange the shredded chicken on the top of the broccoli and pour on the remaining sauce. Top with the cracker crumbs and remaining cheese.

Bake for 20 minutes, and then place the dish under the broiler for no more than 1 minute, until the crackers are golden brown.

Yield: 8 servings
Elena Zenchenko

Nutrition Facts

Serving Size 270 g

Amount Per Serving

Calories 368	Calories from Fat 165
	% Daily Value*
Total Fat 18.4g	28%
Saturated Fat 8.6g	43%
Trans Fat 0.1g	
Cholesterol 109mg	36%
Sodium 1023mg	43%
Total Carbohydrates 11.7g	4%
Dietary Fiber 1.1g	4%
Sugars 1.0g	
Protein 39.6g	
Vitamin A 13%	Vitamin C 51%
Calcium 28%	Iron 11%

Nutrition Grade B
* Based on a 2000 calorie diet

Did you know that broccoli is high in fiber and has been shown to lower cholesterol? It is also rich in sulfur compounds, which are good for the liver, and thus strengthen the body's natural detoxification system.

Chicken and Stuffing

Chicken

2 to 4 chicken breasts, boneless
Water
10 ¾ ounce can cream of chicken soup
¼ cup milk
6 ounce box chicken-flavored stuffing mix
4 tablespoons butter, melted
Parmesan cheese, for sprinkling

Preheat your oven to 350° F. Place the chicken breasts in a Dutch oven on the stove, cover with water, and cook until the juices run clear when pierced with a fork. Drain the chicken, reserving the broth. Cut the chicken in small pieces and place in a 1 ½-quart greased baking dish.

Combine the soup, milk, and ¼ cup of the broth. Pour over the chicken. In a bowl, combine the stuffing seasoning mix packet, butter, and remaining broth. Stir in the dry stuffing and sprinkle on top.

Cover for 30 minutes. Sprinkle with grated Parmesan cheese before serving.

Nutrition Facts

Serving Size 420 g

Amount Per Serving

Calories 762 — Calories from Fat 311

	% Daily Value*
Total Fat 34.5g	**53%**
Saturated Fat 13.4g	**67%**
Cholesterol 240mg	**80%**
Sodium 1327mg	**55%**
Total Carbohydrates 36.8g	**12%**
Dietary Fiber 1.2g	**5%**
Sugars 2.4g	
Protein 73.8g	

Vitamin A 12% • Vitamin C 0%
Calcium 7% • Iron 30%

Nutrition Grade B-

* Based on a 2000 calorie diet

Yield: 4 to 6 servings
Donna Dunn

Brock's Best
Chicken Mole Verde

Yield: 4 servings
Eric Smith

½ cup oil
1 sprig cilantro plus 1 sprig more to be added with the pumpkin seeds later
1 garlic clove
Salt and freshly ground black pepper
4 chicken breasts
½ onion
2 cloves garlic
4 serrano chilies, seeded and chopped
8 tomatillos, peeled and quartered
3 cups chicken broth plus 1 cup more
4 romaine leaves, chopped
4 poblano chilies
3 sprigs epazote* or parsley
¾ cup pumpkin seeds, toasted and ground
1 lemon, sliced, for garnish

Combine the oil, cilantro, and garlic. Pour over the chicken and season with salt and pepper. Allow to marinate at least 2 hours.

Grill the chicken on a char broiler or charcoal grill to 165° F. Arrange the chicken breast in a serving pan.

Heat a saucepan or steam kettle. Add the onion, garlic, and serrano chilies. Cook until the aroma blossoms. Add the tomatillos and cook until heated. Add 3 cups of the chicken broth. Bring the mixture to a boil, then simmer for 5 minutes, or until the tomatillos are soft.

Transfer the mixture to a blender (or use a hand blender in the original pot) to blend tomatillo mixture. Add the romaine and the poblano chilies. Purée until smooth.

Add 1 more sprig of cilantro, the epazote or parsley, and the pumpkin seeds. Purée the mixture again. In the original pot (transfer back if you left it), bring the purée back to a simmer. Add the remaining cup of broth to make a smooth, consistent sauce. Simmer for half an hour, stirring often. Adjust the seasoning with salt and pepper.

Pour the sauce over the chicken breasts and bake at 350° F for 20 minutes, or until the chicken is at 165° F internal temperature. Garnish the chicken with lemon slices and serve.

Nutrition Facts
Serving Size 702 g

Amount Per Serving	
Calories 941	Calories from Fat 556
	% Daily Value*
Total Fat 61.7g	95%
Saturated Fat 11.5g	58%
Trans Fat 0.1g	
Cholesterol 202mg	67%
Sodium 968mg	40%
Total Carbohydrates 20.6g	7%
Dietary Fiber 5.5g	22%
Sugars 4.3g	
Protein 78.8g	
Vitamin A 13%	Vitamin C 96%
Calcium 9%	Iron 46%
Nutrition Grade B	
* Based on a 2000 calorie diet	

*EPAZOTE [eh-paw-ZOH-teh]—A Mexican herb that has a very strong taste and sometimes has a gasoline or perfume-like odor. It has been used in Mexican cuisine for hundreds of years dating back to the Aztecs who used it for cooking as well as for medicinal purposes.

Chicken Sicilian

Chicken

1 Idaho potato, diced in ¼ inch cubes
¼ cup olive oil plus 2 more tablespoons to cook with the tomatoes
½ cup salt and pepper seasoned flour
4 (4 ounce) chicken breasts, ½ inches diced
2 tablespoons minced shallots
½ cup chopped black olives
4 ounces pepperoncini with juice, sliced
4 teaspoons drained capers
¼ cup white wine
¼ cup chicken stock
1 large tomato, firm, diced in ¼ inch cubes
4 cups cooked (8 ounces uncooked) spaghetti
¾ cup flat leaf parsley, chopped
Salt and freshly ground black pepper

Begin by frying the potatoes in olive oil. The oil should be almost smoking. Toss the chicken with the flour mixture. When the potatoes are half done, add the flour-tossed chicken pieces.

While those are frying, first sauté the shallots, then add the olives, pepperoncini and pepperoncini juice, capers, white wine, and chicken stock. Reduce by half.

When the chicken and potatoes are done, transfer them to the pan with the olives. Add the remaining olive oil and tomatoes. Cook till slightly thickened. It's quick, so watch it! If it gets too thick, thin with chicken stock.

Season further with salt and pepper. Place on spaghetti, and sprinkle with parsley.

Nutrition Facts

Serving Size 374 g

Amount Per Serving	
Calories 621	Calories from Fat 218
	% Daily Value*
Total Fat 24.2g	37%
Saturated Fat 4.6g	23%
Cholesterol 142mg	47%
Sodium 834mg	35%
Total Carbohydrates 56.7g	19%
Dietary Fiber 2.7g	11%
Sugars 1.8g	
Protein 42.6g	

Vitamin A 24%	•	Vitamin C 41%
Calcium 6%	•	Iron 34%

Nutrition Grade C
* Based on a 2000 calorie diet

Yield: 4 servings
Gilbert Burns

Brock's Best

Chicken Tingas

4 pounds chicken thighs, boneless, skinless
6 cups chicken broth
2 onions, finely diced
4 teaspoons adobo seasoning
2 cloves garlic
2 tomatoes, diced
1 cup prepared tomato sauce
Salt and freshly ground black pepper
1 (8 ounce) package tostada shells
1 cup (8 ounces) sour cream
1 cup shredded lettuce
1 tablespoon chopped cilantro
2 tablespoons grated Parmesan cheese
Spanish rice (optional)

Boil the chicken with the chicken broth, one of the chopped onions, the adobo seasoning, and the garlic for about 45 minutes, or until it easily shreds.

Remove the chicken and set aside to cool. Once cool, shred with two forks or with your hands.

Sauté the other onion and tomatoes until caramelized, add the tomato sauce and chicken. Bring to a simmer and season with salt and pepper.

Place the shredded chicken mixture on a tostada shell and garnish with sour cream, shredded lettuce, Parmesan cheese, and cilantro. Serve with Spanish rice.

Yield: 8 servings
Paola Crodone

Nutrition Facts

Serving Size 705 g

Amount Per Serving

Calories 804	Calories from Fat 325
	% Daily Value*
Total Fat 36.1g	**56%**
Saturated Fat 14.1g	**70%**
Trans Fat 0.0g	
Cholesterol 251mg	**84%**
Sodium 1486mg	**62%**
Total Carbohydrates 28.5g	**9%**
Dietary Fiber 2.7g	**11%**
Sugars 4.6g	
Protein 85.9g	

Vitamin A 17%	•	Vitamin C 21%
Calcium 18%	•	Iron 27%

Nutrition Grade C+
* Based on a 2000 calorie diet

Chicken

Chinamerica Chicken Pineapple Feast

Yield: 1 serving
Jie Astri

1 chicken breast
White pepper powder
½ teaspoon salt plus and an additional ¼ teaspoon of salt for final seasoning (if needed)
½ teaspoon honey
½ cup chopped pineapple
1 tablespoon cooking wine
Oil
3 tablespoons mayonnaise
½ teaspoon sugar (if needed)

Pound the chicken breast with a wood mallet for a short period of time to soften the breast. Put in a bowl.

Add a little bit of the white pepper powder, salt, and honey. Mix everything thoroughly, turning the chicken over to coat.

Chop the pineapple and add to the bowl. Add the cooking wine. Mix thoroughly and let marinate in the refrigerator for about 60 minutes.

Remove the chicken from the bowl, and set the sauce aside. Cook the chicken with some oil in a pot until brown. (You may use an oven instead if you wish.)

Cook the leftover pineapple sauce. Gradually add 3 tablespoons of mayonnaise, stirring constantly. If needed, add an additional ¼ teaspoon of salt and/or ½ teaspoon of sugar. Pour over the chicken and serve.

Nutrition Facts

Serving Size 337 g

Amount Per Serving

Calories 646	Calories from Fat 311
	% Daily Value*
Total Fat 34.6g	**53%**
Saturated Fat 3.9g	**20%**
Trans Fat 0.0g	
Cholesterol 159mg	**53%**
Sodium 2258mg	**94%**
Total Carbohydrates 26.7g	**9%**
Dietary Fiber 1.2g	**5%**
Sugars 15.9g	
Protein 56.2g	
Vitamin A 3% •	Vitamin C 66%
Calcium 4% •	Iron 15%

Nutrition Grade C
* Based on a 2000 calorie diet

Brock's Best

Grilled Chicken Kabobs With Greek Style Barley Salad

Yield: 8 servings
Gerrard Zolezi

Dressing/Marinade
- 1 teaspoon grated lemon peel
- ½ cup freshly squeezed lemon juice
- ⅓ cup olive oil
- 3 cloves garlic, finely chopped
- 1 tablespoon Dijon style mustard
- 1 teaspoon dried oregano leaves
- ¼ teaspoon salt
- ¼ teaspoon freshly ground black pepper

Salad
- 3 cups cooked pearl barley
- 13 ¾ ounce can artichoke hearts, chopped
- 1 cup pitted Kalamata olives
- 1 cup crumbled feta cheese
- ½ cup finely chopped red onions
- ½ cup chopped parsley

Kabobs
- 16 wooden skewers soaked in water
- 8 chicken breast halves, boneless, skinless

Dressing/Marinade
Combine the dressing/marinade ingredients in a small bowl. Set aside.

Salad
Combine the salad ingredients in a large bowl. Drizzle ½ cup of dressing/marinade (from the recipes above) over the salad and mix well.

Kabobs
Place the chicken in sealable plastic bag. Pour in the remaining dressing/marinade (from the recipes above). Seal the bag and turn over to coat the chicken pieces. Refrigerate for 20 minutes. Remove the chicken from the marinade and thread onto skewers. Grill or broil for 4 to 5 minutes per side, until cooked through. To serve, place a portion of salad (recipe above) on a plate and top with two chicken skewers.

To Cook the Pearl Barley:
In a saucepan with a lid, bring 3 cups of water to a boil. Add 1 cup of pearl barley. Return to a boil. Reduce the heat to low, cover, and cook for 45 minutes, or until the barley is tender and the liquid is absorbed. Add cooked barley to soups, stews, casseroles, and salads for extra fiber and flavor. For best results, bring cooked barley to room temperature before using. It keeps for a week if refrigerated in a closed container.

Nutrition Facts

Serving Size 369 g

Amount Per Serving

Calories 753	Calories from Fat 250
	% Daily Value*
Total Fat 27.8g	43%
Saturated Fat 8.0g	40%
Cholesterol 168mg	56%
Sodium 767mg	32%
Total Carbohydrates 64.4g	21%
Dietary Fiber 14.3g	57%
Sugars 2.5g	
Protein 60.6g	
Vitamin A 13%	Vitamin C 25%
Calcium 18%	Iron 28%

Nutrition Grade B
* Based on a 2000 calorie diet

Chicken

Grilled Chicken Penne Alfredo

1 pound boneless and skinless chicken breast
½ cup balsamic vinaigrette dressing
12 ounces penne
½ cup butter, unsalted
1 tablespoon chopped garlic
½ cup grated Parmesan cheese
⅔ cup heavy cream
Salt and freshly ground black pepper
1 tablespoon chopped fresh basil

Nutrition Facts

Serving Size 293 g

Amount Per Serving

Calories 822	Calories from Fat 419
	% Daily Value*
Total Fat 46.5g	72%
Saturated Fat 23.2g	116%
Trans Fat 0.0g	
Cholesterol 247mg	82%
Sodium 681mg	28%
Total Carbohydrates 52.3g	17%
Sugars 3.1g	
Protein 47.3g	
Vitamin A 24% •	Vitamin C 2%
Calcium 16% •	Iron 22%
Nutrition Grade C+	

* Based on a 2000 calorie diet

Marinate the chicken with the balsamic vinaigrette dressing for at least 2 hours, or overnight.

In a pot of boiling salted water, cook the pasta until al dente. Drain in a colander.

Meanwhile, remove the chicken from the marinade and cook in a large, thick-bottomed sauté pan in the butter until no longer pink. Remove the chicken and cut it into strips.

In the same pan, with the left over butter, sauté the garlic until it is lightly browned. Add the cooked pasta and toss to coat. Add one-half of the cheese along with the cream and the previously cooked chicken. Cook on medium heat until the sauce is thick and all the ingredients are hot. Season with salt and pepper. Garnish with the remaining cheese, and chopped fresh basil.

Yield: 4 servings
Staff of Blue Cross Blue Shield

Brock's Best

Latin Combo—Sky, Sea, and Land

1 pound beef, skirt steak or flank steak—cut in strips
1 pound chicken breast, cut in strips
12 shrimp 16/20
2 packets Goya Sazón
Olive oil
1 cup strip cut onions
1 cup strip cut green peppers
1 bunch, green onions
2 cups cooked rice

Season the beef, chicken, and shrimp with Goya Sazón and oil. Season the onions, green peppers, and green onions in the same manner.

Cook the meat on a charcoal grill. Cook the onions and peppers on the grill. Grill the green onions whole.

Mix all ingredients except the rice together. Serve the mixture over the cooked rice.

Nutrition Facts

Serving Size 427 g

Amount Per Serving

Calories 718 — Calories from Fat 137

% Daily Value*

Total Fat 15.2g — 23%
  Saturated Fat 4.4g — 22%
  Trans Fat 0.0g
Cholesterol 299mg — 100%
Sodium 363mg — 15%
Total Carbohydrates 52.0g — 17%
  Dietary Fiber 2.5g — 10%
  Sugars 2.4g
Protein 88.0g

Vitamin A 11% • Vitamin C 46%
Calcium 13% • Iron 37%

Nutrition Grade A-
* Based on a 2000 calorie diet

Yield: 4 servings
Uvin Figueroa

Chicken

Rotisserie Style Chicken

12 chicken quarters (leg or breast)
2 tbsp McCormick's Rotisserie Seasoning
2 tbsp Worcestershire sauce
2 tbsp brown sugar
⅓ cup chopped parsley
2 tbsp water

Mix all the ingredients except the chicken together to make a marinade. Rub and coat the chicken with the sauce. Marinate for 24 hours. Cook the chicken in a 350° F oven for about 45 minutes, or until the internal temperature of the chicken reaches 165° F.

Yield: 12 servings
John McCrea

Nutrition Facts
Serving Size 240 g
Amount Per Serving
Calories 354 — Calories from Fat 62
% Daily Value*
Total Fat 6.9g — 11%
Saturated Fat 1.9g — 10%
Trans Fat 0.0g
Cholesterol 175mg — 58%
Sodium 925mg — 39%
Total Carbohydrates 2.9g — 1%
Sugars 2.8g
Protein 65.8g
Vitamin A 3% • Vitamin C 3%
Calcium 3% • Iron 12%
Nutrition Grade B-
* Based on a 2000 calorie diet

Tortellini With Chicken, Basil, and Tomato

1 (2 pound) bag of tortellini
1 pound chicken breast, sliced
1 to 2 tablespoons olive oil
¼ cup finely diced red onions
½ teaspoon chopped garlic
2 cups diced tomatoes
½ cup white wine
Basil pesto
¼ cup Parmesan cheese
2 tablespoons chopped parsley
Salt and freshly ground black pepper

Cook the tortellini according to directions. In a warm sauté pan, brown off the chicken in olive oil. When brown, add the onions and garlic. Cook for about 2 minutes. Add the tomatoes and white wine. Season with basil pesto. Once mixture starts to boil, add the cooked tortellini. Decrease the heat. Add the Parmesan and parsley. Season with salt and pepper.

Yield: 8 servings
Nataliya Palash

Nutrition Facts
Serving Size 231 g
Amount Per Serving
Calories 456 — Calories from Fat 107
% Daily Value*
Total Fat 11.9g — 18%
Saturated Fat 3.5g — 17%
Trans Fat 0.0g
Cholesterol 91mg — 30%
Sodium 566mg — 24%
Potassium 258mg — 7%
Total Carbohydrates 48.5g — 16%
Dietary Fiber 4.6g — 18%
Sugars 4.2g
Protein 35.7g
Vitamin A 8% • Vitamin C 12%
Calcium 19% • Iron 23%
Nutrition Grade C+
* Based on a 2000 calorie diet

 Brock's Best

Notes

Desserts And Sweets

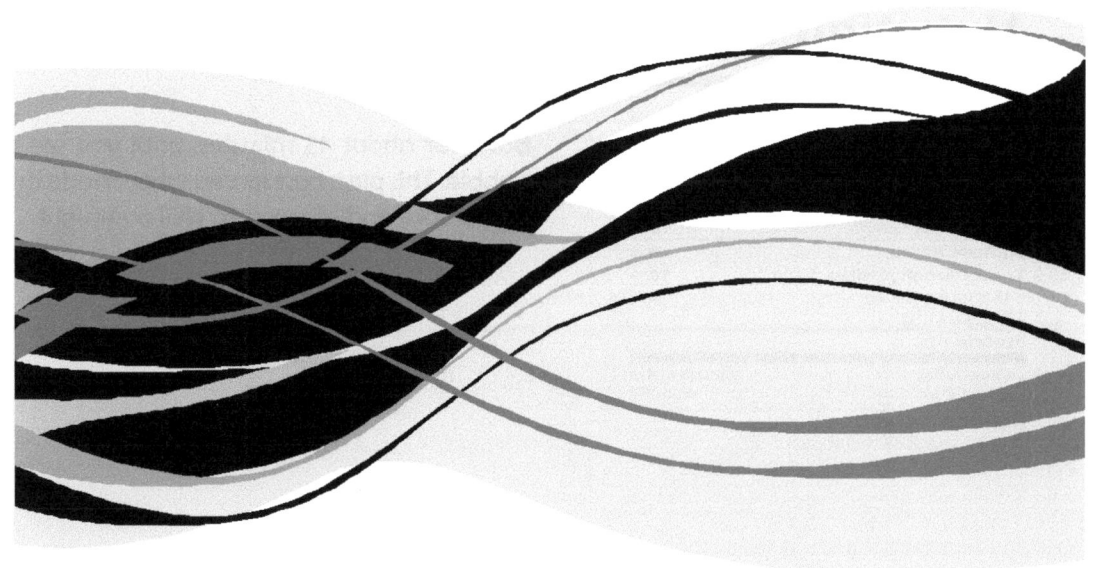

Brock's Best

Brock's Best

Apple Cream Pie

4 cups peeled and sliced apples
½ teaspoon cinnamon
½ teaspoon sugar
⅓ cup (3 ounce package) soft cream cheese
2 eggs
⅔ cup sugar
1 (9-inch) pie crust
2 teaspoons vanilla
½ cup brown sugar
¼ cup flour
¼ cup chopped pecans

Preheat your oven to 350° F. Sprinkle the apples with the cinnamon and sugar and set aside.

Make a cream cheese filling by combining the cream cheese, eggs, sugar, and vanilla and set this aside as well.

Finally prepare the pecans by mixing them with brown sugar and flour, to make a crumbly mixture.

First, add apples to pie crust, then pour the cream cheese filling over the apples. Top with the pecan crumbs.

Bake for about 45 minutes, until you see it bubble. This pie is best served when made the day before and allowed to chill overnight.

Yield: 8 servings
Laura Walther

Nutrition Facts

Serving Size 137 g

Amount Per Serving

Calories 350	Calories from Fat 124
	% Daily Value*
Total Fat 13.8g	21%
Saturated Fat 4.2g	21%
Trans Fat 0.0g	
Cholesterol 53mg	18%
Sodium 200mg	8%
Total Carbohydrates 54.5g	18%
Dietary Fiber 2.2g	9%
Sugars 41.8g	
Protein 4.0g	

Vitamin A 9%	•	Vitamin C 4%
Calcium 4%	•	Iron 7%

Nutrition Grade D

* Based on a 2000 calorie diet

Desserts & Sweets

Apple Crumb Cake

Yield: 12 servings
Maia Maclin

1 box yellow cake mix
1 teaspoons cinnamon, plus 1 teaspoon more to use with the baked crumbs
1 teaspoon clove
3 tablespoons vanilla extract
1 cup brown sugar
1 ½ teaspoons butter, softened plus 1 cup melted more for the crumb layer
6 large apples, sliced paper thin
¾ cup flour
¾ cup sugar

Preheat your oven to 350° F. Follow the directions on the cake box to make the batter and set aside. Mix the cinnamon, clove, vanilla, brown sugar, and softened butter together in a bowl. Toss the apples in this spiced-sugar mixture.

Spray a deep-dish cake pan and layer the batter, then the apples, then batter, and one last layer of apples. Bake as box directions instruct. When done, cool the cake completely.

To make the crumb mixture, mix the flour, sugar, and melted butter. Roll the dough onto a sheet pan in a ½ inch thickness, and bake approximately for 15 minutes until firm. After baking, allow to cool to room temperature and then crumble completely. Mix an additional 1 teaspoon of cinnamon in with the crumbs, and then top the cake with them and serve.

Nutrition Facts

Serving Size 211 g

Amount Per Serving

Calories 519	Calories from Fat 189
	% Daily Value*
Total Fat 21.0g	32%
Saturated Fat 10.8g	54%
Trans Fat 0.0g	
Cholesterol 43mg	14%
Sodium 405mg	17%
Total Carbohydrates 80.7g	27%
Dietary Fiber 3.6g	15%
Sugars 55.2g	
Protein 2.9g	
Vitamin A 11%	Vitamin C 9%
Calcium 9%	Iron 7%

Nutrition Grade D-
* Based on a 2000 calorie diet

Brock's Best

Apple Fritters

Yield: 48 servings-food service version
(8 servings-home version)
Michael Hamilton

6 eggs (1 egg), separated
2 cups (⅓ cup) milk
3 ⅔ cups (⅔ cup) flour
1 tablespoon (½ teaspoon) baking powder
1 teaspoon (1 pinch) salt
2 ounces (2 teaspoons) sugar
½ teaspoon (1 pinch) cinnamon
3 cups (½ cup) peeled, cored and diced apples
Confectioner's (powdered) sugar, for dusting
Oil for frying

Combine the egg yolks and milk in a large mixing bowl and set aside. Sift the flour, baking powder, salt, sugar, and cinnamon in a bowl. Add the dry ingredients to the milk and egg mixture and mix or beat until smooth. Allow to rest for 1 hour.

Stir the apples into the batter. Whip the egg whites and add to the mixture before frying. Scoop the fritters into 350° F oil using the swimming method.* Cook until brown.

Sift powdered sugar on top and serve promptly.

Nutrition Facts

Serving Size 39 g

Amount Per Serving

Calories 57	Calories from Fat 7
	% Daily Value*
Total Fat 0.8g	1%
Trans Fat 0.0g	
Cholesterol 20mg	7%
Sodium 58mg	2%
Total Carbohydrates 10.6g	4%
Dietary Fiber 0.6g	2%
Sugars 3.1g	
Protein 1.9g	

| Vitamin A 1% | • | Vitamin C 1% |
| Calcium 2% | • | Iron 3% |

Nutrition Grade A-
* Based on a 2000 calorie diet

*SWIMMING METHOD FOR FRYING—In the swimming method, the food is gently dropped into hot oil using tongs. Then it falls to the bottom of the fryer. As it cooks, it "swims" back to the surface. It may be necessary to turn it once it reaches the surface to allow it to brown evenly. Remove with skimmer.

Desserts & Sweets

Apple Oat Bars

1 cup whole wheat flour
½ teaspoon baking soda
½ teaspoon salt
1 teaspoon cinnamon
½ cup brown sugar
½ cup rolled oats
½ cup butter, melted
1 egg, beaten
1 ½ teaspoon vanilla
⅓ cup chopped walnuts
2 cups apples, thinly sliced
Confectioner's (powdered) sugar

Preheat your oven to 375° F. Mix the flour, baking soda, salt, and cinnamon until well combined. Add the brown sugar and oats. Add the butter, egg, and vanilla, and mix well.

Place one-half of the mixture in the bottom of a greased square 9-inch pan. Sprinkle walnuts on top of this batter. Arrange the apple slices on the walnuts. Add the remaining batter over the apple slices.

Bake for 25 to 30 minutes. Cool before removing from the pan. Sprinkle confectioner's sugar over the top after cutting into serving-sized pieces.

Nutrition Facts

Serving Size 42 g

Amount Per Serving

Calories 137 — Calories from Fat 70

	% Daily Value*
Total Fat 7.8g	12%
Saturated Fat 3.9g	19%
Trans Fat 0.0g	
Cholesterol 25mg	8%
Sodium 158mg	7%
Total Carbohydrates 14.9g	5%
Dietary Fiber 1.1g	4%
Sugars 6.0g	
Protein 2.2g	

Vitamin A 4% • Vitamin C 1%
Calcium 1% • Iron 4%

Nutrition Grade D
* Based on a 2000 calorie diet

Yield: 12 to 20 servings depending on cut size
Larry Stelitano

Brock's Best

Apple Pie Bars Home Version

Yield: 24 servings
Ted Fekete

Apples
6 Granny Smith or Golden Delicious apples
¼ cup packed brown sugars
1 tablespoon honey
Freshly squeezed lemon juice

Crust
1 cup (2 sticks) unsalted butter
½ cup brown sugar
1 egg
2 ¼ cup flour
½ teaspoon baking powder
¼ teaspoon salt

Streusel Topping
1 cup flour
¼ cup granulated sugar
¼ cup brown sugar
¼ teaspoon cinnamon
¼ teaspoon salt
8 tablespoons (1 stick) unsalted butter
½ cup chopped toasted pecans

Apples
Peel, core, and slice the apples ¼ inches thick. Sauté them in the brown sugar, honey, and lemon juice. Cook until all the liquid in the pan has evaporated. Let the mixture cool.

Crust
Preheat your oven to 325° F. Cream the butter and sugar. Add the egg and blend, then add the remaining dry ingredients. Mix for 1 minute and scrape down the bowl. Mix for 1 minute more. Press the dough into a sheet pan coated with cooking spray. Bake for 15 minutes until lightly spongy.

Streusel Topping
Combine the flour, granulated and brown sugars, cinnamon, and salt. Mix briefly on slow speed. Add the butter and mix on medium speed until the mixture is crumbly and barely holds together when squeezed gently. Stir in the pecans with a large rubber spatula. Set aside.

Baking the Bar
When the crust (recipe above) is done, immediately spread the cooked apples (recipe above) evenly over it while it is still hot. Sprinkle the streusel topping (recipe above) over the apples, gently pressing to adhere. Reduce the oven temperature to 300° F and bake for 15 to 20 minutes, until the topping is lightly browned and crisp.

Nutrition Facts
Serving Size 90 g

Amount Per Serving	
Calories 239	Calories from Fat 121
	% Daily Value*
Total Fat 13.4g	21%
Saturated Fat 7.5g	38%
Trans Fat 0.0g	
Cholesterol 37mg	12%
Sodium 133mg	6%
Total Carbohydrates 28.3g	9%
Dietary Fiber 1.8g	7%
Sugars 13.5g	
Protein 2.3g	

Vitamin A 8%	•	Vitamin C 4%
Calcium 2%	•	Iron 5%

Nutrition Grade C
* Based on a 2000 calorie diet

Desserts & Sweets

Apple Strudel

3 cups all-purpose flour
½ teaspoon salt
½ cup softened butter
1 egg
⅔ cup lukewarm water
2 tablespoons butter, melted
⅔ cup granulated sugar
2 teaspoons cinnamon
6 cups peeled and sliced Granny Smith apples
½ cup raisins
1 egg white, beaten to a stiff
Confectioner's (powdered) sugar

Stir the flour and salt together, and then mix in the butter until crumbly. Mix the egg and water, and add to the flour mixture. Knead the dough for 4 minutes and cut in half. Let the dough rest for 1 hour.

Preheat your oven to 350° F. Sprinkle a countertop with flour (or cover a large table with a plastic covered tablecloth) and sprinkle with flour. Roll half of the dough into a 20-inch square. Brush with 2 tablespoons of melted butter.

Starting from the middle of the dough, work underneath it using the back of your hands and stretch or pull one corner until the dough is paper-thin. Do this for the other 3 corners as well. Brush with more melted butter. Cut this now very large square into four equal squares and stack them on top of each other. Repeat the process with the other half of the dough, giving you 2 stacks of 4 sheets.

Mix the sugar and cinnamon. Spread half of the apples filling evenly over one of the stacks of dough leaving ½ an inch clean on the border on all sides. Sprinkle over the apples with half the sugar/cinnamon mixture and the raisins. Roll the dough to make a log. Tuck the ends under the pastry. Repeat with the other stack of dough.

Place on a lightly greased baking pan. Brush the top with the egg whites. Bake the strudel at 350° F for about 45 minutes. Cool the strudel to room temperature and sprinkle with powdered sugar. Note: a good substitute for making the dough is phyllo dough.

Nutrition Facts

Serving Size 104 g

Amount Per Serving

Calories 252 — Calories from Fat 79

% Daily Value*

Total Fat 8.8g — 14%
Saturated Fat 5.3g — 27%
Trans Fat 0.0g
Cholesterol 33mg — 11%
Sodium 150mg — 6%
Total Carbohydrates 40.8g — 14%
Dietary Fiber 2.2g — 9%
Sugars 17.6g
Protein 3.7g

Vitamin A 6% • Vitamin C 4%
Calcium 2% • Iron 8%

Nutrition Grade C+
* Based on a 2000 calorie diet

Yield: 14 servings
Peter Gruenfelder

Brock's Best

Banana Granola Cookies

½ cup butter
1 cup brown sugar
1 egg
½ teaspoon vanilla
1 cup mashed banana
1 ½ cup flour
1 teaspoon cinnamon
1 ½ teaspoon baking soda
1 ½ teaspoon salt
1 cup granola

Preheat your oven to 375° F. Grease two cookie sheets. Cream the butter and sugar. Add the egg, vanilla, bananas, and blend. Next, mix in the flour, cinnamon, baking soda, and salt. Stir in granola.

Drop the batter by teaspoons onto a greased cookie sheet. Bake for 12 minutes until done.

Yield: 10 servings
Larry Stelitano

Nutrition Facts

Serving Size 90 g

Amount Per Serving	
Calories 254	Calories from Fat 142
	% Daily Value*
Total Fat 15.8g	**24%**
Saturated Fat 7.0g	**35%**
Trans Fat 0.0g	
Cholesterol 41mg	**14%**
Sodium 620mg	**26%**
Total Carbohydrates 45.2g	**15%**
Dietary Fiber 3.2g	**13%**
Sugars 20.9g	
Protein 6.4g	

Vitamin A 6%	•	Vitamin C 4%
Calcium 4%	•	Iron 13%

Nutrition Grade D-
* Based on a 2000 calorie diet

Desserts & Sweets

Bavarian Apple Torte

½ cup butter, at room temperature
⅓ cup sugar
¼ teaspoon vanilla or almond flavoring
1 cup flour
1 cup (8 ounces) cream cheese, softened
¼ cup sugar
1 egg
½ teaspoon vanilla or almond flavoring
⅓ cup sugar
½ teaspoon cinnamon
4 cups peeled and thinly sliced apples
¼ cup chopped walnuts or almonds
Caramel sauce (optional)

Preheat your oven to 450° F. Cream the butter, sugar, and vanilla. Blend in the flour by hand. Spread the dough onto the bottom and sides of a torte or springform pan.

Combine the softened cream cheese and sugar. Mix well. Add the egg and vanilla or almond flavoring. Mix well with a hand mixer. Pour into the pastry-lined pan.

Combine the sugar and cinnamon. Toss the apples in sugar and cinnamon. Arrange the slices around the top of the cream cheese filling. Sprinkle with nuts.

Bake for 10 minutes. Decrease the heat to 400° F. Bake for 30 minutes more. Cool to room temperature. Chill for 3 hours. Drizzle caramel sauce over the torte and serve.

Yield: 8 servings
Larraine Santa

Nutrition Facts

Serving Size 145 g

Amount Per Serving

Calories 408	Calories from Fat 218
	% Daily Value*
Total Fat 24.2g	37%
Saturated Fat 8.4g	42%
Trans Fat 0.0g	
Cholesterol 52mg	17%
Sodium 226mg	9%
Total Carbohydrates 43.8g	15%
Dietary Fiber 2.1g	8%
Sugars 28.8g	
Protein 5.5g	

Vitamin A 19%	•	Vitamin C 4%
Calcium 4%	•	Iron 8%

Nutrition Grade D-
* Based on a 2000 calorie diet

Brock's Best

Cedar Planked Apples With Walnut Praline Stuffing

¾ cup firmly packed light brown sugar
¼ cup flour
¼ cup oats
½ teaspoon cinnamon
¼ teaspoon salt
¼ teaspoon ginger
¼ teaspoon nutmeg
3 tablespoons butter, cubed, with 3 more tablespoons, for topping
½ cup chopped walnuts
3 apples, unpeeled

Light the grill or smoker and stabilize the temperature to 300° F.

In a bowl, stir the brown sugar, flour, oats, cinnamon, salt, ginger, and nutmeg until blended.

With a fork or pastry cutter, cut 3 tablespoons of the butter into the flour mixture. Also fold the chopped walnuts into the mixture.

Core the apples. Divide the filling between them, and place them on a cedar plank. Top with the remaining butter and place on the grill. Cook for about 10 minutes, until the apples are softened and the tops are golden brown.

Yield: 6 servings
Molly Hamlin

Nutrition Facts

Serving Size 286 g

Amount Per Serving

Calories 631 — Calories from Fat 324

	% Daily Value*
Total Fat 36.0g	55%
Saturated Fat 15.4g	77%
Trans Fat 0.0g	
Cholesterol 61mg	20%
Sodium 371mg	15%
Total Carbohydrates 75.9g	25%
Dietary Fiber 7.0g	28%
Sugars 54.5g	
Protein 7.3g	

Vitamin A 16%	•	Vitamin C 15%
Calcium 7%	•	Iron 11%

Nutrition Grade C
* Based on a 2000 calorie diet

Desserts & Sweets

Cheesecake Supreme

Yield: 12 servings
Renee Bloch

Crust
1 cup flour
¼ cup sugar
1 teaspoon grated lemon peel
½ cup butter or margarine
1 egg yolk, slightly beaten
¼ teaspoon vanilla

Filling
5 cups (40 ounces—5 packages), cream cheese
¼ teaspoon vanilla
Lemon peel
¾ cup sugar
3 teaspoons flour
¼ teaspoon salt
1 cup eggs (4 to 5 eggs)
2 egg yolks
¼ cup whipping cream

Crust
Preheat your oven to 400° F. Combine the flour, sugar, and grated lemon peel. Cut in the butter until the mixture is crumbly. Add the egg yolk and vanilla. Blend thoroughly. Pat one-third of the dough on the bottom of a 9-inch springform pan (with its sides removed). Bake in the oven for about 8 minutes, or until golden. Cool. Attach the sides to the cooked bottom, butter, and pat the remaining dough on sides. Don't cook again just yet.

Filling
Let the cream cheese stand at room temperature to soften (1 to 1 ½ hours). Beat cream cheese, and then add vanilla, and lemon peel. Mix sugar, flour, and salt, in a bowl and then gradually blend the mixture into the cheese. Add eggs and egg yolks one at a time, beating after each just to blend. Gently stir in the whipping cream.

Baking
Add filling to crust (recipes above). Increase oven temperature to 450° F and bake for 12 minutes, then decrease heat to 300° F, and continue baking for 55 minutes. Remove from the oven and let cool. Loosen the sides with spatula after ½ hour, then loosen again at the end of 1 hour. Allow to cool 2 hours longer, and serve.

Nutrition Facts

Serving Size 160 g

Amount Per Serving

Calories 551 — Calories from Fat 402

	% Daily Value*
Total Fat 44.6g	**69%**
Saturated Fat 27.2g	**136%**
Cholesterol 255mg	**85%**
Sodium 416mg	**17%**
Total Carbohydrates 28.1g	**9%**
Sugars 17.1g	
Protein 11.6g	

| Vitamin A 34% | • | Vitamin C 1% |
| Calcium 10% | • | Iron 12% |

Nutrition Grade D-
* Based on a 2000 calorie diet

Brock's Best
Cherry or Cranberry Pie

4 eggs
1 cup sugar
½ cup (1 stick) butter, softened
1 cup flour
½ teaspoon baking powder
½ teaspoon vinegar
1 ¼ cup cherries or cranberries
½ cup walnuts
1 tablespoon confectioner's (powdered) sugar

Preheat your oven to 325° F. Add the eggs to the sugar and mix well. Add butter to the sugar mixture and mix well again. Add the flour and baking soda. Mix. Spritz the vinegar on the top of the dough. Put the walnuts and berries in an oiled pie pan and top with the dough mixture. Bake for 50 minutes. Cool and top with powdered sugar.

Yield: 8 servings
Gennadiy Shats

Nutrition Facts
Serving Size 102 g

Amount Per Serving	
Calories 352	Calories from Fat 167
	% Daily Value*
Total Fat 18.5g	28%
Saturated Fat 8.2g	41%
Trans Fat 0.0g	
Cholesterol 112mg	37%
Sodium 113mg	5%
Total Carbohydrates 42.1g	14%
Dietary Fiber 1.3g	5%
Sugars 29.0g	
Protein 6.6g	
Vitamin A 10%	Vitamin C 2%
Calcium 4%	Iron 8%

Nutrition Grade C
* Based on a 2000 calorie diet

Cherry-O Cream Cheese Pie

1 (8 ounce) package cream cheese
1 (15 ounce) can sweetened condensed milk
⅓ cup freshly squeezed lemon juice
1 teaspoon vanilla extract
1 (9-inch) graham cracker crumb crust
1 (21 ounce) can cherry pie filling

Soften the cream cheese to room temperature, then whip until fluffy. Gradually add the condensed milk while continuing to beat until well blended. Add the lemon juice and vanilla. Blend well. Pour into the crust and refrigerate for 2 to 3 hours before garnishing with the cherry pie filling.

Yield: 8 servings
Debbie O'Donovan

Nutrition Facts
Serving Size 167 g

Amount Per Serving	
Calories 359	Calories from Fat 132
	% Daily Value*
Total Fat 14.6g	23%
Saturated Fat 9.2g	46%
Cholesterol 49mg	16%
Sodium 167mg	7%
Potassium 322mg	9%
Total Carbohydrates 50.8g	17%
Sugars 29.3g	
Protein 6.7g	
Vitamin A 14%	Vitamin C 15%
Calcium 18%	Iron 3%

Nutrition Grade D
* Based on a 2000 calorie diet

Desserts & Sweets

Desserts & Sweets

Chocolate Chip Cheeseball

1 (8 ounce) package cream cheese
½ cup butter, softened
¼ teaspoon vanilla extract
¾ cup confectioner's (powdered) sugar
2 tablespoons brown sugar
¾ cup miniature semi-sweet chocolate chips
¾ cup finely chopped pecans or pretzels

In a mixing bowl, beat the cream cheese, butter, and vanilla until fluffy. Gradually add the sugars. Beat just until combined. Stir in the chocolate chips. Cover and refrigerate for 2 hours. Shape into a ball. Refrigerate for 1 hour more. Roll the cheese ball in pecans or pretzels. Serve with vanilla wafers, graham crackers, or any other type of sweet treat.

Yield: 12 servings
Larry Stelitano

Nutrition Facts
Serving Size 63 g
Amount Per Serving
Calories 299 — Calories from Fat 183
% Daily Value*
Total Fat 20.3g — 31%
Saturated Fat 9.8g — 49%
Trans Fat 0.0g
Cholesterol 41mg — 14%
Sodium 127mg — 5%
Total Carbohydrates 26.9g — 9%
Dietary Fiber 3.8g — 15%
Sugars 24.7g
Protein 2.3g
Vitamin A 10% • Vitamin C 0%
Calcium 2% • Iron 3%
Nutrition Grade F
* Based on a 2000 calorie diet

Coconut Mango Rice Pudding

2 cups short grain rice (sushi rice or Arborio)
5 cups water
1 vanilla bean, split
1 cup sugar
3 cans coconut milk
3 diced mangoes
Mint sprig, for garnish

Combine the rice, water, sugar, and vanilla bean in a pot. Cover and bring to a boil. Reduce heat and simmer covered until almost all the water is absorbed. Remove from heat and pour in the coconut milk. Allow to cool, stirring occasionally to incorporate the coconut milk. Refrigerate.

To serve, scoop chilled pudding (it can be heated slightly if desired) into a serving dish. Top with mango and garnish with a sprig of fresh mint.

Yield: 8 servings
Jen Foy

Nutrition Facts
Serving Size 382 g
Amount Per Serving
Calories 504 — Calories from Fat 196
% Daily Value*
Total Fat 21.8g — 34%
Saturated Fat 19.1g — 95%
Cholesterol 0mg — 0%
Sodium 19mg — 1%
Total Carbohydrates 76.1g — 25%
Dietary Fiber 3.5g — 14%
Sugars 39.6g
Protein 5.5g
Vitamin A 12% • Vitamin C 40%
Calcium 3% • Iron 9%
Nutrition Grade C
* Based on a 2000 calorie diet

Brock's Best

Brock's Best

Cream Cheese Flan

Yield: 16 servings
Jose Belteton

1 teaspoon sugar
3 tablespoons water
4 eggs
18 ounces cream cheese
1 teaspoon vanilla
1 can evaporated milk
1 can sweetened condensed milk

Preheat your oven to 400° F. On the stovetop, heat the sugar and water to caramelize. Pour the caramelized mixture into an 8 by 8-inch baking dish or mold, covering the bottom and sides. Once the mold is covered, remove from heat and allow to cool and harden.

Place the remaining ingredients in a mixer and incorporate thoroughly. Pour the mixture into the caramel-lined mold.

Place the mold or baking dish in a larger pan. Fill the larger pan halfway up the side of the mold. Place this double pan in your preheated oven.

Bake for 30 to 35 minutes. Check doneness with a toothpick, which should come out clean when the flan is ready. Remove the dishes from the oven. Allow to cool completely and then refrigerate for 2 hours. Cut 2 by 2-inch squares giving 16 portions.

Nutrition Facts

Serving Size 90 g

Amount Per Serving	
Calories 236	Calories from Fat 144
	% Daily Value*
Total Fat 16.0g	25%
Saturated Fat 9.7g	49%
Cholesterol 91mg	30%
Sodium 164mg	7%
Total Carbohydrates 16.4g	5%
Sugars 15.7g	
Protein 7.2g	

Vitamin A 12%	•	Vitamin C 2%
Calcium 16%	•	Iron 4%

Nutrition Grade D+
* Based on a 2000 calorie diet

Desserts & Sweets

Dirt

1 (8 ounce) box cream cheese
1 (1 pound, 2 ounce) bag Oreo cookies
1 (3.4 ounce) box chocolate or vanilla pudding
2 (8 ounce) containers Cool Whip
Gummy worms (optional)

Let the cream cheese sit out, until it reaches room temperature. Blend cookies in a blender, until they are in small crumbs.

Mix together cream cheese, cookies, pudding, and Cool Whip, into one bowl. When combined, let sit in the refrigerator for 2 to 4 hours before serving.

Serve and enjoy! For kids' dessert, also add gummy worms.

Yield: 12 servings
Britney Thompson

Nutrition Facts
Serving Size 71 g

Amount Per Serving	
Calories 244	Calories from Fat 155
	% Daily Value*
Total Fat 17.2g	27%
Saturated Fat 12.6g	63%
Trans Fat 0.2g	
Cholesterol 21mg	7%
Sodium 223mg	9%
Total Carbohydrates 20.9g	7%
Sugars 17.1g	
Protein 2.4g	
Vitamin A 6%	Vitamin C 0%
Calcium 2%	Iron 3%
Nutrition Grade D	

* Based on a 2000 calorie diet

Brock's Best

Donut Bread Pudding With Chocolate

Yield: 6 servings
Rosanne DiGiovanni

4 stale glazed donuts
1 cup semi-sweet chocolate chips
2 eggs, room temperature
2 cups whole milk
3 tablespoons white sugar
1 teaspoon vanilla extract
¼ teaspoon almond extract
1 teaspoon ground cinnamon
¼ teaspoon ground nutmeg
1 teaspoon orange zest
Vanilla ice cream (optional)
Whipped cream (optional)

Preheat your oven to 350° F. Lightly grease a small glass baking dish. Tear the donuts into bite-sized pieces. Combine donut pieces and chocolate chips in the dish.

In a bowl, mix the eggs, milk, sugar, vanilla extract, and almond extract. Also mix in the cinnamon, nutmeg, and orange zest. Pour the mixture over the donuts in the dish, and press down lightly to help absorption. Let stand for 15 minutes, or cover and refrigerate overnight.

Place the baking dish inside a larger baking dish, and fill the outer dish with enough water to go about halfway up the sides.

Bake for 35 to 40 minutes, until a knife inserted near the center comes out clean. Serve warm with fresh whipped cream or vanilla ice cream.

Nutrition Facts

Serving Size 212 g

Amount Per Serving

Calories 461	Calories from Fat 212
	% Daily Value*
Total Fat 23.6g	36%
Saturated Fat 9.1g	45%
Trans Fat 0.0g	
Cholesterol 63mg	21%
Sodium 409mg	17%
Total Carbohydrates 55.6g	19%
Dietary Fiber 2.2g	9%
Sugars 34.3g	
Protein 8.0g	

Vitamin A 4%	•	Vitamin C 1%
Calcium 11%	•	Iron 11%

Nutrition Grade D-
* Based on a 2000 calorie diet

Desserts & Sweets

Fresh Berry Trifle

16 slices of lemon pound cake
2 ounces simple syrup
2 tablespoons Grand Marnier
2 cups (1 pint) blueberries
2 cups (1 pint) blackberries
2 cups (1 pint) sliced strawberries
3 cups whipped cream
4 mint sprigs, for garnish
4 rolled chocolate cookie sticks, for garnish

Place 1 slice of pound cake on each of four, 6-inch plates. Drizzle with simple syrup and Grand Marnier. Top with berries and whipped cream.

Repeat three more times, finishing with a drizzle of simple syrup and Grand Marnier. Garnish with mint and cookie stick.

Nutrition Facts
Serving Size 778 g

Amount Per Serving
Calories 2,068 — Calories from Fat 948

	% Daily Value*
Total Fat 105.3g	**162%**
Saturated Fat 37.5g	**187%**
Trans Fat 0.0g	
Cholesterol 454mg	**151%**
Sodium 2361mg	**98%**
Total Carbohydrates 259.0g	**86%**
Dietary Fiber 17.6g	**70%**
Sugars 146.6g	
Protein 24.6g	

Vitamin A 23% • Vitamin C 141%
Calcium 10% • Iron 16%

Nutrition Grade D+
* Based on a 2000 calorie diet

Yield: 4 servings
Gilbert Burns

Brock's Best

Gluten Free Banana-Oatmeal Chocolate Chip Cookies

1 ripe banana, mashed
½ cup packed brown sugars
¼ cup butter, softened
¼ cup sugar
1 teaspoon vanilla extract
1 egg
1 ¼ cup gluten free flour
2 cups old fashioned oats
1 teaspoon baking soda
1 tablespoon ground cinnamon
¾ cup chocolate chips
½ cup sliced almonds

Preheat your oven to 350° F. Combine banana, brown sugar, butter, sugar, and vanilla in a large bowl. Beat with a mixer until smooth. Next, add the egg and beat well.

Combine the flour, oats, baking soda, and cinnamon in another bowl. Stir well. Add the flour mixture to the banana mixture. Beat on medium speed with the mixer until well-blended. Stir in the chocolate chips and almonds.

Drop the batter onto cookie sheets by heaping spoonfuls. Bake for 12 to 15 minutes, until golden. Cool on pans for two minutes, then remove cookies and cool them on a wire rack.

Yield: 2 dozen cookies
Cary Callahan

Nutrition Facts

Serving Size 105 g

Amount Per Serving

Calories 161	Calories from Fat 50
	% Daily Value*
Total Fat 5.5g	8%
Saturated Fat 2.6g	13%
Trans Fat 0.0g	
Cholesterol 13mg	4%
Sodium 76mg	3%
Total Carbohydrates 24.4g	8%
Dietary Fiber 2.0g	8%
Sugars 9.0g	
Protein 3.2g	
Vitamin A 2%	Vitamin C 1%
Calcium 4%	Iron 6%

Nutrition Grade C-
* Based on a 2000 calorie diet

Did you know that oatmeal helps you to produce serotonin, a calming hormone that helps fight anxiety's negative effect? Oatmeal is high in fiber, which mean that your body will absorb it slowly. In one fell swoop, you'll prolong the serotonin boost.

Desserts & Sweets

Jell-O Pie

1 package Jell-O
2 ice cubes
1 cup whipped cream
1 ready-made pie crust, baked

Prepare the Jell-O according to the package directions. Place the ice in the Jell-O to cool it down. Mix the whipped cream and Jell-O in a mixer. Pour into the pre-baked pie shell. Refrigerate for 4 hours or until firm.

Yield: 8 servings
Brandon Heard

Lemon Basil Smoothie

2 cups lemon sorbet or sherbet
1 cup fat free milk
6 ounces vanilla yogurt—about 3/4 cup
1 teaspoon grated lemon zest
1/3 cup freshly squeezed lemon juice
2 tablespoons chopped fresh basil
1 cup ice cubes
Lemon curls, for garnish

In a blender, combine until smooth, the sorbet/sherbet, milk, yogurt, lemon zest, lemon juice, basil, and ice. Scrape the sides once during blending. Pour into three glasses, and garnish with the lemon curl and basil. Serve immediately.

Yield: 3 servings
Celeste Durr/Sharon Houck

 Brock's Best

Mexican Flan

1 ½ cup sugar
4 eggs
1 (14 ounce) can sweetened condensed milk
1 teaspoon vanilla or rum extract

Yield: 5 servings
Daniel Urias

Nutrition Facts

Serving Size 135 g

Amount Per Serving

Calories 383 — Calories from Fat 94

% Daily Value*

Total Fat 10.4g — 16%
Saturated Fat 5.4g — 27%
Cholesterol 158mg — 53%
Sodium 150mg — 6%
Total Carbohydrates 63.6g — 21%
Sugars 63.6g
Protein 10.7g

Vitamin A 8% • Vitamin C 3%
Calcium 24% • Iron 4%

Nutrition Grade C-
* Based on a 2000 calorie diet

Preheat your oven to 350° F. Caramelize the sugar by pouring it into a heavy saucepan and stirring continuously with a wooden spoon over a low flame until sugar melts and turns golden brown.

Pour the sugar immediately into a 1-quart baking dish, coating the bottom and sides evenly (this can be accomplished by holding the baking dish in your hands and carefully tilting to coat the sides). Be careful while pouring hot sugar, as it can cause severe burns! Allow the sugar to cool.

Prepare the custard by beating the eggs, then adding the milk and vanilla. Mix well. Next pour the mixture into the caramel-lined baking dish. Set this dish into a larger pan containing 1 inch of hot water.

Bake for 1 to 1 ½ hours, until a knife inserted in the center comes out clean. It should be golden brown on top.

Loosen around the sides with a spatula and turn upside-down onto a serving dish. The caramel should have formed a syrupy layer on top. Refrigerate for 4 hours and serve.

Desserts & Sweets

Mini Peanut Butter Cup Cheese Cakes

Preheat oven to 350° F.

Crust
2 tablespoons margarine or butter, melted
2 tablespoons sugar
¾ cup graham cracker crumbs

Cheesecake
8 ounce package cream cheese, softened
½ cup sugar
2 tablespoons cup flour
1 egg
½ teaspoon vanilla
1 bags miniature peanut butter cups

Crust
With a fork, combine the melted butter or margarine, the sugar, and the graham cracker crumbs.

With enough to cover bottom of the cups, press the sugar-buttered crumbs into paper-lined miniature muffin tins.

Cheesecake
Cream together the cream cheese, sugar, flour, egg, and vanilla.

Over top of the crumb crust mixture (recipe above), place one peanut butter cup in each muffin cup. Drop 1 teaspoon of the cream cheese batter on top of the peanut butter cups. Bake for 12 minutes.

Yield: 2 ½ dozen
Colleen Grimplin

Nutrition Facts
Serving Size 26 g

Amount Per Serving	
Calories 113	Calories from Fat 73
	% Daily Value*
Total Fat 8.1g	12%
Saturated Fat 2.7g	14%
Trans Fat 0.0g	
Cholesterol 14mg	5%
Sodium 53mg	2%
Total Carbohydrates 8.2g	3%
Dietary Fiber 0.7g	3%
Sugars 5.4g	
Protein 3.1g	
Vitamin A 3% • Vitamin C 0%	
Calcium 1% • Iron 2%	

Nutrition Grade D
* Based on a 2000 calorie diet

Brock's Best

Brock's Best
Oatmeal Raisin Spice Cookies

1 cup (2 sticks) butter
1 cup brown sugar
½ cup sugar
2 eggs, beaten
1 ½ teaspoon vanilla
1 ½ cup flour
1 teaspoon baking soda
1 ½ tablespoon cinnamon
¼ teaspoon allspice
3 cups old fashioned oatmeal
1 ½ cup raisins

Preheat your oven to 350° F. Beat the butter and two sugars together. Add the eggs and vanilla until incorporated. Add the flour, baking soda, cinnamon, and allspice. Mix thoroughly. Add the oats and raisins and mix until evenly distributed.

Drop by heaping tablespoons onto an ungreased sheet pan lined with parchment paper.

Bake for 10 to 12 minutes. Cool on pans for two minutes, then remove cookies and cool them on a wire rack.

Yield: 36 cookies
Douglas Vezzosi

Nutrition Facts

Serving Size 35 g

Amount Per Serving

Calories 141	Calories from Fat 54
	% Daily Value*
Total Fat 6.0g	9%
Saturated Fat 3.4g	17%
Trans Fat 0.0g	
Cholesterol 23mg	8%
Sodium 77mg	3%
Total Carbohydrates 20.8g	7%
Dietary Fiber 1.3g	5%
Sugars 10.5g	
Protein 2.0g	

Vitamin A 3%	•	Vitamin C 0%	
Calcium 1%	•	Iron 4%	

Nutrition Grade D-
* Based on a 2000 calorie diet

Desserts & Sweets

Peanut Butter Bars

⅓ cup cool water
2 large eggs
¾ cup creamy peanut butter
3 ½ ounces brown sugar
1 box yellow cake mix
3 Snickers bars, crushed

Preheat a convection oven to 325° F (or 350° F for a conventional oven). Place all ingredients in a mixing bowl. Mix on low speed for 1 minute. Scrape bowl. Mix for an additional 2 minutes.

Spread the batter evenly in a greased sheet pan. Bake for 15 minutes. Turn the sheet pan around and bake for an additional 5 to 15 minutes. Check the bar cake for doneness with a toothpick or knife.

Spread chopped Snickers bars on the top when it first comes out of the oven, and cool completely. When cooled, ice like a brownie with frosting. Cut up and serve.

Yield: 24 servings
Ted Fekete

Nutrition Facts

Serving Size 45 g

Amount Per Serving

Calories 200	Calories from Fat 81
	% Daily Value*
Total Fat 9.1g	14%
Saturated Fat 2.1g	10%
Trans Fat 0.0g	
Cholesterol 17mg	6%
Sodium 219mg	9%
Total Carbohydrates 27.0g	9%
Dietary Fiber 0.9g	4%
Sugars 17.5g	
Protein 4.0g	

| Vitamin A 1% | • | Vitamin C 0% |
| Calcium 4% | • | Iron 7% |

Nutrition Grade B-
* Based on a 2000 calorie diet

Brock's Best

Poppy Seed Cake

Yield: 14 to 16 servings
Dawn Corder

3 cups flour
½ teaspoon salt
1 ½ teaspoon baking soda
2 cups sugar
1 cup cooking oil
4 eggs
1 (12 or 13 ounce) can evaporated milk
1 teaspoon vanilla
1 (10 ounce) jar poppy seeds
1 cup chopped nuts
Confectioner's (powdered) sugar, for sprinkling

Preheat your oven to 350° F. In a large mixing bowl, add the flour, salt, baking soda, sugar, oil, eggs, evaporated milk and vanilla. Mix well. Fold in the poppy seeds and chopped nuts. Bake in a greased Bundt pan for 50 to 60 minutes. Sprinkle with powdered sugar before serving.

Nutrition Facts
Serving Size 132 g

Amount Per Serving	
Calories 510	Calories from Fat 272
	% Daily Value*
Total Fat 30.2g	46%
Saturated Fat 4.2g	21%
Trans Fat 0.0g	
Cholesterol 46mg	15%
Sodium 297mg	12%
Total Carbohydrates 54.1g	18%
Dietary Fiber 3.4g	14%
Sugars 31.2g	
Protein 9.9g	
Vitamin A 1%	Vitamin C 1%
Calcium 32%	Iron 19%

Nutrition Grade C
* Based on a 2000 calorie diet

Pound Cake

3 cups flour
¼ teaspoon baking soda
6 eggs
1 cup butter
3 cups sugar
2 teaspoons vanilla
1 cup sour cream

Preheat your oven to 350° F. Sift the flour with the baking soda into a bowl and set aside. Beat the eggs lightly in a large mixing bowl. Add the flour mix, butter, sugar, vanilla, and sour cream. Mix well. Grease and flour a tube or Bundt pan. Pour in the ingredients and bake for 65 minutes.

Yield: 12 servings
Evelyn Bitner

Nutrition Facts
Serving Size 142 g

Amount Per Serving	
Calories 511	Calories from Fat 197
	% Daily Value*
Total Fat 21.9g	34%
Saturated Fat 13.0g	65%
Cholesterol 131mg	44%
Sodium 178mg	7%
Potassium 96mg	3%
Total Carbohydrates 74.9g	25%
Dietary Fiber 0.8g	3%
Sugars 50.4g	
Protein 6.8g	
Vitamin A 14%	Vitamin C 0%
Calcium 4%	Iron 10%

Nutrition Grade D-
* Based on a 2000 calorie diet

Desserts & Sweets

Russian Cheese Wheels

Yield: 6 servings
Veta Mesh

Dash vanilla extract
1 egg
Pinch baking soda
1 large farmer's cheese* (not cottage cheese)
1 tablespoon sugar
2 tablespoons flour
6 tablespoons of vegetable oil
1 container sour cream or jam of choice

In a bowl, whip by hand the vanilla, egg, and baking soda. Add the farmer's cheese, sugar, and flour. Mix well.

Take a cutting board and lightly dust with flour. Form by hand, wheels or disks about 1 ½ inch in diameter by ½ inch thick. Lightly cover both sides in flour.

Heat a skillet and add 2 tablespoons of oil. Fry the wheels in the skillet, until golden brown on both sides. Add more oil as needed.

Serve the cheese wheels with the sour cream or your favorite jam for a delicious breakfast treat.

Note: you can use Mexican queso blanco as a replacement for the farmer's cheese as it is made the exact same way. Also in a pinch it's acceptable to use cottage cheese but try to drain it with cheese cloth or an equivalent.

Nutrition Facts

Serving Size 89 g

Amount Per Serving

Calories 438	Calories from Fat 418
	% Daily Value*
Total Fat 46.4g	71%
Saturated Fat 13.2g	66%
Trans Fat 0.0g	
Cholesterol 48mg	16%
Sodium 91mg	4%
Total Carbohydrates 3.7g	1%
Sugars 2.1g	
Protein 3.3g	

Vitamin A 7%	•	Vitamin C 1%
Calcium 7%	•	Iron 1%

Nutrition Grade F
* Based on a 2000 calorie diet

---

*FARMER'S CHEESE—A type of soft cheese which is made all over the world. Provided by goat, sheep, and cow's milk.

Brock's Best

Brock's Best

Sand Dessert

2 boxes vanilla cookies
1 (8 ounce) package cream cheese, softened
½ cup (1 stick) butter, softened
1 cup confectioner's (powdered) sugar
12 ounce Jell-O Instant French Vanilla Pudding package
3 ½ cup milk
1 (12 ounce) container Cool Whip
A cleaned 8-inch children's sand bucket with plastic shovel

In a bowl, crumble the cookies into fine crumbs and set aside.

In another bowl, combine the cream cheese, butter, and powdered sugar. Beat until smooth, and set aside.

In a third bowl (this time a large one), mix the pudding and milk until smooth. Fold in the Cool Whip and the earlier prepared cream cheese mixture. Mix thoroughly.

Butter the sides of the sand bucket. Alternate layers of cookie crumbs and the pudding mixture. End with at least 1-inch of cookies on top. Chill in the refrigerator for 2 hours.

Use a large spoon or even the bucket's plastic shovel for effect (if you have cleaned it!), to spoon out the pudding into bowls.

Yield: 18 servings
Debbie O'Donovan

Desserts & Sweets

Shoo-Fly Pie

1 ⅓ cup flour
⅔ cup sugar
⅓ cup Crisco shortening
Pinch salt
⅔ cup Maple, Pancake, or Corn Syrup
⅔ cup hot water
⅔ teaspoon baking soda
1 eggs
1 (8-inch) pie shell

Preheat your oven to 350° F. Using a large bowl, add the flour, sugar, shortening, and a pinch of salt. Mix thoroughly with your hands to make a crumb-like mixture.

In another bowl, add the syrup. Boil the water and add it to the syrup, then add the baking soda. Mix until liquefied.

In a small bowl, beat the eggs then add it to the syrup mixture. Add half of the crumbs to the liquid mixture. Pour into the pie shell. Sprinkle the remaining crumbs on top of the pie.

Bake for 45 minutes, or until a toothpick comes out clean.

Yield: 1 pie of eight servings
Renee Bloch

Nutrition Facts

Serving Size 96 g

Amount Per Serving	
Calories 371	Calories from Fat 131
	% Daily Value*
Total Fat 14.5g	22%
Saturated Fat 3.6g	18%
Cholesterol 20mg	7%
Sodium 236mg	10%
Total Carbohydrates 58.0g	19%
Dietary Fiber 0.7g	3%
Sugars 33.1g	
Protein 3.5g	

Vitamin A 1%	•	Vitamin C 0%
Calcium 3%	•	Iron 10%

Nutrition Grade C
* Based on a 2000 calorie diet

Brock's Best

Strawberry Topping

1 cup water
1 cup sugar
3 tablespoons cornstarch
2 tablespoons corn syrup
Pinch of salt
Small amount of red food coloring
2 tablespoons strawberry Jell-O
4 cups (2 pints) fresh strawberries, halved

In a saucepan, boil together, until clear and thick, the water, sugar, cornstarch, corn syrup, and salt. Add a small amount of red food coloring and the strawberry Jell-O. Cool and add the berries. Serve with pancakes, crepes, french toast, waffles, ice cream, etc.

Nutrition Facts
Serving Size 85 g

Amount Per Serving	
Calories 96	Calories from Fat 1
	% Daily Value*
Total Fat 0.1g	0%
Cholesterol 0mg	0%
Sodium 20mg	1%
Total Carbohydrates 24.6g	8%
Dietary Fiber 3.7g	15%
Sugars 19.9g	
Protein 0.5g	
Vitamin A 0%	Vitamin C 47%
Calcium 1%	Iron 1%

Nutrition Grade A
* Based on a 2000 calorie diet

Yield: 12 servings
Renee Bloch

Sweet and Spicy Pecans

¼ cup sugar + 2 tablespoons more for mixing with the chili powder and pepper
1 cup warm water
1 cup pecan halves
1 tablespoon chili powder
Pinch of ground red pepper

Preheat your oven to 350° F. Stir together the sugar and water until the sugar dissolves. Add the pecan halves, and soak for 10 minutes. Drain, discarding the sugar mixture.

Combine on a plate or in a bowl, 2 tablespoons more of sugar, the chili powder, and the red pepper. Add the pecans, tossing to coat. Place the coated pecans on a lightly greased baking sheet. Bake for 10 minutes, or until the nuts are golden brown, stirring once.

Nutrition Facts
Serving Size 107 g

Amount Per Serving	
Calories 262	Calories from Fat 178
	% Daily Value*
Total Fat 19.8g	30%
Saturated Fat 1.7g	9%
Cholesterol 0mg	0%
Sodium 21mg	1%
Total Carbohydrates 23.3g	8%
Dietary Fiber 3.2g	13%
Sugars 19.7g	
Protein 2.7g	
Vitamin A 12%	Vitamin C 3%
Calcium 3%	Iron 5%

Nutrition Grade B-
* Based on a 2000 calorie diet

Use in the Baby Blue Salad in the Salads Section (page 139) or just as a healthy snack!

Yield: 4 servings of one-quarter cup
Debbie O'Donovan

Desserts & Sweets

Swiss Apple Pie

2 eggs, well-beaten
¾ cup granulated sugar
½ cup flour
1 tablespoon vanilla
1 tablespoon baking powder
Pinch of salt
1 cup peeled and diced, apples
½ cup walnuts

Preheat oven to 350° F. Mix together all the ingredients in a bowl. Pour into a greased pie plate.

Bake for 30 minutes. Let cool, as the apples will be hot!

Note: Do not use a pastry shell for this recipe!

Yield: 8 servings
Doris Barton

Nutrition Facts

Serving Size 63 g

Amount Per Serving

Calories 176	Calories from Fat 52
	% Daily Value*
Total Fat 5.8g	9%
Saturated Fat 0.6g	3%
Trans Fat 0.0g	
Cholesterol 41mg	14%
Sodium 37mg	2%
Total Carbohydrates 28.5g	10%
Dietary Fiber 1.1g	4%
Sugars 20.6g	
Protein 4.1g	

| Vitamin A 1% | • | Vitamin C 1% |
| Calcium 9% | • | Iron 5% |

Nutrition Grade C+
* Based on a 2000 calorie diet

Brock's Best

Tiramisu*

Yield: 12 servings
Lori Testa

6 egg yolks
¾ cup sugar
⅔ cup milk
1 pound mascarpone cheese
1 ¼ cup heavy cream
½ teaspoon vanilla extract
¼ cup sugar
1 cup strong brewed coffee, room temperature
2 tablespoons Kahlúa Liqueur
2 (3 ounce) packages hard lady fingers
1 tablespoon sweetened cocoa

In a saucepan, whisk together the egg yolks and sugar until well-blended. Whisk in milk and cook over medium heat until the mixture boils, stirring constantly. Boil gently for 1 minute, remove from heat, and cool slightly. Cover and refrigerate for 1 hour. After the hour, whisk in the mascarpone cheese until smooth.

In a separate bowl beat the cream, vanilla, and sugar until stiff peaks form. In an additional small bowl, combine the coffee and Kahlúa. Dip one-half of the lady fingers in the coffee-Kahlúa mix and layer in a 7 by 11-inch pan, cutting them in half in order to fit in the pan if necessary. Spread with one-half of the mascarpone mixture, then one-half of the whipped cream. Repeat with a second layer.

Cover with plastic wrap and refrigerate for 2 to 8 hours. Sprinkle with cocoa and serve.

Nutrition Facts

Serving Size 107 g

Amount Per Serving

Calories 270 — Calories from Fat 113

	% Daily Value*
Total Fat 12.6g	19%
Saturated Fat 7.0g	35%
Trans Fat 0.0g	
Cholesterol 142mg	47%
Sodium 47mg	2%
Total Carbohydrates 31.7g	11%
Sugars 18.4g	
Protein 7.4g	

| Vitamin A 10% | • | Vitamin C 0% |
| Calcium 11% | | Iron 2% |

Nutrition Grade D-

* Based on a 2000 calorie diet

---

*TIRAMISU [tih-ruh-mee-SOO, tih-ruh-MEE-soo]—The translation for tiramisu is "carry me up," and many who taste this ethereal dessert assume the unspoken continuation must surely be "to heaven." Tiramisu is a light composition of sponge cake or ladyfingers dipped in a coffee-marsala mixture, then layered with mascarpone (an ultra-rich Italian cream cheese) and grated chocolate. The dessert is refrigerated for several hours before serving to allow the flavors to intermingle. Although tiramisu is sometimes referred to as an Italian trifle, its texture is much lighter than that dessert.

Desserts & Sweets

Tookies

Yield: 24 cookies
Ted Fekete

Cake
½ cup—8 ounces—margarine or butter
1 box yellow cake mix
2 tablespoons vanilla extract
⅓ cup sliced almonds
½ cup water

Topping
¾ cup confectioner's/powdered sugar
¼ cup cornstarch

Preheat a convection oven to 325° F (or 350° F for a conventional oven). Cream the margarine or butter in a mixing bowl. Add the cake mix and vanilla extract. Mix on low speed for 3 to 5 minutes. Add the almonds and the water, and mix for an additional 2 minutes.

Scoop the cookie dough into tablespoon-sized balls. Portion the balls 1 inch apart on a parchment-lined sheet pan. Gently flatten the cookies with the palm of your hand, until each cookie is ½ inch thick.

Bake for 12 to 15 minutes, until golden brown. (The bake time is the same regardless of whether you are using a convection or conventional oven.) Remove the cookies from the oven. Cool for 20 to 25 minutes.

Place powdered sugar and cornstarch in a small bowl and hand mix until well combined. Gently toss cooled cookies in the mixture until they are lightly but completely coated.

Nutrition Facts

Serving Size 34 g

Amount Per Serving

Calories 162	Calories from Fat 69
	% Daily Value*
Total Fat 7.6g	12%
Saturated Fat 1.1g	6%
Trans Fat 0.0g	
Cholesterol 0mg	0%
Sodium 188mg	8%
Total Carbohydrates 22.3g	7%
Dietary Fiber 0.6g	2%
Sugars 13.0g	
Protein 1.6g	

Vitamin A 3%	•	Vitamin C 0%
Calcium 4%	•	Iron 2%

Nutrition Grade C
* Based on a 2000 calorie diet

Brock's Best

Brock's Best

Warm Nutty Caramel Brownies

1 (18 to 21 ounce) package brownie mix
½ cup packed brown sugar plus ¾ cup more for the topping
1 ½ cup miniature chocolate chips plus ½ cup more for the topping
½ cup chopped mixed salted nuts plus ½ cup more for sprinkling on baked brownies
12 caramels
Ice cream (optional)

Preheat your oven to 375° F. Prepare the brownie mix according to its directions. Add the first ½ cup of brown sugar. Mix well. Also fold in the first 1 ½ cups of chocolate chips. Pour batter into a bar pan and spread evenly.

Combine the nuts, the rest of the chocolate chips, and the remaining ¾ cup of brown sugar in a bowl. Sprinkle evenly over the brownie batter. Bake 20 to 22 minutes, until a toothpick inserted in the center of the brownies comes out clean.

Cut the caramels in half. Once the brownies are removed from the oven, immediately press the twenty-four caramel pieces evenly into four rows of six caramels each. Cut the brownies into 24 squares. Serve warm. Serve with ice cream if desired.

Yield: 24 servings
Renee Bowman

Nutrition Facts

Serving Size 59 g

Amount Per Serving

Calories 276	Calories from Fat 111
	% Daily Value*
Total Fat 12.4g	19%
Saturated Fat 4.2g	21%
Cholesterol 4mg	1%
Sodium 126mg	5%
Total Carbohydrates 40.3g	13%
Dietary Fiber 1.0g	4%
Sugars 17.8g	
Protein 3.8g	

Vitamin A 1%	•	Vitamin C 0%
Calcium 5%	•	Iron 6%

Nutrition Grade C-
* Based on a 2000 calorie diet

Dips And Sauces

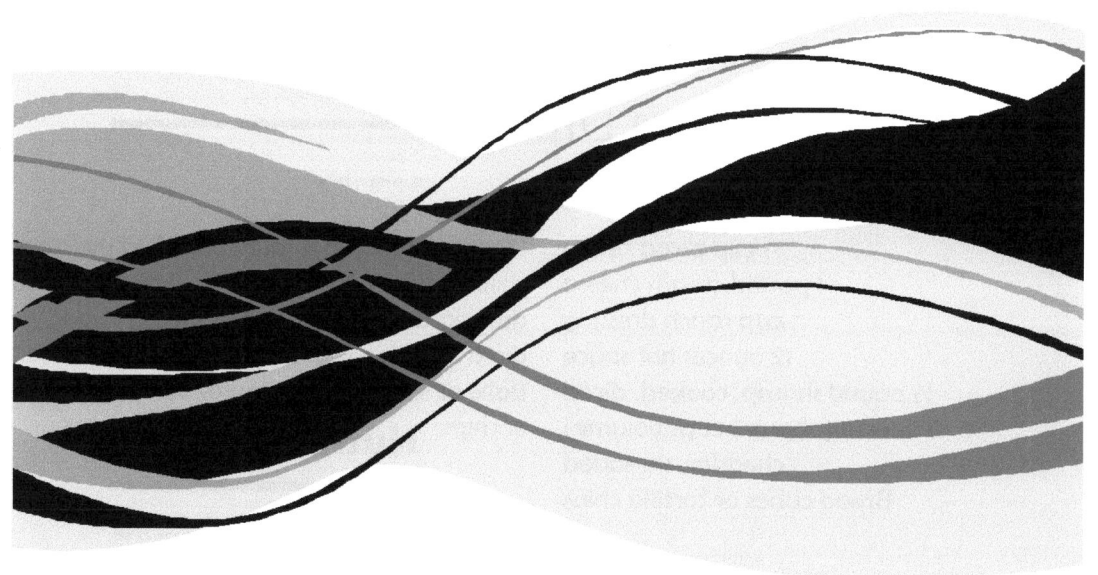

Brock's Best

Brock's Best

Artichoke Crab Spread

Yield: 24 servings
Teresa Flebbe

Cooking spray
14 ounces artichoke heart quarters, drained and coarsely chopped
8 ounces (1 cup) cream cheese, cubed
¼ cup sliced green onions
1 cup shredded imitation crabmeat
½ cup grated Parmesan cheese
4 teaspoons freshly squeezed lemon juice
French baguette or cocktail rye bread slices for serving (optional)

Spray the inside of a small slow cooker with cooking spray. Place all the ingredients except the bread in the cooker. Cover and cook on a low heat setting, for 1 to 1 ¼-hours, until the cream cheese is melted. Stir until the cheese is smooth. Scrape down the sides of the cooker with a rubber spatula to help prevent the edge of the spread from scorching. Serve warm.

Nutrition Facts
Serving Size 33 g

Amount Per Serving	
Calories 47	Calories from Fat 33
	% Daily Value*
Total Fat 3.7g	6%
Saturated Fat 2.3g	12%
Cholesterol 12mg	4%
Sodium 106mg	4%
Total Carbohydrates 1.9g	1%
Dietary Fiber 0.6g	3%
Protein 1.7g	
Vitamin A 3%	Vitamin C 2%
Calcium 3%	Iron 2%

Nutrition Grade C
* Based on a 2000 calorie diet

Buffalo Shrimp Dip

½ cup diced celery
1 pound cream cheese
1 cup ranch dressing
12 ounces hot sauce
½ pound shrimp, cooked, diced
8 ounces (about 2 cups volume) cheddar, shredded
Bread cubes or tortilla chips

Yield: 12 servings
Dermott McGroarty

Place the celery in a sauté pan. Add the cream cheese. When the cheese is soft, add ranch dressing and hot sauce. Mix well and add the diced shrimp. Top with the cheddar cheese. Bake at 350° F for 15 minutes. Serve with bread or chips.

Nutrition Facts
Serving Size 131 g

Amount Per Serving	
Calories 201	Calories from Fat 135
	% Daily Value*
Total Fat 15.1g	23%
Saturated Fat 9.2g	46%
Cholesterol 85mg	28%
Sodium 1140mg	48%
Total Carbohydrates 4.3g	1%
Sugars 1.2g	
Protein 12.3g	
Vitamin A 18%	Vitamin C 37%
Calcium 13%	Iron 4%

Nutrition Grade D
* Based on a 2000 calorie diet

Dips & Sauces

Celeste's Best BBQ Sauce

Yield: 16 to 18 servings
Celeste Durr/Sharon Houck

2 cups ketchup
2 ½ tablespoon yellow mustard
2 ½ tablespoon Worcestershire sauce
½ teaspoon liquid smoke
2 teaspoons smoked paprika
2 tablespoons white sugar
2 tablespoons brown sugar
2 tablespoons honey
2 teaspoons apple cider vinegar
½ teaspoon garlic powder

Set a pot on low heat. Simmer all ingredients for 20 to 30 minutes.

Serve on any of your favorite grilled foods.

Nutrition Facts
Serving Size 39 g

Amount Per Serving	
Calories 49	Calories from Fat 2
	% Daily Value*
Total Fat 0.2g	0%
Trans Fat 0.0g	
Cholesterol 0mg	0%
Sodium 366mg	15%
Total Carbohydrates 12.4g	4%
Sugars 11.4g	
Protein 0.7g	
Vitamin A 8%	Vitamin C 7%
Calcium 1%	Iron 1%

Nutrition Grade B+
* Based on a 2000 calorie diet

Cranberry Salsa

1 (12 ounce) bag fresh cranberries
½ cup granulated sugar
⅓ cup freshly squeezed lime juice
2 large cloves garlic, minced
½ cup fresh minced cilantro leaves
1 small jalapeño pepper, seeded, finely chopped
3 scallions, finely chopped
Salt
Baked tortilla and pita chips (optional)

Yield: 12 servings
Kim Stayrook

Place the cranberries in a saucepan with unheated water and bring to a boil. Drain well. Combine the sugar and lime juice in a bowl. Add the cranberries and stir gently. Add garlic, cilantro, jalapeño, and scallions. Season with salt. Let "marinate" for 20 minutes. Serve with chips or atop cooked chicken/pork.

Nutrition Facts
Serving Size 50 g

Amount Per Serving	
Calories 49	Calories from Fat 0
	% Daily Value*
Total Fat 0.1g	0%
Cholesterol 0mg	0%
Sodium 13mg	1%
Potassium 47mg	1%
Total Carbohydrates 13.0g	4%
Dietary Fiber 1.5g	6%
Sugars 9.8g	
Protein 0.2g	
Vitamin A 2%	Vitamin C 12%
Calcium 1%	Iron 1%

Nutrition Grade A
* Based on a 2000 calorie diet

Brock's Best

Hot Artichoke Heart Dip

1 (14 ounce) can artichoke hearts, drained and chopped
1 cup mayonnaise
1 cup grated Parmesan cheese
1 (4 ounce) can chopped green chilies
1 clove garlic, chopped
¼ cup scallion, for garnish
2 plum tomatoes, diced, for garnish
Tortilla chips (optional)
Crackers (optional)
Cocktail bread slices (optional)

Preheat your oven to 350° F. In a bowl, combine the artichoke hearts, mayonnaise, Parmesan cheese, green chilies, and garlic. Spoon into a lightly greased pie plate.

Bake for 20 to 25-minutes, until lightly browned. Garnish with chopped scallion and plum tomatoes. Serve with tortilla chips, crackers, or cocktail bread slices.

Yield: 10 servings
Brian Poff

Nutrition Facts

Serving Size 108 g

Amount Per Serving	
Calories 172	Calories from Fat 88
	% Daily Value*
Total Fat 9.8g	**15%**
Saturated Fat 2.1g	**10%**
Trans Fat 0.0g	
Cholesterol 10mg	**3%**
Sodium 271mg	**11%**
Total Carbohydrates 19.4g	**6%**
Dietary Fiber 5.7g	**23%**
Sugars 7.6g	
Protein 4.9g	

Vitamin A 66%	•	Vitamin C 24%
Calcium 8%	•	Iron 8%

Nutrition Grade B+
* Based on a 2000 calorie diet

Dips & Sauces

Maple Chipotle BBQ Sauce

6 cups (1 ½ cup) Vermont maple syrup
4 ounces (2 tablespoons) chipotle peppers in adobo sauce
2 cups (½ cup) apple cider vinegar
1 ½ cup (⅓ cup) brown sugar
2 tablespoons (1 ½ teaspoon) Worcestershire sauce
4 tablespoons (1 tablespoon) dry rub mix
8 cups (2 cup) ketchup

Dry Rub
4 tablespoons (1 tablespoon) brown sugar
2 tablespoons (1 ½ teaspoon) kosher salt
2 tablespoons (1 ½ teaspoon) chili powder
1 tablespoon (¾ teaspoon) freshly ground black pepper
1 tablespoon (¾ teaspoon) onion powder
1 tablespoon (¾ teaspoon) garlic powder
1 tablespoon (¾ teaspoon) red pepper flakes

Combine the maple syrup and chipotle peppers in a thick-bottomed stainless steel pot. Cook on medium-low heat for 20 minutes, or until the syrup has reduced by half.

Add the vinegar, brown sugar, Worcestershire sauce, dry rub (recipe follows), and ketchup, and let simmer for 30 minutes. Remove from heat and purée with a hand held mixer or stick blender. Serve with chicken or pork.

Dry Rub
Combine the dry rub ingredients in a bowl and mix well.

Yield: 8 cups-food service version
(2 cups-home version)
Craig Locarno

Nutrition Facts
Serving Size 70 g

Amount Per Serving	
Calories 87	Calories from Fat 2
	% Daily Value*
Total Fat 0.2g	0%
Trans Fat 0.0g	
Cholesterol 0mg	0%
Sodium 801mg	33%
Total Carbohydrates 22.1g	7%
Dietary Fiber 0.6g	2%
Sugars 20.4g	
Protein 0.8g	

Vitamin A 14% • Vitamin C 10%
Calcium 2% • Iron 3%

Nutrition Grade B
* Based on a 2000 calorie diet

Brock's Best

Nacho Bake

1 box Velveeta Shells & Cheese Dinner
1 pound ground beef
1 package taco seasoning mix
¾ cup water
¾ cup sour cream
¾ cup shredded cheese
¾ cup salsa
¼ cup Tortilla chips, crushed

Preheat oven to 400° F. Cook the Velveeta Shells & Cheese Dinner according to its directions. Mix the sour cream into the dinner. Separately, brown the ground beef. Add the taco seasoning mix and water. Cook for 5 minutes on medium. Put half of the cheese dinner into a baking dish. Next, layer with the beef mixture, then half of the cheese, and then the remaining dinner. Top with salsa, the rest of cheese, and crushed tortilla chips. Cover. Bake for 15 minutes. Bake uncovered for an additional 5 minutes.

Yield: 3 servings
Amanda Brown

Nutrition Facts
Serving Size 501 g

Amount Per Serving	
Calories 966	Calories from Fat 391
	% Daily Value*
Total Fat 43.5g	67%
Saturated Fat 20.6g	103%
Trans Fat 0.0g	
Cholesterol 210mg	70%
Sodium 2112mg	88%
Potassium 948mg	27%
Total Carbohydrates 70.2g	23%
Dietary Fiber 4.2g	17%
Sugars 6.4g	
Protein 69.8g	
Vitamin A 21%	Vitamin C 3%
Calcium 32%	Iron 218%

Nutrition Grade C+
* Based on a 2000 calorie diet

Peach Salsa

2 pounds (1 ½ cup) sliced peaches, diced
1 (⅓ cup) red bell pepper, diced
1 bunch (¼ cup) green onions, sliced
1 (2 ½ teaspoon) jalapeño pepper, diced, no seeds
4 (⅔ cup) vine-ripened tomatoes, deseeded and diced
Freshly squeezed juice of two limes
3 tablespoons (1 tablespoon) cilantro
Salt

Yield: 10 servings
Michael Hamilton

Combine all the ingredients, and adjust the seasoning with salt. Let stand overnight. Serve with crab cakes (page 165).

Nutrition Facts
Serving Size 185 g

Amount Per Serving	
Calories 58	Calories from Fat 3
	% Daily Value*
Total Fat 0.3g	0%
Cholesterol 0mg	0%
Sodium 147mg	6%
Potassium 243mg	7%
Total Carbohydrates 14.1g	5%
Dietary Fiber 3.0g	12%
Sugars 10.6g	
Protein 1.8g	
Vitamin A 21%	Vitamin C 52%
Calcium 3%	Iron 4%

Nutrition Grade A
* Based on a 2000 calorie diet

Dips & Sauces

Dips & Sauces

Pepperoni Dip

1 can condensed cream of mushroom soup
1 (8 ounce) package light cream cheese
1 (4 ounce) package turkey pepperoni, chopped

Place the soup and cream cheese into a microwaveable bowl. Cover and heat on high for 1 minute, and then stir and heat until melted together, approximately another 1 to 2 minutes.

Add chopped pepperoni. Stir. Cover and microwave for another minute. Serve with crackers, pita chips, or mini bagels.

Yield: 10 to 12 servings
Chuck Staab

Nutrition Facts
Serving Size 65 g
Amount Per Serving
Calories 132 Calories from Fat 101
% Daily Value*
Total Fat 11.2g — 17%
Saturated Fat 6.0g — 30%
Trans Fat 0.0g
Cholesterol 40mg — 13%
Sodium 506mg — 21%
Total Carbohydrates 2.6g — 1%
Sugars 0.5g
Protein 5.6g
Vitamin A 7% • Vitamin C 0%
Calcium 2% • Iron 5%
Nutrition Grade F
* Based on a 2000 calorie diet

Yield: 12 servings.
William Daniel Hall

Pizza Dip

8 ounces cream cheese
2 ounces tomato sauce
1 tablespoon garlic powder
8 ounces mozzarella cheese, shredded
1 tbsp oregano

Preheat your oven to 350° F. Soften the cream cheese in a microwave for 15 to 20 seconds, then spread it in a small 9 by 13-inch casserole or sauce baking dish.

In a bowl, mix the tomato sauce with the garlic powder. Spread the mixture on top of cream cheese. Sprinkle mozzarella cheese and oregano on top of the tomato mix. Bake for 12 to 15 minutes, until golden brown and bubbly.

Nutrition Facts
Serving Size 44 g
Amount Per Serving
Calories 128 Calories from Fat 94
% Daily Value*
Total Fat 10.4g — 16%
Saturated Fat 6.6g — 33%
Cholesterol 31mg — 10%
Sodium 181mg — 8%
Potassium 70mg — 2%
Total Carbohydrates 2.2g — 1%
Sugars 0.5g
Protein 6.6g
Vitamin A 8% • Vitamin C 1%
Calcium 16% • Iron 3%
Nutrition Grade B-
* Based on a 2000 calorie diet

Brock's Best

Brock's Best

Pizza Sauce

3 cups crushed tomato
1 tablespoon chopped fresh basil
1 tablespoon sugar
1 tablespoon fresh chopped garlic
1 tablespoon grated Parmesan cheese
¾ teaspoon kosher salt
1 tablespoon olive oil

Blend all the ingredients and refrigerate. Use 8 ounces of the sauce for a 22-ounce dough ball. Can be made with the Pizza Dough recipe (page 38).

Yield: 16 ounces of sauce for two large pizzas
Tony Paterno

Southwest American Indian Salsa Salad

11 tomatillos, finely chopped
4 large tomatoes, finely chopped
¾ cup finely chopped red onion
3 serrano chili peppers, finely chopped
3 jalapeño peppers, finely chopped
⅓ cup finely chopped cilantro
1 teaspoon freshly squeezed lime juice
½ cup chopped roasted pine nuts

In a large bowl, toss together all the ingredients. Allow to marinate about 2 hours. Serve cold. Salsa can be used as a condiment for dishes like, tacos, burritos, wraps, etc.

Yield: 4 servings
Patrick Baca

Dips & Sauces

Dips & Sauces

Spinach Dip

Yield: 12 servings
Debbie O'Donovan

1 package Knorr Vegetable Recipe Mix
1 large container of sour cream
1 cup mayonnaise
1 small box frozen chopped spinach—thawed and drained
1 small can tiny shrimp
1 small can crabmeat
1 large round loaf of bread
Green onions, chopped (optional)
Cheddar cheese, cut into sticks (optional)
Vegetable sticks (optional)

Combine all ingredients except the bread. Cut the top off the bread, remove most of the inside bread to form a "bowl." Reserve the top for dipping pieces. Add the dip to the bread, replace the lid, refrigerate for 2 hours. Serve the creation with vegetable sticks, cheese sticks, or bread cubes.

Nutrition Facts
Serving Size 188 g

Amount Per Serving	
Calories 392	Calories from Fat 155
	% Daily Value*
Total Fat 17.2g	27%
Saturated Fat 7.5g	37%
Trans Fat 0.0g	
Cholesterol 72mg	24%
Sodium 877mg	37%
Potassium 2mg	0%
Total Carbohydrates 45.9g	15%
Dietary Fiber 6.9g	28%
Sugars 5.0g	
Protein 12.7g	
Vitamin A 37%	Vitamin C 10%
Calcium 9%	Iron 15%

Nutrition Grade D+
* Based on a 2000 calorie diet

Spring Pea Dip

1 pound bag frozen petite peas, thawed
2 cloves of garlic
⅓ cup extra virgin olive oil
⅓ cup Parmesan cheese

Place the thawed peas and garlic in a food processor with steel blade. Pulse until blended, while slowly adding the extra virgin olive oil. Then season with the Parmesan cheese. Refrigerate for 2 hours.

Serve this dip with fresh vegetables, roasted potato slices, Indian Naan bread, raw carrots, radishes, asparagus, crostini, grilled pita bread, etc.

Nutrition Facts
Serving Size 47 g

Amount Per Serving	
Calories 90	Calories from Fat 56
	% Daily Value*
Total Fat 6.3g	10%
Saturated Fat 1.2g	6%
Trans Fat 0.0g	
Cholesterol 2mg	1%
Sodium 71mg	3%
Potassium 2mg	0%
Total Carbohydrates 5.6g	2%
Dietary Fiber 1.8g	7%
Sugars 2.2g	
Protein 2.8g	
Vitamin A 4%	Vitamin C 11%
Calcium 4%	Iron 5%

Nutrition Grade C
* Based on a 2000 calorie diet

Yield: 12 servings
Christine Trapaga

Brock's Best

Vidalia Onion Relish

5 pounds (3 ½ cup chopped) Vidalia onions, peeled and finely diced
6 tablespoons (4 ½ teaspoon) kosher or pickling salt
½ teaspoon (1 pinch) turmeric
½ cup (2 tablespoons) roasted red peppers
1 teaspoon (¼ teaspoon) celery seed
1 teaspoon (¼ teaspoon) dry mustard
2 cups (½ cup) sugar
2 cups (½ cup) cider vinegar

In a ceramic dish like a lasagne dish or casserole, layer the onions with the salt applied over each layer. Let stand in the refrigerator, covered for 2 hours, up to 24 hours.

Drain the juice from the onions and rinse them well. Place in a large heavy-bottomed pot, and cook over medium-high heat. Cook the onions down without letting them brown.

Add all remaining ingredients and incorporate well. Bring to a simmer and continue to simmer for 30 minutes. Adjust seasoning as necessary.

You can refrigerate the resulting relish. It can also be jarred or frozen. Put on hot dogs, hamburgers, or use as a general summertime condiment.

Yield: 8 cups-food service version
(2 cups-home version)
Eric Smith

Nutrition Facts

Serving Size 104 g

Amount Per Serving

Calories 82	Calories from Fat 1
	% Daily Value*
Total Fat 0.1g	0%
Trans Fat 0.0g	
Cholesterol 0mg	0%
Sodium 1088mg	45%
Total Carbohydrates 19.5g	6%
Dietary Fiber 1.6g	6%
Sugars 15.7g	
Protein 0.6g	
Vitamin A 2% •	Vitamin C 25%
Calcium 0% •	Iron 1%
Nutrition Grade B-	

* Based on a 2000 calorie diet

Family Heirlooms

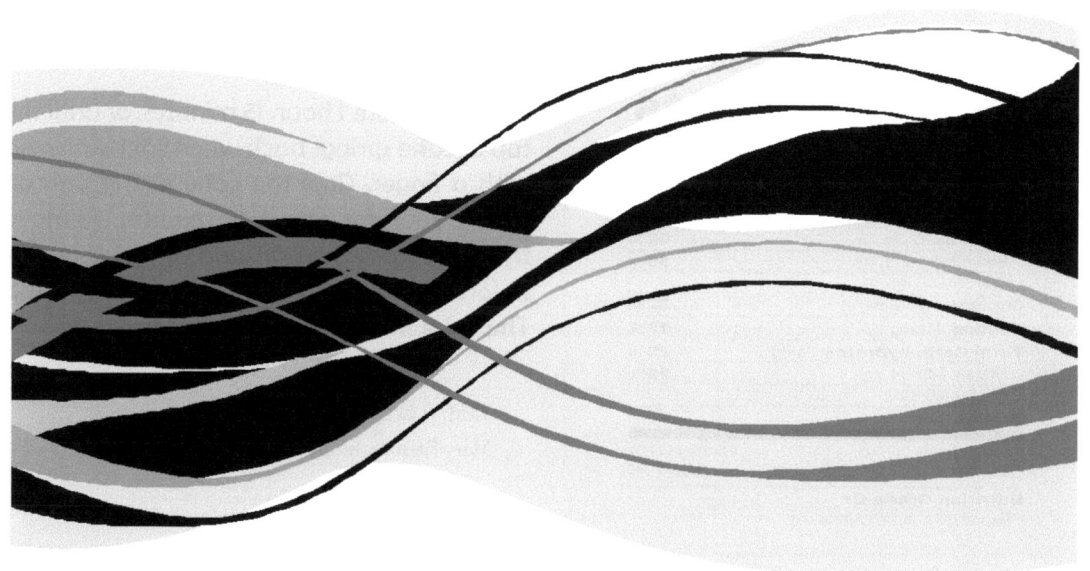

Brock's Best

Brock's Best

Carrot Cake

4 eggs
1 ½ cup sugar
1 ½ cup vegetable oil
3 cup whole wheat flour, plus ½ cup more for tossing with the pecans and dates
2 teaspoons baking powder
2 teaspoons baking soda
½ teaspoon salt
1 teaspoon ground cinnamon
1 can (8 ounce) crushed pineapple in juice, drained
4 large (2 cups) carrots, grated
1 cup pecans
1 cup dates

Preheat oven to 350° F. Grease a 10-inch tube pan, then lightly flour. Beat the eggs in a large mixing bowl. Gradually beat in the sugar. Stir in the oil.

Combine the first 3 cups of the whole wheat flour with the baking powder, baking soda, salt, and cinnamon in another bowl. Stir into egg mixture. Add the drained pineapple and carrots. Mix well.

Toss the pecans and dates with the remaining ½ cup of flour and stir into the batter, then transfer it into a prepared cake pan.

Bake for about 1 hour, 15 minutes, or until the top of cake springs back when lightly pressed with a finger. Cool the cake in the pan on a wire rack for about 15 minutes. Remove the cake from the pan and completely cool before wrapping in aluminum foil or plastic. The cake keeps well in a refrigerator.

Yield: 12 to 14 servings
Mary Parsons, mother of Debbie O'Donovan

Nutrition Facts

Serving Size 207 g

Amount Per Serving	
Calories 739	Calories from Fat 385
	% Daily Value*
Total Fat 42.8g	66%
Saturated Fat 7.7g	39%
Trans Fat 0.0g	
Cholesterol 65mg	22%
Sodium 415mg	17%
Total Carbohydrates 85.6g	29%
Dietary Fiber 4.7g	19%
Sugars 46.8g	
Protein 8.6g	

Vitamin A 7%	Vitamin C 8%
Calcium 8%	Iron 19%

Nutrition Grade C+
* Based on a 2000 calorie diet

Family Heirlooms
Cream Cheese Pie

Pie Filling
2 (8 ounce) packages cream cheese, softened
3 eggs, beaten one at a time
⅓ cup sugar
¼ teaspoon almond extract

Icing
1 cup sour cream
3 tablespoons sugar
1 teaspoon vanilla extract

Preheat your oven to 325° F. Beat the pie filling ingredients together until smooth. Butter an 8 or 9-inch pie plate. Pour the mixture into the pie plate and bake for 40 minutes. Remove from the oven and cool for 20 minutes.

While cooling, mix the icing ingredients to a creamy consistency. Pour the icing on top of the pie and bake in the oven at the same temperature for an additional 15 minutes. Let cool and refrigerate at least 2 hours prior to serving.

Yield: 8 servings
Susan McLaughlin, mother of Tracey Woomer

Nutrition Facts
Serving Size 120 g

Amount Per Serving	
Calories 355	Calories from Fat 254
	% Daily Value*
Total Fat 28.2g	43%
Saturated Fat 16.9g	84%
Trans Fat 0.0g	
Cholesterol 136mg	45%
Sodium 215mg	9%
Total Carbohydrates 19.2g	6%
Sugars 16.4g	
Protein 7.3g	

Vitamin A 21%	•	Vitamin C 0%
Calcium 9%	•	Iron 6%

Nutrition Grade D-
* Based on a 2000 calorie diet

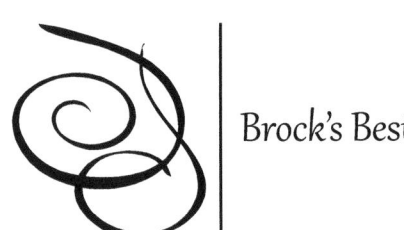

Brock's Best

Granny Sullivan's Pineapple Upside Down Cake

⅓ cup butter or margarine
1 cup firmly packed dark brown sugar
7 slices of canned pineapple
7 maraschino cherries
1 package of yellow cake mix

Nutrition Facts
Serving Size 151 g

Amount Per Serving	
Calories 451	Calories from Fat 138
	% Daily Value*
Total Fat 15.3g	24%
Saturated Fat 6.0g	30%
Cholesterol 22mg	7%
Sodium 491mg	20%
Total Carbohydrates 77.2g	26%
Dietary Fiber 1.5g	6%
Sugars 52.5g	
Protein 3.3g	
Vitamin A 6% •	Vitamin C 40%
Calcium 11% •	Iron 7%

Nutrition Grade C
* Based on a 2000 calorie diet

Preheat your oven to 325° F. Melt the butter/margarine in a 9-inch round skillet or baking pan. Add the brown sugar and stir over low heat until dissolved.

Cut the pineapple slices in half and arrange with the cherries in the bottom and around sides of a cake pan.

Prepare the cake mix according to its directions. Fill the prepared pan three-quarters full and bake for 30 to 40 minutes, until a toothpick comes out clean. (Any remaining batter may be used for cupcakes.)

To make it an upside down cake, when the cake is done and still hot, run a knife around its edge, and invert it onto a serving plate.

Yield: 8 servings
Don Direso's Grandmother

Family Heirlooms

Green and Red Peppers with Crabmeat

3 green peppers
3 red peppers
1 cup light cream
4 teaspoons butter
¼ teaspoon ground nutmeg
2 tablespoons cornstarch
¼ cup dry white wine
1 teaspoon freshly squeezed lemon juice
1 teaspoon salt plus 1 additional teaspoon salt, for seasoning
2 cups cooked crabmeat
1 cup cooked rice
White pepper, for seasoning
Paprika, for garnish

Preheat your oven to 350° F. Cut the tops off the peppers and remove their seeds. Steam them for 2 to 4 minutes, and drain.

Heat the cream and butter in a saucepan. Add the nutmeg.

In a separate small bowl, mix the cornstarch, wine, lemon juice, and salt. Add to the cream-butter mixture. Cook until thickened, stirring constantly. Combine with the crabmeat and rice. Spoon into the peppers.

Season with salt and white pepper. Garnish with paprika. Bake in a greased baking dish for 20 minutes.

Yield: 6 servings
Staff of The Park School

Nutrition Facts
Serving Size 121 g

Amount Per Serving

Calories 181	Calories from Fat 63
	% Daily Value*
Total Fat 7.0g	11%
Saturated Fat 4.2g	21%
Cholesterol 25mg	8%
Sodium 648mg	27%
Total Carbohydrates 24.7g	8%
Dietary Fiber 1.3g	5%
Sugars 2.1g	
Protein 3.6g	

Vitamin A 11%	•	Vitamin C 101%
Calcium 5%	•	Iron 8%

Nutrition Grade C
* Based on a 2000 calorie diet

Brock's Best

Hungarian Beef Paprika

½ cup vegetable oil
1 cup diced onions
1 diced green pepper
1 tomato, diced
2 rounded tablespoons Hungarian paprika
1 pound stew beef, cut into ¾-inch cubes (chicken can be substituted for the beef)
¼ to ½ cup beef stock
Salt

In large frying pan, heat the oil, then sauté the onions to light brown over medium heat. Add the green pepper and tomato, and sauté another 10 minutes. Add a little water to avoid burning. Turn the heat to low, add the paprika, beef (you can use chicken instead), and ¼ cup beef stock.

Cook for 1 to 2 hours, stirring frequently until the beef is tender, adding beef stock as needed to make a sauce. You can also use a slow cooker instead of the stove. (Cook for 4 hours on low if choose to use a slow cooker.)

This dish is best prepared a day before serving. Serve over noodles.

Yield: 4 to 6 servings
Joseph Smik, father of Suzanne Smik

Nutrition Facts

Serving Size 156 g

Amount Per Serving	
Calories 293	Calories from Fat 208
	% Daily Value*
Total Fat 23.1g	35%
Saturated Fat 3.6g	18%
Cholesterol 0mg	0%
Sodium 2mg	0%
Total Carbohydrates 4.7g	2%
Dietary Fiber 1.8g	7%
Sugars 2.0g	
Protein 17.5g	
Vitamin A 26%	Vitamin C 40%
Calcium 1%	Iron 5%

Nutrition Grade C
* Based on a 2000 calorie diet

Family Heirlooms

Family Heirlooms

Mary's Easter Bread

12 eggs, extra-large
2 cups milk plus 1 cup milk, warm more, for activating the yeast
4 cups sugar plus 1 more tablespoon for activating the yeast
1 ½ cup oil
1 teaspoon vanilla or
2 teaspoons anisette seed oil
2 envelopes dry yeast
5 pounds flour

In a large bowl, combine the eggs, milk, sugar, oil, and vanilla or anisette seed oil.

In a separate small bowl, add the yeast into the 1 cup warm milk (about 108 ° F) and mix well. Also add the last 1 tablespoon of sugar. Let the yeast sit and activate, which is indicated by bubbling after about 10 minutes. After activation, mix into the larger bowl.

Make a well with the flour on a cutting board or other kneading surface. Slowly add the liquid mix from the large bowl to the flour. When it is well mixed, knead the dough for about 8 minutes and then, let set under a towel in a warm place until the dough doubles. (You can create a warm place by setting your oven to 125 or 150 ° F, then turning it off and allowing it to cool down to 100 to 110 ° F and leaving the light on to maintain the 100° F temperature.)

Knead again, and put in individual greased and floured pans to rise again in a warm place. Bake at 325° F for 25 to 30 minutes.

Nutrition Facts
Serving Size 134 g

Amount Per Serving	
Calories 443	Calories from Fat 107
	% Daily Value*
Total Fat 11.9g	18%
Saturated Fat 2.0g	10%
Trans Fat 0.0g	
Cholesterol 58mg	19%
Sodium 31mg	1%
Total Carbohydrates 74.0g	25%
Dietary Fiber 1.9g	8%
Sugars 24.6g	
Protein 9.5g	
Vitamin A 1%	Vitamin C 0%
Calcium 2%	Iron 19%

Nutrition Grade C-
* Based on a 2000 calorie diet

Yield: 5 loaves

Mary Alleva, mother of Angie Gonsorick

Brock's Best

Mary's Zucchini Bread

3 cups flour
2 teaspoons baking soda
1 teaspoon salt
¼ teaspoon baking powder
1 ½ teaspoon cinnamon
¾ teaspoon nutmeg
3 eggs
1 cup oil
2 cups sugar
2 teaspoons vanilla
2 cups shredded zucchini
1 cup snipped dates
1 cup broken walnuts
1 small can crushed pineapple, well drained

Preheat oven to 350° F. In a large mixing bowl, combine and mix the flour, baking soda, salt, baking powder, cinnamon, and nutmeg. Add eggs and oil. Beat until thick. Add sugar and vanilla, and mix. Stir in shredded zucchini, dates, broken walnuts, and well-drained pineapple.

Pour into two greased loaf pans (5 by 9-inch) and bake for 1 hour, or until testing shows the bread is done.

Yield: 12 to 14 servings
Mary Parsons, mother of Debbie O'Donovan

Nutrition Facts

Serving Size 150 g

Amount Per Serving
Calories 538 — Calories from Fat 233

% Daily Value*

Total Fat 25.9g	40%
Saturated Fat 3.1g	16%
Trans Fat 0.1g	
Cholesterol 41mg	14%
Sodium 423mg	18%
Total Carbohydrates 72.0g	24%
Dietary Fiber 3.2g	13%
Sugars 44.8g	
Protein 7.8g	

Vitamin A 2%   •   Vitamin C 7%
Calcium 3%   •   Iron 13%

Nutrition Grade D+
* Based on a 2000 calorie diet

Did you know that walnuts have been shown to help lower blood pressure which is critical for those whose hearts are already working overtime thanks to high adrenaline levels? Research so strongly backs their health benefits that the U.S. Food and Drug Administration goes so far as to recommend 1 ½ ounces (42 grams) of walnuts or other nuts per day.

Family Heirlooms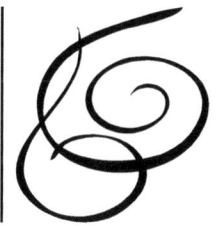

Mom's Meatloaf

2 to 3 pounds ground beef
3 cups breadcrumbs
¾ cup chopped onions
¼ cup chopped green pepper (optional)
6 teaspoons prepared horseradish
1 teaspoon salt
1 teaspoon dry mustard
2 eggs
¼ cup milk
¼ cup ketchup mixed into the meatloaf plus ¼ cup more used to make the sauce
1 tablespoon water

Preheat your oven to 400° F. Mix the ground beef and breadcrumbs in a large bowl. Add to this the chopped onions and green pepper, and mix thoroughly. Next, add the horseradish, salt, and dry mustard. Finally add the eggs, the milk, and the first ¼ cup of ketchup and thoroughly blend with the rest of the beef mixture.

Form the mixture into a meatloaf shape, and center it in an oven-safe glass dish (9 by 13-inch).

In a separate bowl, place ¼ cup of ketchup and the water, and stir until blended. Pour on top of meatloaf before placing in oven. Bake for 40 minutes.

Yield: 4 to 6 servings
Mary Parsons, mother of Debbie O'Donovan

Nutrition Facts

Serving Size 350 g

Amount Per Serving

Calories 692 — Calories from Fat 170

	% Daily Value*
Total Fat 18.9g	29%
Saturated Fat 6.6g	33%
Cholesterol 258mg	86%
Sodium 1196mg	50%
Total Carbohydrates 46.7g	16%
Dietary Fiber 3.1g	12%
Sugars 9.6g	
Protein 78.9g	

Vitamin A 5%	Vitamin C 15%
Calcium 12%	Iron 254%

Nutrition Grade A-
* Based on a 2000 calorie diet

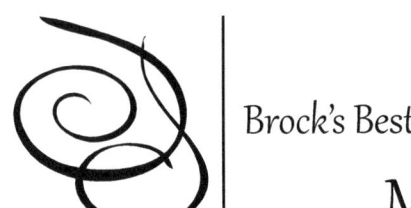

Brock's Best

Mom's Peach Cobbler

½ cup (1 stick) melted butter
4 cups peaches
2 tablespoons freshly squeezed lemon juice
1 cup flour
1 cup sugar
3 teaspoons baking powder
1 cup milk
Vanilla ice cream (optional)

Preheat your oven to 350° F. In a large saucepot, combine the peaches and lemon juice. Bring to a boil and simmer for 10 minutes. Set aside.

In a different bowl, combine the flour, sugar, baking powder, and milk. Stir well.

In a round ceramic baking or casserole dish, pour in the melted butter. Pour the batter over the butter. Top with the warm peaches.

Bake for 30 minutes. Best served with vanilla ice cream while still warm from the oven.

Yield: 8 servings
Mary Parsons, mother of Debbie O'Donovan

Nutrition Facts

Serving Size 145 g

Amount Per Serving

Calories 291	Calories from Fat 107
	% Daily Value*
Total Fat 11.9g	18%
Saturated Fat 7.3g	37%
Cholesterol 30mg	10%
Sodium 84mg	4%
Total Carbohydrates 46.0g	15%
Dietary Fiber 1.8g	7%
Sugars 32.2g	
Protein 2.5g	

Vitamin A 13%	Vitamin C 12%
Calcium 9%	Iron 6%

Nutrition Grade C+

* Based on a 2000 calorie diet

Family Heirlooms

Pork Adobo

1 pound pork meat (any part, fatty is good)
2 tablespoons salt
¼ teaspoon freshly ground black pepper
2 tablespoons crushed fresh garlic
½ cup vinegar
Water

Cut the meat into 1 by 1-inch cubes. Place all the ingredients in a saucepot and add enough water to cover the meat. Boil uncovered for about 5 minutes.

Cover the pot and boil until the meat is tender. Remove and save half of the broth. Set aside. Continue boiling the meat until it fries in its own oil. Fry it until it is crisp on all sides. Add the reserved broth.

Variations:
1. Add chicken or replace pork with chicken.
2. Add hard-boiled eggs.
3. Add a bay leaf.
4. Replace salt with soy sauce.

Yield: 3 to 4 servings
Eric Rappaport's mother-in-law,
San Andres family of Nueva Ecija, Philippines

Nutrition Facts

Serving Size 183 g

Amount Per Serving	
Calories 207	Calories from Fat 41
	% Daily Value*
Total Fat 4.5g	7%
Saturated Fat 1.6g	8%
Trans Fat 0.0g	
Cholesterol 95mg	32%
Sodium 4116mg	172%
Total Carbohydrates 0.1g	0%
Protein 33.9g	
Vitamin A 0% •	Vitamin C 0%
Calcium 1% •	Iron 9%

Nutrition Grade B+
* Based on a 2000 calorie diet

Brock's Best

Ratatouille

3 cups cubed eggplant
1 zucchini, cubed
¼ teaspoon salt to desiccate the eggplant and zucchini and more to use for seasoning later
½ cup chopped onions
1 clove of garlic, minced
1 tablespoon olive oil
½ cup sweet pepper
1 cup skinned and drained tomatoes (canned tomatoes may be used but drain well)
3 tablespoons dry wine, chicken broth or vegetable broth
Pinch of freshly ground black pepper
1 tablespoon finely chopped fresh basil or oregano

Sprinkle the eggplant and zucchini with salt. Let sit for 30 minutes, while the salt pulls moisture out from the vegetables. Rinse the eggplant and zucchini, and dry well.

In a large skillet, cook the onions and garlic in hot oil over medium heat, until the onions are tender. Stir in the eggplant, zucchini, sweet pepper, tomatoes and wine/broth. Bring to a boil, and then decrease the heat. Cover and cook 15 to 20 minutes, until done but not soft and mushy, being careful not to overcook.

Uncover and cook about 5 minutes more, or until most of the liquid evaporates, stirring occasionally.

Season ratatouille with additional salt and the black pepper. Stir in basil just before serving.

Nutrition Facts
Serving Size 190 g

Amount Per Serving	
Calories 79	Calories from Fat 34
	% Daily Value*
Total Fat 3.8g	6%
Saturated Fat 0.5g	3%
Cholesterol 0mg	0%
Sodium 157mg	7%
Total Carbohydrates 9.2g	3%
Dietary Fiber 3.7g	15%
Sugars 4.4g	
Protein 1.9g	
Vitamin A 10%	Vitamin C 58%
Calcium 1%	Iron 9%
Nutrition Grade B+	

* Based on a 2000 calorie diet

Yield: 4 servings
Mary Parsons, mother of Debbie O'Donovan

Pasta

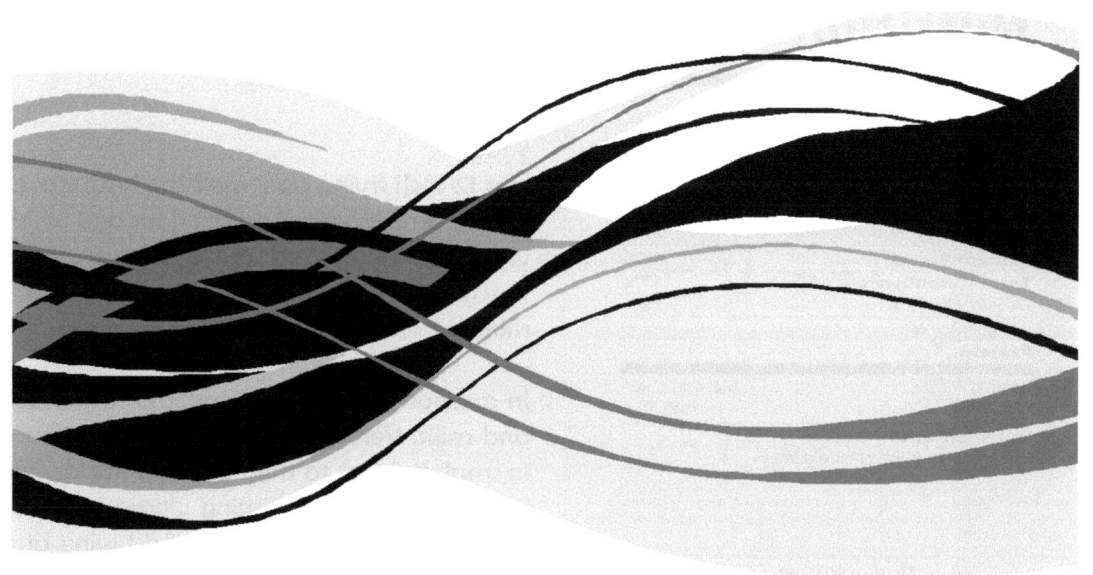

Brock's Best

Brock's Best

20-Minute Tuna Casserole

½ to 1 teaspoons of salt
12 ounces extra wide egg noodles
1 cup frozen petite green peas
6 ounces chunk light tuna in water, drained

Sauce
2 tablespoons butter
3 tablespoons flour
1 ¾ cup chicken broth
12 ounces evaporated milk
¼ cup dry white wine

Nutrition Facts
Serving Size 252 g

Amount Per Serving	
Calories 405	Calories from Fat 106
	% Daily Value*
Total Fat 11.8g	18%
Saturated Fat 6.2g	31%
Trans Fat 0.0g	
Cholesterol 97mg	32%
Sodium 417mg	17%
Total Carbohydrates 52.0g	17%
Dietary Fiber 2.1g	9%
Sugars 9.0g	
Protein 21.5g	

Vitamin A 7%	•	Vitamin C 4%
Calcium 15%	•	Iron 15%

Nutrition Grade C-
* Based on a 2000 calorie diet

Yield: 6 servings
Debbie O'Donovan

In a 5 to 6 quart saucepan over high heat, bring about 3 quarts of salted water to a boil. Add the noodles and cook according to their package directions.

About a minute before the noodles are ready, add the peas to the pasta and water and cook until the peas are bright green and tender. Drain the noodles and peas, and return them to the saucepan. Stir in the tuna.

Pour the sauce (recipe follows) over the tuna-noodle mixture and gently stir to mix well. Serve immediately.

Sauce
In a 12-inch frying pan, melt the butter over medium-high heat. Add the flour and whisk vigorously until a smooth paste forms. Stir the mixture until it simmers after about 1 minute.

In a separate bowl, mix together the broth and milk. Very gradually, add this mixture in small batches to the flour and butter mix in the frying pan, whisking vigorously after each addition until smooth. Add wine and cook until the sauce simmers and thickens, about 2 minutes.

Cheaty Ziti

Pasta

1 pound pasta (ziti or ziti rigati)
1 (32 ounce) jar spaghetti sauce
1 pound mozzarella cheese, shredded
¼ cup grated Pecorino Romano cheese
1 pound ricotta cheese
2 to 3 tablespoons chopped parsley

Preheat your oven to 350° F. Boil the pasta as per the instructions on its box. When done, drain the pasta and return it to the pot.

Add the other ingredients except the parsley, reserving a little of the sauce, mozzarella, and grated cheese to later top the casserole with.

Transfer the pot's contents to a disposable aluminum pan or casserole dish, spread the leftover sauce on top and then sprinkle with the remaining mozzarella and grated cheese. Finally, sprinkle with chopped parsley and cover with aluminum foil. Bake for approximately 45 minutes.

Yield: 8 servings
Debbie O'Donovan

Nutrition Facts

Serving Size 288 g

Amount Per Serving

Calories 745	Calories from Fat 173
	% Daily Value*
Total Fat 19.2g	**30%**
Saturated Fat 11.5g	**57%**
Cholesterol 93mg	**31%**
Sodium 10044mg	**419%**
Total Carbohydrates 109.2g	**36%**
Dietary Fiber 3.4g	**14%**
Sugars 0.6g	
Protein 35.5g	

Vitamin A 14%	•	Vitamin C 7%
Calcium 81%	•	Iron 30%

Nutrition Grade B-

* Based on a 2000 calorie diet

Brock's Best

Easy Add-In Macaroni and Cheese

1 (7 ¼ ounce) package macaroni and cheese dinner
1 (10 ¾ ounce) can condensed cream of mushroom soup
¼ cup butter or margarine plus ¼ cup melted for later pouring over crackers
3 tablespoons sour cream
1 cup shredded cheddar cheese
12 buttery round crackers

Preheat your oven to 350° F. In a saucepan, cook the macaroni according to the directions on the box. Don't add the cheese packet. Remove from heat, and drain. Return the pasta to the saucepan.

Add the soup, ¼ cup of butter/margarine, sour cream, shredded cheese, and the cheese packet from the mac and cheese package to the pasta. (Do not use milk as directed on the box.)

Pour this mixture into a small casserole dish and top with crumbled crackers. Melt the remaining butter/margarine and pour over the crackers. Bake for 25 minutes.

Yield: 6 servings
Debbie O'Donovan

Nutrition Facts

Serving Size 209 g

Amount Per Serving	
Calories 453	Calories from Fat 318
	% Daily Value*
Total Fat 35.3g	54%
Saturated Fat 9.2g	46%
Trans Fat 0.0g	
Cholesterol 24mg	8%
Sodium 1056mg	44%
Total Carbohydrates 27.9g	9%
Sugars 3.0g	
Protein 9.0g	
Vitamin A 19%	Vitamin C 0%
Calcium 21%	Iron 13%
Nutrition Grade C-	

* Based on a 2000 calorie diet

Fettuccine Carbonara

Pasta

Yield: 6 to 8 servings
Marlena Tavenner

2 cloves garlic
2 fresh parsley sprig
½ pound Pancetta
3 tablespoons butter
¼ cup dry white wine
4 eggs
3 tablespoons heavy cream
¾ cup grated Parmesan cheese
Salt and freshly ground black pepper
1 pound fettuccine

Chop the garlic, and strip the leaves from the parsley and chop. Set aside. Also, slice the Pancetta crosswise into strips.

Melt the butter in a sauté pan on medium heat. Add the garlic and Pancetta. Sauté for 2 to 3 minutes. Add the wine and then reduce. When reduced, remove from heat and keep warm.

Beat the eggs with a fork in a large bowl. Add the cream and Parmesan cheese and season with salt and pepper.

Cook the fettuccine according to its package and drain. When cooked, add the fettuccine to the egg mixture in the large bowl. The pasta needs to be very hot. It will cook the egg as you toss it. Toss quickly to coat evenly.

Add the Pancetta mixture and toss some more as before. Add the chopped parsley, and toss lightly. Add more salt and pepper if needed.

Nutrition Facts

Serving Size 155 g

Amount Per Serving

Calories 506	Calories from Fat 244
	% Daily Value*
Total Fat 27.1g	42%
Saturated Fat 11.6g	58%
Trans Fat 0.0g	
Cholesterol 206mg	69%
Sodium 961mg	40%
Total Carbohydrates 37.2g	12%
Protein 26.2g	

Vitamin A 10%	•	Vitamin C 1%
Calcium 13%	•	Iron 17%

Nutrition Grade D-

* Based on a 2000 calorie diet

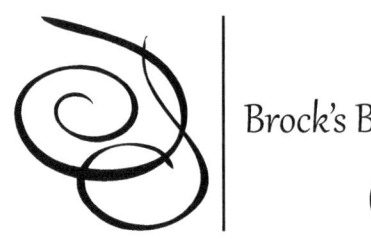

Brock's Best

Orecchiette with Mixed Greens and Goat Cheese

Yield: 1 serving
Debbie O'Donovan

1 cup dried orecchiette* pasta
2 cups Mediterranean-style mixed salad greens
2 tablespoons chopped, olive oil packed, sun-dried tomatoes
1 tablespoon crumbled goat cheese
2 tablespoons grated Parmesan cheese plus more for garnish
Pinch of salt
Pinch of pepper

Bring a pot of salted water to a boil over high heat. Add the orecchiette and cook for 8 to 10 minutes, until tender but still firm to the bite, stirring occasionally. Drain the pasta, reserving ½ cup of the water.

In a bowl, mix the salad greens with the sun-dried tomatoes, goat cheese, and Parmesan.

Top with the warm pasta and ½ cup of the reserved pasta water. Toss to combine and wilt the greens. Season with a pinch each of salt and pepper.

Garnish with additional Parmesan, if desired, and serve.

*ORECCHIETTE [oh-rayk-kee-EHT-tay]—Italian for "little ears," referring culinary to tiny disk-shaped pasta.

Nutrition Facts

Serving Size 496 g

Amount Per Serving

Calories 866 — Calories from Fat 279

	% Daily Value*
Total Fat 31.1g	48%
Saturated Fat 15.2g	76%
Trans Fat 0.0g	
Cholesterol 157mg	52%
Sodium 926mg	39%
Total Carbohydrates 103.5g	34%
Dietary Fiber 8.9g	36%
Sugars 16.6g	
Protein 45.9g	

Vitamin A 54%	•	Vitamin C 366%
Calcium 72%	•	Iron 79%

Nutrition Grade B
* Based on a 2000 calorie diet

Pasta

Pasta Primavera*

1 pound penne pasta
1 cup broccoli florets
1 cup diced zucchini
1 cup sliced mushrooms
1 cup diced tomatoes
2 tablespoons shredded fresh basil
2 tablespoons Parmesan cheese, for garnish

Sauce
4 tablespoons butter
2 ounces flour
1 pint heavy cream
Salt
3 tablespoons Parmesan cheese

Cook the penne pasta in salted boiling water until al dente. Once cooked, shock by running under cold water.

Blanch the broccoli starting with boiling water in a saucepan, cooking for 2 to 5 minutes and then shocking in cold water.

In a large frying pan, sauté the zucchini and mushrooms until tender. Add the pasta, broccoli, tomatoes, and sauce (recipe follows). Continue to sauté until all ingredients are well incorporated and hot. Garnish with fresh basil and Parmesan cheese.

Sauce
In a saucepan under medium heat, add the butter and flour. Melt and mix to a smooth consistency. Decrease the heat to low and cook for 5 minutes. Stir occasionally.

In a separate saucepan, heat the cream to a simmer. Add it to the butter-flour mixture. Whip to a smooth consistency. Add salt and the Parmesan cheese and bring to a simmer again. Cook the sauce for 10 minutes.

Nutrition Facts

Serving Size 378 g

Amount Per Serving

Calories 949	Calories from Fat 549
	% Daily Value*
Total Fat 61.0g	94%
Saturated Fat 36.8g	184%
Trans Fat 0.0g	
Cholesterol 285mg	95%
Sodium 302mg	13%
Total Carbohydrates 81.0g	27%
Dietary Fiber 1.9g	8%
Sugars 2.3g	
Protein 22.0g	
Vitamin A 56%	Vitamin C 52%
Calcium 21%	Iron 33%

Nutrition Grade C
* Based on a 2000 calorie diet

Yield: 4 servings
Jerry Goard

> *PRIMAVERA, alla [pree-muh-VEHR-uh]—This Italian phrase means "spring style" and culinarily refers to the use of fresh vegetables (raw or blanched) as a garnish to various dishes. One of the most popular dishes prepared in this manner is pasta primavera, pasta tossed or topped with diced or julienned cooked vegetables.

Brock's Best

Brock's Best

Philly Mac and Cheese Steak

Yield: 8 to 10 servings
Debbie O'Donovan

16 ounces mini penne pasta
2 tablespoons olive oil
½ cup finely chopped Vidalia onions
½ cup finely chopped green bell peppers
½ cup of the caps of sliced fresh mushrooms
½ pound sirloin steak, trimmed of excess fat and sliced very thinly
½ teaspoon minced garlic
½ teaspoon salt
½ teaspoon ground freshly ground black pepper
4 tablespoons butter plus 2 tablespoons, for the topping
6 ounces cream cheese
1 cup whole milk
1 cup half and half cream
2 cup shredded provolone or mozzarella cheese
⅓ cup panko* breadcrumbs

Preheat your oven to 375° F. Bring a large pot of lightly salted water to a boil. Add the pasta and cook for 6 to 8 minutes, until al dente. Drain well.

Meanwhile, preheat a large skillet on medium-high heat. Add the olive oil, onions, green peppers, and mushrooms. Sauté over medium heat for about 10 minutes, stirring occasionally. Add the sirloin, garlic, salt, and pepper to the skillet. Continue to cook for another 5 to 7 minutes, until the meat is browned. Remove from heat and set aside momentarily.

In a large saucepan over medium heat, melt 4 tablespoons butter. Add the cream cheese. Heat and stir with a wire whisk until completely melted and smooth. Add the milk and cream a little at a time. Continue to whisk quickly in order to avoid lumps. Add the provolone/mozzarella. Continue to whisk until thoroughly blended and smooth. Add the cooked macaroni and then the beef mixture. Stir well until thoroughly combined.

Pour into a lightly greased 9 by 13-inch glass baking dish. In a small bowl, mix together the breadcrumbs and the remaining 2 tablespoons of melted butter. Sprinkle the topping over the macaroni mixture. Bake uncovered for 25 to 30 minutes, until the top is golden brown.

Nutrition Facts

Serving Size 237 g

Amount Per Serving

Calories 633	Calories from Fat 323
	% Daily Value*
Total Fat 35.9g	55%
Saturated Fat 19.7g	99%
Cholesterol 109mg	36%
Sodium 637mg	27%
Total Carbohydrates 51.0g	17%
Dietary Fiber 2.6g	10%
Sugars 3.8g	
Protein 28.6g	

Vitamin A 23%	•	Vitamin C 14%
Calcium 35%	•	Iron 34%

Nutrition Grade B-
* Based on a 2000 calorie diet

*PANKO [PAHN-koh]—Breadcrumbs sold in Asian markets and used in Japanese cooking for coating fried foods. Coarser than those from the United States. They create a crunchy crust.

Pasta

Skillet Lasagna

1 (28 ounce) can diced tomatoes
Water
1 tablespoon olive oil
1 onion, minced
Salt
3 cloves garlic, minced and pressed through a garlic press—about 1 tablespoon
Pinch of red pepper flakes
1 pound Italian sausage, remove from casing
10 curly edged lasagna noodles, broken into 2-inch lengths
1 (8 ounce) can tomato sauce
½ cup grated Parmesan cheese, plus 2 tablespoons for garnish
1 cup ricotta cheese
3 tablespoons chopped fresh basil, for garnish

Pour the tomatoes with their juices into a 4 cup (1-quart) liquid measuring cup. Add water until the mixture measures 1 quart.

Heat the oil in large non-stick skillet over medium heat until simmering. Add the onion and ½ teaspoon of salt, and cook for about 5 minutes until it begins to brown. Stir in the garlic and pepper flakes, and cook until fragrant (about 30 seconds). Add the sausage and cook, breaking apart the meat, until it is no longer pink (about 4 minutes).

Scatter the pasta over the sausage but do not stir. Pour the diced tomatoes with their juices and tomato sauce over the pasta. Cover and bring to a simmer. Reduce the heat to medium-low and simmer, stirring occasionally, until the pasta is tender (about 20 minutes).

Remove the skillet from the heat and stir in ½ cup of Parmesan cheese. Season with salt and pepper. Dot with heaping tablespoons of ricotta cheese, cover, and let stand off the heat for 5 minutes.

To garnish, sprinkle with basil and the remaining 2 tablespoons of Parmesan cheese. Serve.

Yield: 4 to 6 servings
Tracey Woomer

Nutrition Facts

Serving Size 544 g

Amount Per Serving

Calories 788	Calories from Fat 385
	% Daily Value*
Total Fat 42.7g	66%
Saturated Fat 14.7g	74%
Trans Fat 0.3g	
Cholesterol 117mg	39%
Sodium 1311mg	55%
Total Carbohydrates 60.3g	20%
Dietary Fiber 5.5g	22%
Sugars 10.4g	
Protein 40.7g	
Vitamin A 45%	Vitamin C 64%
Calcium 24%	Iron 32%

Nutrition Grade B
* Based on a 2000 calorie diet

 Brock's Best

Notes

Pork

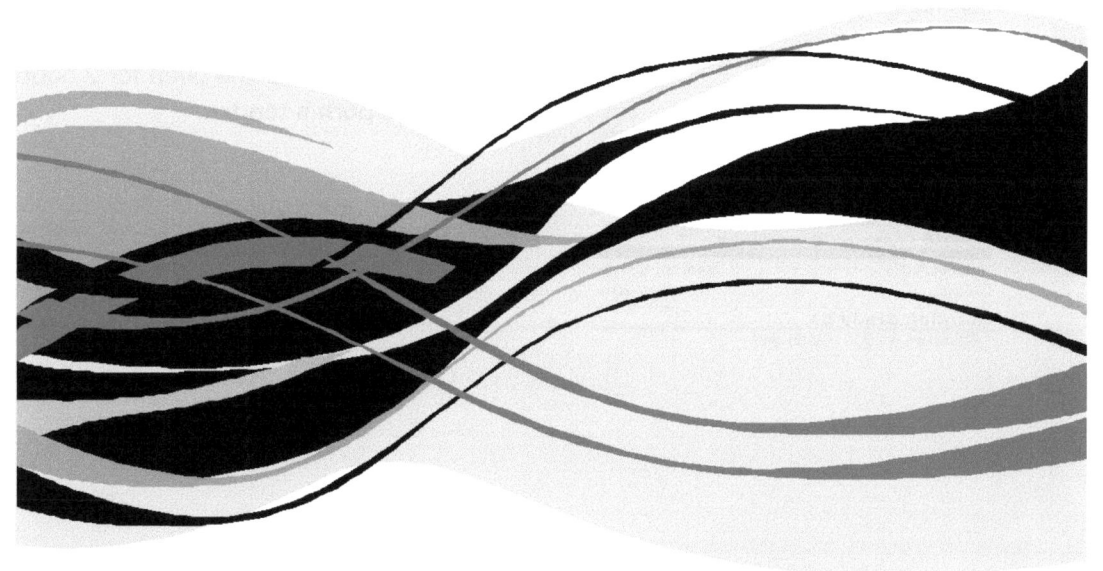

Brock's Best

Brock's Best

Apple Butter Pork Loin

2 (1 ½ pound) pork tenderloins
Seasoning salt
2 cups apple juice
½ cup apple butter
¼ cup brown sugar
2 tablespoons water
¼ teaspoon ground cinnamon
¼ teaspoon ground cloves

Preheat your oven to 350° F. Season the pork tenderloins with seasoning salt, and place them in a 9 by 13-inch baking dish or small roasting pan. Pour apple juice over the pork, and cover the dish with a lid or aluminum foil.

Bake for 1 hour. While the pork is roasting, mix together the apple butter, brown sugar, water, cinnamon, and cloves. When the time is up, remove the pork tenderloins from the oven, and spread the apple butter mixture over them.

Cover, and return to the oven for 2 hours, or until the pork is tender.

Yield: 6 servings
Debbie O'Donovan

Nutrition Facts

Serving Size 344 g

Amount Per Serving

Calories 559	Calories from Fat 167
	% Daily Value*
Total Fat 18.6g	**29%**
Saturated Fat 6.7g	**33%**
Trans Fat 0.0g	
Cholesterol 213mg	**71%**
Sodium 180mg	**8%**
Total Carbohydrates 25.7g	**9%**
Dietary Fiber 0.5g	**2%**
Sugars 23.2g	
Protein 67.9g	

Vitamin A 0%	•	Vitamin C 61%
Calcium 3%	•	Iron 20%

Nutrition Grade B+
* Based on a 2000 calorie diet

Pork

Apricot Pork Chops

6 pork chops
1 (1 ounce) package dry onion soup mix
10 ounces Russian-style salad dressing
1 cup apricot preserves

Preheat your oven to 350° F. Place the pork chops in a casserole dish.

Mix the onion soup mix, Russian dressing, and apricot preserves together in a bowl. Pour the mixture over the chops. Bake for 1 hour.

Yield: 6 servings
Debbie O'Donovan

Nutrition Facts
Serving Size 185 g

Amount Per Serving	
Calories 631	Calories from Fat 409
	% Daily Value*
Total Fat 45.4g	70%
Saturated Fat 11.4g	57%
Cholesterol 82mg	27%
Sodium 715mg	30%
Total Carbohydrates 37.7g	13%
Sugars 25.7g	
Protein 19.0g	
Vitamin A 2%	Vitamin C 9%
Calcium 4%	Iron 6%

Nutrition Grade C
* Based on a 2000 calorie diet

Heaven on a Bun

1 pound ground pork
1 pound ground beef
Seasoning blend
1 pint (2 cups) sour cream
6 ounces cream cheese
6 to 8 hamburger buns
Jalapeño pepper cheese, sliced (optional)
Lettuce (optional)
Tomato (optional)

Brown the pork and beef in a frying pan. Drain off the grease. Season with a seasoning blend. Add the sour cream and cream cheese. Stir the mixture over medium-low heat until blended and warmed.

Spoon the meat mixture onto the bottom half of the hamburger buns. Top with a slice of jalapeño pepper cheese, if desired. Broil just until cheese is melted. Add the top of the bun and serve. Some people also like lettuce and tomato with their sandwich.

Yield: 6 to 8 servings
Debbie O'Donovan

Nutrition Facts
Serving Size 287 g

Amount Per Serving	
Calories 605	Calories from Fat 293
	% Daily Value*
Total Fat 32.5g	50%
Saturated Fat 17.7g	89%
Trans Fat 0.0g	
Cholesterol 182mg	61%
Sodium 418mg	17%
Total Carbohydrates 24.9g	8%
Dietary Fiber 0.9g	4%
Sugars 2.9g	
Protein 51.0g	
Vitamin A 16%	Vitamin C 1%
Calcium 16%	Iron 94%

Nutrition Grade B
* Based on a 2000 calorie diet

Brock's Best

Home-Style Asian Burger

1 pound ground pork sausage
1 small onion, chopped
4 to 5 cloves garlic, chopped
½ teaspoon salt
½ teaspoon pepper
1 teaspoon ground ginger
¼ cup dry sherry
1 (6 ounce) can water chestnuts, finely diced
8 hamburger buns
Bean sprouts
1 cup sweet and sour sauce

In a large bowl, mix together the ground pork sausage, onion, garlic, salt, pepper, ginger, sherry, and water chestnuts.

Form the meat mixture into eight burger patties and grill over a medium heat.

Place on a hamburger bun and serve topped with the bean sprouts and sweet and sour sauce.

Yield: 8 servings
Keith Leder

Nutrition Facts
Serving Size 142 g

Amount Per Serving
Calories 270 — Calories from Fat 25
% Daily Value*
Total Fat 2.7g — 4%
Saturated Fat 0.9g — 4%
Trans Fat 0.0g
Cholesterol 2mg — 1%
Sodium 284mg — 12%
Total Carbohydrates 49.9g — 17%
Dietary Fiber 9.7g — 39%
Sugars 12.5g
Protein 13.1g

Vitamin A 3% • Vitamin C 21%
Calcium 8% • Iron 25%
Nutrition Grade A
* Based on a 2000 calorie diet

Pork

Pork Roast With Ginger Peach Glaze

2 teaspoons Season-All seasoned salt
1 teaspoon ground thyme
2 pounds pork loin roast, boneless
½ cup peach preserves
2 teaspoons Worcestershire sauce
¾ teaspoon ground ginger

Preheat your oven to 350° F. In a small bowl, mix the seasoned salt and thyme. Place the roast in an aluminum foil-lined roasting pan. Rub the seasoned salt–thyme mix on all sides of the roast.

Roast the pork for 1 ¼ hours, or until the desired doneness is achieved. Mix the preserves, Worcestershire Sauce, and ginger in small bowl. Spoon this sauce over the pork during the last 10 minutes of cooking and serve.

Yield: 8 servings
Joshua Stayrook

Brock's Best

Pork Stew

2 (1 ½ pound) pork tenderloins, trimmed of fat
1 yellow or white onion, chopped
1 can beef stock or beef bouillon
1 large can diced tomatoes
Salt and freshly ground black pepper
1 can large butter beans
1 to 2 tablespoons A.1. or Tabasco sauce (optional)

Layer the meat, onion, stock, and tomatoes into a crockpot, making sure the meat is completely covered. Season with salt and pepper now and/or later. Cover and set on high for at least 4 ½ hours.

When the meat is tender, break it up with a fork, and then add the butter beans. Simmer until serving time. The beans will turn mushy if they are left in the pot too long or stirred too often. Add A.1. or Tabasco if desired.

Serve with sourdough bread.

Yield: 4 to 5 servings
Debbie O'Donovan

Nutrition Facts

Serving Size 599 g

Amount Per Serving	
Calories 785	Calories from Fat 257
	% Daily Value*
Total Fat 28.5g	44%
Saturated Fat 10.2g	51%
Cholesterol 320mg	107%
Sodium 595mg	25%
Total Carbohydrates 17.7g	6%
Dietary Fiber 4.5g	18%
Sugars 3.7g	
Protein 107.8g	
Vitamin A 16% • Vitamin C 51%	
Calcium 5% • Iron 44%	
Nutrition Grade A-	

* Based on a 2000 calorie diet

Pork

Roast Pork Tenderloin With Balsamic Reduction, Fall Fruit Compote

Yield: 6 servings
Christine Trapaga

2 pork tenderloins
2 tablespoons olive oil
Salt and freshly ground black pepper
2 rosemary sprigs, minced
6 figs, diced and dried, for garnish
2 tablespoons butter
2 shallots, diced
1 pear, peeled and diced
1 green apple, peeled and diced
1 apricot, diced
¼ cup raisins
½ cup white wine
1 tablespoon chiffonade* of basil
1 cup balsamic vinegar
½ cup honey

Nutrition Facts
Serving Size 205 g

Amount Per Serving	
Calories 323	Calories from Fat 93
	% Daily Value*
Total Fat 10.3g	16%
Saturated Fat 3.7g	19%
Trans Fat 0.0g	
Cholesterol 28mg	9%
Sodium 47mg	2%
Total Carbohydrates 50.3g	17%
Dietary Fiber 3.9g	15%
Sugars 42.2g	
Protein 6.8g	
Vitamin A 7%	Vitamin C 7%
Calcium 5%	Iron 7%

Nutrition Grade C-
* Based on a 2000 calorie diet

*CHIFFONADE [shihf-uh-NAHD, shihf-uh-NAYD]—Literally translated, this French phrase means "made of rags." Culinarily, it refers to thin strips or shreds of vegetables (classically, sorrel and lettuce), either lightly sautéed or used raw to garnish soups.

Preheat your oven to 450° F. Rub the tenderloins with olive oil, and season with salt and pepper. Sear the tenderloins on a hot skillet, and then roast in the oven for 20 minutes.

Once removed from the oven, sprinkle with minced fresh rosemary and then let sit for 5 minutes before slicing (see the serve step). The pork can be slightly pink inside.

Sear the figs in a hot pan, and then dice into small pieces. Slice the pork tenderloins into medallions, drizzle with the balsamic reduction (recipe follows) and serve with the fruit compote (recipe follows). Use the figs as a garnish on the serving plate.

Balsamic Reduction
Combine the vinegar and honey in a saucepan and reduce to a thick, syrupy consistency after 20 to 25 minutes (please note this sauce will thicken as it cools).

Fruit Compote
In a skillet over medium heat, sauté the shallots in butter. Add the diced fruit and raisins. Cook for about 15 minutes until the fruit softens. Add the white wine, and continue cooking for another 10 minutes until the wine is reduced into the fruit. Stir in the fresh basil.

Brock's Best

Brock's Best

Root Beer–Glazed Ham

24 ounces—2 cans—(½ cup) Barq's Root Beer
4 ½ teaspoon (1 teaspoon) Tabasco sauce or similar
6 cloves (1 ½ cloves)
1 stick (1 pinch) cinnamon
1 (Pinch of crushed) bay leaf
½ peel of orange (dash of orange extract)
Freshly squeezed juice from 1 orange (5 teaspoons orange juice)
½ peel of lemon (dash of lemon extract)
12 pound (3 pound) smoked ham
¾ cup (3 tablespoons) dark brown sugar
½ teaspoon (1 pinch) dry mustard
½ cup (2 tablespoons) water

Preheat oven to 350° F. Combine the first eight ingredients (up to and including the lemon peel) in a large saucepan for the glaze. Bring the mixture to a boil, then lower to a simmer, and cook for about 30 minutes. Strain the pan contents and discard the strained solids. Return the liquid to the saucepan and reduce to about ½ cup. Refrigerate if doing this in advance. (For doing this in the home version, mix the eight ingredients in a mini-blender and uses this as the glaze.)

Place the ham on a rack in a disposable aluminum pan. Cut shallow gashes in a crisscross pattern across the top half of the meat. Spoon just enough of the glaze over the ham to completely cover the surface. Combine the brown sugar and mustard together and pat it all over the ham. Pour ½ cup of water into the pan. (2 tablespoons for the home version.)

Bake the ham, spooning some of the glaze over it every 15 minutes until the glaze is used up. Try to get some glaze on all parts of the ham. Continue baking for a total of 3 ½ to 4 hours, until the ham reaches an internal temperature on a meat thermometer, of 160° F.

Remove from the oven and allow to rest for 30 minutes before carving.

Nutrition Facts

Serving Size 260 g

Amount Per Serving

Calories 386 — Calories from Fat 169

	% Daily Value*
Total Fat 18.8g	29%
Saturated Fat 6.4g	32%
Trans Fat 0.0g	
Cholesterol 124mg	41%
Sodium 2856mg	119%
Total Carbohydrates 16.4g	5%
Dietary Fiber 2.9g	12%
Sugars 7.6g	
Protein 36.2g	

Vitamin A 0%	•	Vitamin C 18%
Calcium 6%	•	Iron 13%

Nutrition Grade B

* Based on a 2000 calorie diet

Yield: 25 to 30 servings-food service version (6 to 8 servings-home version)
Renee Bloch

South Carolina Style Pulled Pork Sandwich

Pork

Yield: 18 servings
Derek Chimel

Pork
1 (5 to 8 pound) pork butt, bone in
3 ounces chili powder
3 ounces salt
3 ounces brown sugar
4 cups cider vinegar
24 ounces (2 bottles) lager beer
2 cups BBQ sauce

Coleslaw
1 head green cabbage, shredded
2 carrots, grated
1 red onion, thinly sliced
1 ½ cup mayonnaise
¼ cup Dijon mustard
1 tablespoon cider vinegar
Freshly squeezed juice from 1 lemon
Pinch of sugar
½ teaspoon celery seed
Kosher salt and freshly ground black pepper

Pork
Preheat your oven to 300° F. Combine the chili powder, salt, and sugar together, and rub them into the pork, then place the pork in a deep pan or pot. Add vinegar and beer, cover with plastic wrap and then aluminum foil, or a tight fitting lid, taking care that no plastic wraps hangs out from under the foil or cover as it might melt away.

Cook in the oven for 4 to 6 hours, until the pork is tender and falling off the bone. When the pork is done, reserve the cooking liquid and allow the meat to cool in the refrigerator for about 1 ½ hours, then pull it apart, removing any fat or bone.

Finish the meat by mixing in about half of the cooking liquid along with the BBQ sauce. Season further with kosher salt and pepper if needed. Serve the pork warm on a potato roll topped with the coleslaw (recipe follows).

Coleslaw
Combine the cabbage, carrots, and red onion in a large bowl. In another bowl, stir together the mayonnaise, mustard, vinegar, lemon juice, and sugar. Pour the dressing over the cabbage mixture and toss gently to mix. Season the coleslaw with the celery seed, salt, and black pepper. Chill for 2 hours in the refrigerator before serving.

Nutrition Facts
Serving Size 339 g

Amount Per Serving

Calories 440	Calories from Fat 144

	% Daily Value*
Total Fat 16.0g	25%
Saturated Fat 3.9g	20%
Trans Fat 0.0g	
Cholesterol 121mg	40%
Sodium 2462mg	103%
Total Carbohydrates 27.9g	9%
Dietary Fiber 3.3g	13%
Sugars 15.6g	
Protein 41.0g	

Vitamin A 32%	•	Vitamin C 36%
Calcium 7%	•	Iron 16%

Nutrition Grade B-
* Based on a 2000 calorie diet

Brock's Best

Southwest Roasted Pork Loin

Yield: 12 servings
Samuel Cole

½ teaspoon chili powder
½ teaspoon salt
½ teaspoon garlic salt
4 pounds boneless rolled pork loin

Jelly Sauce
1 cup apple jelly
1 cup ketchup
2 tablespoons white vinegar
2 teaspoons more chili powder

Preheat your oven to 350° F. In a bowl, combine the chili powder, salt, and garlic salt, and then rub over the roast. Place the roast fat side up on a rack in a shallow roasting pan. Bake uncovered for 1 ½ hours.

Brush ¼ cup of the jelly sauce (recipe follows) over the roast. Bake for 10 to 15 minutes longer, until a meat thermometer reads 160° F. Remove the roast onto a serving platter and let stand for 10 to 15 minutes.

Skim the fat from the pan drippings and discard. Stir the remaining jelly sauce into the drippings to make a gravy. Heat it thoroughly and serve with the sliced roast loin.

Jelly Sauce

In a saucepan, combine the jelly, ketchup, vinegar, and chili powder. Bring to a boil, then cook and stir until the jelly is melted and the mixture is smooth. Reduce heat and simmer, uncovered, for 2 minutes.

Nutrition Facts

Serving Size 201 g

Amount Per Serving	
Calories 462	Calories from Fat 191
	% Daily Value*
Total Fat 21.2g	33%
Saturated Fat 7.9g	40%
Trans Fat 0.0g	
Cholesterol 121mg	40%
Sodium 428mg	18%
Total Carbohydrates 23.8g	8%
Dietary Fiber 0.5g	2%
Sugars 17.6g	
Protein 41.9g	
Vitamin A 7%	Vitamin C 11%
Calcium 4%	Iron 9%

Nutrition Grade B-
* Based on a 2000 calorie diet

Salads

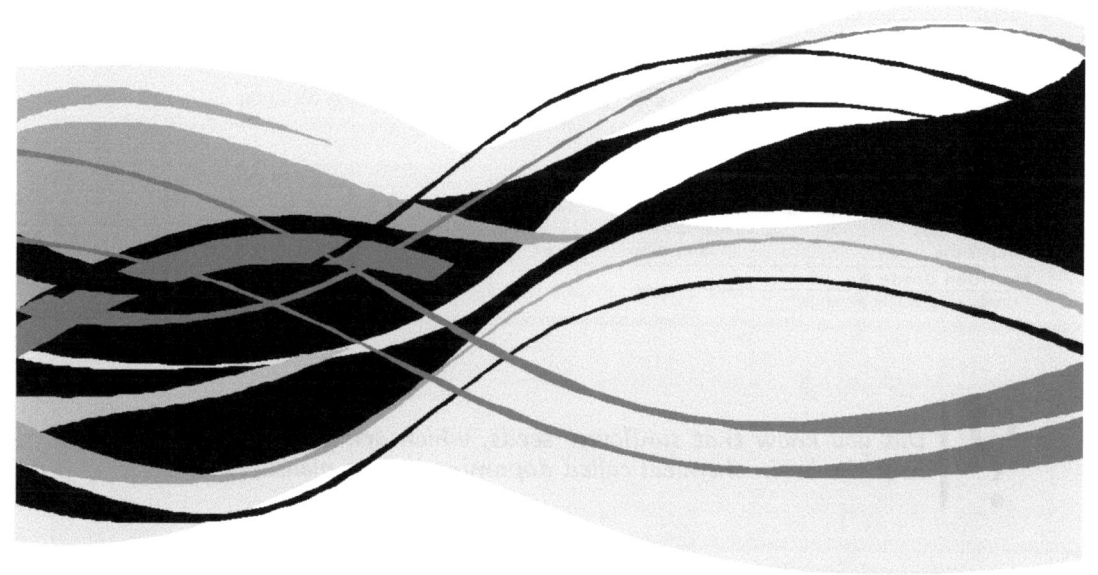

Brock's Best

Brock's Best

Apple Spinach Salad

1 bag fresh spinach
2 Granny Smith apples
1 cup sunflower seeds
⅓ cup apple vinegar
¼ teaspoon salt
1 teaspoon garlic salt
1 teaspoon celery salt

Wash the spinach and apples. Skin and slice the apples. Drain and add the spinach to a bowl along with the apples and sunflower seeds.

In a separate bowl, combine the vinegar, salt, garlic salt and celery salt for a dressing. Toss the spinach, apples, and sunflower seeds with the dressing.

Nutrition Facts
Serving Size 122 g

Amount Per Serving	
Calories 89	Calories from Fat 37
	% Daily Value*
Total Fat 4.1g	6%
Trans Fat 0.0g	
Cholesterol 0mg	0%
Sodium 137mg	6%
Total Carbohydrates 12.0g	4%
Dietary Fiber 3.2g	13%
Sugars 6.8g	
Protein 3.0g	

Vitamin A 90%	•	Vitamin C 27%
Calcium 6%	•	Iron 10%

Nutrition Grade A
* Based on a 2000 calorie diet

Yield: 6 to 8 servings

Larry Stelitano

Did you know that sunflower seeds, which are a good source of folate, help the brain chemical called dopamine induce pleasure?

Salads

Baby Blue Salad

10 to 12 ounce mixed salad green package
Balsamic Vinaigrette (ingredients follow)
1 cup crumbled (4 ounces) bleu cheese
2 oranges, peeled and cut into thin slices
2 cups (1 pint) quartered strawberries
Sweet and Spicy Pecans (ingredients follow)

Balsamic Vinaigrette
½ cup balsamic vinegar
3 tablespoons Dijon mustard
3 tablespoons honey
2 cloves garlic, minced
2 small shallots, minced
¼ teaspoon salt
¼ teaspoon pepper
1 cup olive oil

Sweet and Spicy Pecans
¼ cup sugar plus 2 tablespoons more for mixing with the chili powder & red pepper
1 cup warm water
1 cup pecan halves
1 tablespoon chili powder
Pinch of ground red pepper

Toss greens with Balsamic Vinaigrette (recipe follows) and crumbled bleu cheese. Place on 6 individual plates.

Arrange orange slices over greens. Sprinkle with strawberries. Top with Sweet-and-Spicy Pecans (recipe follows).

Balsamic Vinaigrette
Whisk the balsamic vinegar, Dijon mustard, honey, minced garlic, minced shallots, salt, and pepper together until blended,. Gradually whisk in olive oil.

Sweet and Spicy Pecans
Preheat your oven to 350° F. In a bowl, stir together ¼ cup sugar and 1 cup warm water until sugar dissolves. Add pecan halves, and soak for 10 minutes. Drain, discarding the sugar mixture.

Combine 2 tablespoons sugar, chili powder, and red pepper. Add the pecans, tossing to coat. Place on a lightly greased baking sheet.

Bake for 10 minutes, or until pecans are golden brown, stirring once.

Yield: 6 servings
Debbie O'Donovan

Nutrition Facts
Serving Size 328 g

Amount Per Serving	
Calories 640	Calories from Fat 476
	% Daily Value*
Total Fat 52.9g	81%
Saturated Fat 9.5g	47%
Trans Fat 0.0g	
Cholesterol 14mg	5%
Sodium 456mg	19%
Total Carbohydrates 40.3g	13%
Dietary Fiber 9.5g	38%
Sugars 30.6g	
Protein 7.9g	
Vitamin A 7%	Vitamin C 114%
Calcium 16%	Iron 6%

Nutrition Grade C+
* Based on a 2000 calorie diet

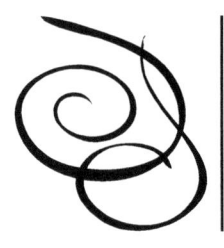

Brock's Best
Baby Mixed Greens With Apple Pear, Pecans, and Feta

3 tablespoons extra virgin olive oil
2 tablespoons red wine vinegar
2 tablespoons freshly squeezed orange juice
3 tablespoons finely chopped pecan halves
2 tablespoons honey
Sea salt and freshly ground black pepper
6 cups loosely packed baby mixed greens
1 Apple Pear, halved, cored, and sliced into thin wedges
⅓ cup pomegranate seeds or dried cranberries
⅓ cup feta cheese

To prepare the dressing, combine the olive oil, vinegar, orange juice, pecans, and honey in a salad bowl. Mix until well blended. Season with sea salt and pepper.

Add the greens and toss to coat with the dressing. Divide the salad among four plates. Top with the Apple Pear slices. Sprinkle with the pomegranate seeds or dried cranberries and feta cheese.

Yield: 4 servings
Gerry Guthridge

Nutrition Facts
Serving Size 279 g

Amount Per Serving
Calories 262 — Calories from Fat 151
% Daily Value*
Total Fat 16.8g — 26%
Saturated Fat 3.7g — 18%
Trans Fat 0.0g
Cholesterol 11mg — 4%
Sodium 201mg — 8%
Total Carbohydrates 24.9g — 8%
Dietary Fiber 5.6g — 23%
Sugars 12.6g
Protein 6.8g

Vitamin A 61% • Vitamin C 40%
Calcium 13% • Iron 8%
Nutrition Grade B-
* Based on a 2000 calorie diet

Salads

Barley and Mushroom Salad

Yield: 10 to 12 side servings
Chris Gearin

2 cups barley
4 cups vegetable stock
1 pound fresh baby spinach
½ cup olive oil
2 pounds fresh button mushrooms, quartered
1 tablespoon chopped garlic
4 cups half-sliced cherry tomatoes
Salt and freshly ground black pepper

Place the barley in a saucepan and cover with the vegetable stock. Bring to a boil for 25 to 30 minutes until the barley gets soft. Drain and rinse the barley in cold water and transfer to a large bowl. Cover the barley in the bowl with the fresh spinach leaves.

Add the oil to a sauté pan and heat until it begins to smoke. Add the quartered mushrooms and garlic. Sauté at high heat until mushrooms sear slightly. As the mushrooms begin to brown, add the halved cherry tomatoes. Let this mixture cook for 7 to 12 minutes depending on how soft you want the tomatoes.

When the tomatoes are done, pour the entire mixture over the barley and spinach leaves and toss. The hot oil will wilt the spinach. Season with salt and pepper. Serve as a side salad.

Nutrition Facts

Serving Size 254 g

Amount Per Serving	
Calories 259	Calories from Fat 104
	% Daily Value*
Total Fat 11.5g	18%
Saturated Fat 1.7g	8%
Cholesterol 0mg	0%
Sodium 53mg	2%
Total Carbohydrates 34.4g	11%
Dietary Fiber 9.1g	36%
Sugars 3.7g	
Protein 9.4g	
Vitamin A 95%	Vitamin C 40%
Calcium 6%	Iron 34%

Nutrition Grade A
* Based on a 2000 calorie diet

Brock's Best

Broccoli Slaw Salad

2 (3 ounce) bags ramen noodle soup, any flavor
6 tablespoons (¾ stick) butter
¼ cup slivered almonds
¼ cup sunflower seeds
½ cup whole cashews
2 (12 ounce) bags broccoli slaw
Green onions, chopped, for garnish

Dressing
¾ cup canola oil
¼ cup brown or white sugar
¼ cup apple cider vinegar
1 ramen noodle seasoning packet

Leave the ramen noodles in their package and crush them with a rolling pin. Meanwhile, melt the butter in a large skillet over low/medium heat.

Add the dry crushed noodles, slivered almonds, cashews, and sunflower seeds to the skillet and sauté (it's not necessary to brown the nuts and seeds if you prefer them raw), stirring occasionally. Keep the temperature at low/medium heat.

Meanwhile, whisk together all the dressing ingredients in a small bowl.

Place the shredded broccoli in a separate salad bowl and toss with the noodles, almonds, cashews, and sunflower seeds.

Pour the dressing over the salad and toss to coat. Garnish with chopped green onion.

Yield: 6 to 8 servings
Larry Stelitano

Nutrition Facts
Serving Size 222 g

Amount Per Serving	
Calories 646	Calories from Fat 469
	% Daily Value*
Total Fat 52.1g	80%
Saturated Fat 12.9g	65%
Trans Fat 0.1g	
Cholesterol 30mg	10%
Sodium 736mg	31%
Total Carbohydrates 39.7g	13%
Dietary Fiber 5.4g	22%
Sugars 12.9g	
Protein 9.8g	
Vitamin A 22%	Vitamin C 170%
Calcium 8%	Iron 17%

Nutrition Grade C
* Based on a 2000 calorie diet

? Did you know that parsley gives great flavor and is nutritious in salads? Just 1 ounce provides 43% of the Recommended Dietary Allowance for Vitamin C and 18% and RDA for iron in men and 12% in women, plus 1 mg of beta carotene.

Salads

Brown Rice Salad
With Citrus-Basil Vinaigrette

Citrus-Basil Vinaigrette
¾ cup freshly squeezed orange juice
¼ cup freshly squeezed lime juice
½ cup chopped fresh basil leaves
1 teaspoon kosher salt
¼ teaspoon freshly ground black pepper
1 tablespoon heaping tablespoons of honey
½ cup canola oil or olive oil

Brown Rice Salad
2 cups cooked brown rice
2 carrots, grated
1 small red onion, halved and minced
6 green onions, thinly sliced on an angle
Chopped fresh, cilantro, basil, and/or mint leaves, for garnish

Yield: 4 servings
Gerrard Zolezi

Combine the vinaigrette ingredients in a bowl and set aside.

Combine the rice, carrots, red onion and green onion, in a large bowl. Add the citrus-basil vinaigrette and stir to combine.

Let the salad sit at room temperature for 30 minutes before serving. Garnish with desired herbs.

Nutrition Facts
Serving Size 294 g

Amount Per Serving	
Calories 636	Calories from Fat 252
	% Daily Value*
Total Fat 28.0g	43%
Saturated Fat 4.1g	21%
Trans Fat 0.0g	
Cholesterol 0mg	0%
Sodium 612mg	25%
Total Carbohydrates 91.6g	31%
Dietary Fiber 5.4g	22%
Sugars 11.7g	
Protein 8.6g	
Vitamin A 14%	Vitamin C 104%
Calcium 6%	Iron 18%

Nutrition Grade B
* Based on a 2000 calorie diet

Brock's Best

Brock's Best

California Mango Chicken Salad

6 pounds (1 pound) chicken, cooked and diced
3 cups (½ cup) diced mangoes
½ cup (4 teaspoons) chopped cilantro
½ cup (4 teaspoons) chopped jalapeños
1 tablespoon (½ teaspoon) salt and pepper
2 tablespoons (1 teaspoon) chili powder
1 teaspoon (¼ teaspoon) cumin
1 tablespoon (½ teaspoon) coriander
2 sweet (3 tablespoons) red peppers, finely diced
¼ cup (2 teaspoons) honey
½ cup (4 teaspoons) Dijon mustard
¾ cup (2 tablespoons) mayonnaise

Yield: 40 sandwiches-food service version
(6 to 7 sandwiches-home versions)
Eric Lindholm

Mix all the ingredients well.

Serve with your favorite bread or sandwich roll.

Nutrition Facts

Serving Size 94 g

Amount Per Serving	
Calories 133	Calories from Fat 27
	% Daily Value*
Total Fat 3.0g	5%
Saturated Fat 0.7g	4%
Trans Fat 0.0g	
Cholesterol 53mg	18%
Sodium 273mg	11%
Total Carbohydrates 5.4g	2%
Dietary Fiber 0.6g	2%
Sugars 4.3g	
Protein 20.1g	

Vitamin A 6%	•	Vitamin C 10%
Calcium 1%	•	Iron 4%

Nutrition Grade B
* Based on a 2000 calorie diet

Salads

Carolina Cabbage

1 large head green cabbage
1 red bell pepper
1 green bell pepper
1 onion, large
1 head of broccoli
½ cup vegetable oil
½ pound turkey bacon
Mrs. Dash seasoning
Salt and freshly ground black pepper

Finely dice the cabbage. Remove the seeds from the peppers and dice. Dice the onion. Remove the broccoli florets from the stalk.

Combine all the ingredients except the seasonings. Adjust seasoning with Mrs. Dash and/or salt and pepper.

Allow to set in the refrigerator until the flavors have combined. Serve.

Nutrition Facts

Serving Size 84 g

Amount Per Serving

Calories 72	Calories from Fat 44
	% Daily Value*
Total Fat 4.9g	8%
Saturated Fat 0.9g	5%
Trans Fat 0.0g	
Cholesterol 6mg	2%
Sodium 84mg	4%
Total Carbohydrates 4.3g	1%
Dietary Fiber 1.7g	7%
Sugars 2.3g	
Protein 2.7g	

Vitamin A 8%	•	Vitamin C 60%
Calcium 2%	•	Iron 2%

Nutrition Grade B
* Based on a 2000 calorie diet

Yield: 24 servings
Antoine Lee

Brock's Best

Celyodka pod Shuboy— Herring Under a "Fur Coat"

Yield: 6 or more servings
Leonid Shteyman

2 beets
2 potatoes
3 carrots
3 eggs
1 onion
10 ounces pickled or salted herring fillet
2 sour Granny Smith apples
1 pound mayonnaise (use more if necessary)

Boil the beets, potatoes, and carrots, until done. Meanwhile boil the eggs, until they are hardboiled. Cool and peel the vegetables and eggs. Separate the egg whites from the yolks. Mince the onion.

Cut the herring fillets into small pieces. Grate the beets, potatoes, carrots, egg whites, and apples on a fine grater.

Place all the herring fillet pieces on the bottom of a flat dish. Next layer all of the grated potato. Then make a layer of all the minced onion. On top of these three layers, spread one-third of the mayonnaise.

Next make a layer of all of the shredded carrots, then make a layer of the shredded hardboiled egg whites, then spread with another one-third of the mayonnaise.

Make another layer with the apples. Top with the beets and then with the last one-third of the mayonnaise. Decorate with grated boiled egg yolks.

Nutrition Facts

Serving Size 359 g

Amount Per Serving	
Calories 538	Calories from Fat 298
	% Daily Value*
Total Fat 33.1g	51%
Saturated Fat 5.7g	28%
Trans Fat 0.0g	
Cholesterol 138mg	46%
Sodium 674mg	28%
Total Carbohydrates 45.7g	15%
Dietary Fiber 5.1g	20%
Sugars 17.0g	
Protein 16.5g	

| Vitamin A 13% | • | Vitamin C 40% |
| Calcium 7% | • | Iron 13% |

Nutrition Grade B-
* Based on a 2000 calorie diet

Salads

Couscous Salad

4 boxes couscous, cooked as instructed on box
1 cup green chopped onions
2 cups crumbled feta cheese
2 cups diced tomatoes
2 cups diced cucumbers
2 cups diced peppers
Freshly squeezed juice from 7 fresh lemons
¼ cup oil
Salt and freshly ground black pepper

After couscous has cooled and chilled, mix it with the rest of the ingredients except the salt and pepper. Use the salt and pepper to adjust the seasoning if needed.

Yield: 18 servings
Laura Walther

Nutrition Facts
Serving Size 129 g

Amount Per Serving	
Calories 242	Calories from Fat 64
	% Daily Value*
Total Fat 7.1g	11%
Saturated Fat 3.0g	15%
Trans Fat 0.0g	
Cholesterol 15mg	5%
Sodium 194mg	8%
Total Carbohydrates 37.7g	13%
Dietary Fiber 4.4g	17%
Sugars 2.1g	
Protein 8.4g	
Vitamin A 6%	Vitamin C 37%
Calcium 12%	Iron 14%

Nutrition Grade B
* Based on a 2000 calorie diet

Crabmeat Salad

12 ounces imitation crabmeat
¼ bunch celery
⅓ bunch green onions
2 cucumbers
3 hardboiled eggs
4 ounces sweet fish roe
2 to 3 tablespoons mayonnaise
Salt and freshly ground black pepper (optional)

Cut the crabmeat, celery, onions, cucumber, and hardboiled eggs into small pieces. Add sweet fish roe and mayonnaise. Mix well. Adjust the seasoning with salt and pepper if needed.

Yield: 4 servings
Leonid Shteyman

Nutrition Facts
Serving Size 377 g

Amount Per Serving	
Calories 237	Calories from Fat 77
	% Daily Value*
Total Fat 8.6g	13%
Saturated Fat 1.6g	8%
Trans Fat 0.0g	
Cholesterol 247mg	82%
Sodium 877mg	37%
Potassium 536mg	15%
Total Carbohydrates 24.0g	8%
Dietary Fiber 2.8g	11%
Sugars 7.5g	
Protein 18.6g	
Vitamin A 16%	Vitamin C 31%
Calcium 7%	Iron 25%

Nutrition Grade A-
* Based on a 2000 calorie diet

Brock's Best

Cucumber Salad

Yield: 15 servings
Gail Hollinger

5 cucumbers

Dressing
1 cup sour cream
¼ to ⅓ cup apple cider vinegar
1 teaspoon dill
½ teaspoon hot sauce
2 onions, chopped
Salt and freshly ground black pepper

Slice the cucumbers and add them to a salad bowl. Toss with the dressing (recipe follows). Chill for an hour and serve.

Dressing
In a bowl, combine the sour cream, vinegar, dill, hot sauce, and onions. Season with salt and pepper.

Nutrition Facts
Serving Size 136 g

Amount Per Serving	
Calories 56	Calories from Fat 31
	% Daily Value*
Total Fat 3.4g	5%
Saturated Fat 2.0g	10%
Trans Fat 0.0g	
Cholesterol 7mg	2%
Sodium 19mg	1%
Total Carbohydrates 5.8g	2%
Dietary Fiber 0.9g	4%
Sugars 0.7g	
Protein 1.2g	
Vitamin A 2%	Vitamin C 11%
Calcium 2%	Iron 11%

Nutrition Grade B+
* Based on a 2000 calorie diet

Dan's Country Style Coleslaw

75 (8 small apples) small apples
50 cups (5 cups) chopped fresh cabbage
4 pounds (1 ¼ cup) raisins
6 cups (⅔ of a cup) shredded carrots
1 cup (5 teaspoons) freshly squeezed lemon juice
Cinnamon

Yield: 80 to 100 servings-food service version
(8 to 10 servings-home version)
Dan Cuccia

Core, and then slice the apples. Add to the chopped cabbage, raisins, and shredded carrots. Toss in lemon juice. Season with cinnamon. Refrigerate for 2 hours. Serve chilled.

Nutrition Facts
Serving Size 202 g

Amount Per Serving	
Calories 143	Calories from Fat 2
	% Daily Value*
Total Fat 0.2g	0%
Trans Fat 0.0g	
Cholesterol 0mg	0%
Sodium 17mg	1%
Potassium 388mg	11%
Total Carbohydrates 37.3g	12%
Dietary Fiber 5.2g	21%
Sugars 27.4g	
Protein 1.2g	
Vitamin A 2%	Vitamin C 45%
Calcium 3%	Iron 7%

Nutrition Grade A
* Based on a 2000 calorie diet

Salads

Deconstructed Chicken Ratatouille Salad

Yield: 8 servings
Jonathan A. Berger

⅓ cup dry oregano
½ cup dry basil leaves
¼ cup dry marjoram
¼ cup rubbed sage
Kosher salt and freshly ground black pepper
Blended olive oil
2 zucchini squash, cut into 1-inch cubes
2 yellow squash, cut into 1-inch cubes
½ eggplant, cut into 1-inch cubes
1 large red pepper, thin julienned
1 red onion, cut into ½-inch cubes
1 large Portobello cap, cut into 1-inch cubes
8 ounces garlic, minced (1 cup minced)
3 tomatoes, cut into 1-inch cubes
Salt and freshly ground black pepper
1 pound chicken breast
5 to 6 cups mixed greens—spring mix or baby arugula
5 ounces shredded Parmesan cheese, for garnish

White Balsamic Vinaigrette
1 tablespoon Dijon mustard
1 tablespoon minced garlic
Salt and freshly ground black pepper
1 tablespoon freshly squeezed lemon or lime juice
½ cup white balsamic vinegar
1 cup blended olive oil

Preheat your oven to 425° F. Mix the dry spices, and add salt and pepper to taste. Add the mix to the vegetables listed in the ingredients up to and including the Portobello mushroom. Top the veggies with a little olive oil. Transfer them to a sheet pan. Roast for about 12 minutes, or until they begin to show color. Remove from the oven. Cool.

Add the garlic and tomatoes to a saucepot. Cook until the tomatoes just begin to break down. Remove from the heat and cool. Season the chicken with salt and pepper and roast until done. While the meat is still warm, julienne. In a large salad bowl, toss the chicken, vegetables, and tomatoes with the white balsamic vinaigrette (recipe follows). Add greens. Garnish with Parmesan cheese.

White Balsamic Vinaigrette
Mix all the ingredients except the oil with a hand blender. While blending, slowly add the oil until fully mixed. Season with salt and pepper.

Nutrition Facts
Serving Size 558 g

Amount Per Serving	
Calories 466	Calories from Fat 188
	% Daily Value*
Total Fat 20.9g	32%
Saturated Fat 4.2g	21%
Trans Fat 0.0g	
Cholesterol 72mg	24%
Sodium 462mg	19%
Potassium 1016mg	29%
Total Carbohydrates 39.6g	13%
Dietary Fiber 11.2g	45%
Sugars 9.6g	
Protein 34.1g	
Vitamin A 142%	Vitamin C 92%
Calcium 36%	Iron 35%

Nutrition Grade A
* Based on a 2000 calorie diet

Brock's Best

French Green Lentil Salad

2 cups French green lentils
1 cup diced red peppers
1 cup micro diced carrots
1 cup chopped scallions
1 cup olive oil
⅓ cup white balsamic vinegar
Salt and freshly ground black pepper
½ cup chopped fresh tarragon
2 cups crumbled feta cheese

Place the lentils in a saucepan and cover with water. Bring to boil and continue boiling for approximately 12 to 15 minutes. Water will turn slightly cloudy. Test the lentils for doneness. After 15 minutes of boiling, if they are not soft enough, cover and turn off the heat. Let them steep for 10 minutes and test again. When they are at the desired texture, drain and rinse with cold water.

In a large salad bowl combine lentils, peppers, carrots, and scallions. Mix thoroughly.

In a smaller bowl whisk together the oil and vinegar. Season with salt and pepper. Pour this vinaigrette over the lentil-vegetable mixture and blend. Add in the tarragon and feta. Toss until combined and serve.

Yield: 10 to 12 side dishes
Christopher Gearin

Nutrition Facts

Serving Size 128 g

Amount Per Serving	
Calories 427	Calories from Fat 249
	% Daily Value*
Total Fat 27.6g	42%
Saturated Fat 7.4g	37%
Trans Fat 0.0g	
Cholesterol 27mg	9%
Sodium 347mg	14%
Total Carbohydrates 31.9g	11%
Dietary Fiber 10.5g	42%
Sugars 2.8g	
Protein 14.9g	
Vitamin A 8% •	Vitamin C 8%
Calcium 21% •	Iron 28%

Nutrition Grade B-
* Based on a 2000 calorie diet

Salads

Georgian Style Bean Salad

1 large can of dark red kidney beans
1 bunch cilantro
1 white onion
1 cup shelled walnuts
4 cloves of garlic, peeled
2 tablespoons vegetable oil
2 tablespoons white vinegar
Pinch of salt

Empty the can of beans into a colander and drain. Wash the cilantro and add to the colander.

Grind the beans, cilantro, onion, walnuts, and garlic through a meat grinder. Transfer the ground mixture to a bowl. Add the vegetable oil, vinegar, and salt. Mix well using a mixing spoon. Chill and serve.

Yield: 8 servings
Veta Mesh

Nutrition Facts
Serving Size 110 g

Amount Per Serving	
Calories 387	Calories from Fat 121
	% Daily Value*
Total Fat 13.4g	21%
Saturated Fat 1.3g	7%
Trans Fat 0.0g	
Cholesterol 0mg	0%
Sodium 11mg	0%
Total Carbohydrates 48.9g	16%
Dietary Fiber 12.7g	51%
Sugars 2.2g	
Protein 20.9g	
Vitamin A 3%	Vitamin C 10%
Calcium 8%	Iron 31%

Nutrition Grade A
* Based on a 2000 calorie diet

 Did you know that all kinds of nuts are very healthy for you? First it takes more time to chew than to chew french fries, plus it contains fat and fiber that needs more time to digest, so your stomach stays fuller and you feel satisfied longer, and you'll end up eating less at your next meal.

Brock's Best

Kielbasa and Lentil Salad
With Warm Mustard Fennel Dressing

Yield: 6 servings
Mark Gazo

1 pound package dried lentils
3 carrots, peeled thinly sliced
2 celery stalks, chopped
½ teaspoon of salt
⅓ cup malt vinegar
2 tablespoons coarse grain Dijon mustard
1 ½ teaspoon sugar
2 tablespoons olive oil for cooking the kielbasa plus ½ cup for later in the recipe
1 pound fully cooked smoked kielbasa
3 cloves garlic, peeled and flattened
1 large fennel bulb with fronds*, bulb and fronds chopped, fronds used for garnish
5 green onions, chopped
2 heads frisée** lettuce or curly endive

Place the lentils, carrots, and celery in a heavy large saucepan. Add enough cold water to cover. Stir in the salt and bring to a boil. Reduce heat, cover, and simmer about 20 minutes until tender. Drain the vegetables and transfer to a bowl.

Whisk the vinegar, mustard, and sugar in a small bowl to blend. Heat 2 tablespoons of oil in a heavy skillet over medium-high heat and sauté the kielbasa for about 5 minutes until brown. Transfer the sausage to a plate lined with paper towels, and cover to keep warm.

Pour off any fat from the skillet. Add the remaining ½ cup olive oil and decrease the heat to medium. Add the garlic, and stir and cook for about 2 minutes until golden. Add the fennel bulb and sauté for about 4 minutes more. Add the green onions and stir 1 more minute. Whisk in the vinegar mixture and bring to a boil. Pour this fennel and dressing mix over the lentils and toss to coat. Season with salt and pepper.

Line a serving platter with frisée leaves, spoon on the lentil salad, and arrange the kielbasa on top of lentils. Garnish with chopped fennel.

Nutrition Facts
Serving Size 395 g

Amount Per Serving

Calories 770	Calories from Fat 421
	% Daily Value*
Total Fat 46.8g	72%
Saturated Fat 10.5g	53%
Trans Fat 0.0g	
Cholesterol 47mg	16%
Sodium 893mg	37%
Total Carbohydrates 60.1g	20%
Dietary Fiber 27.0g	108%
Sugars 8.0g	
Protein 31.3g	
Vitamin A 117%	Vitamin C 27%
Calcium 11%	Iron 41%

Nutrition Grade B
* Based on a 2000 calorie diet

*FENNEL BULB WITH FRONDS—The fronds resemble ferns. It has bright green feathery leaf also resembling dill. The fronds can be used as a seasoning, eaten alone, or in salads, or even used to make a tea.

**FRISÉE [free-ZAY]—Another feathery vegetable, it has a mildly bitter flavor often used in the special salad mix, mesclun. Choose crisp leaf frisée with no sign of wilting. Refrigerate in a plastic bag for up to 5 days. Wash just before using.

Salads

Panzanella* (Bread Salad)

4 ciabatta rolls (4 by 4 inches)
3 tablespoons balsamic vinegar
3 tablespoons extra virgin olive oil
¼ teaspoon kosher salt
¼ teaspoon coarse black pepper
4 tomatoes, peeled, seeded, and diced in 1-inch cubes
1 red onion, cut into julienne
1 small zucchini, cut into 1-inch cubes
1 cup fresh basil chiffonade**
¾ cup chopped fresh Italian parsley
2 cloves garlic diced and sautéed
5 cups cleaned baby arugula

Cut bread lengthwise into 4 by 2-inch strips and place them on a hot grill. Lightly grill both sides of the bread.

To make the dressing, stir together the vinegar, oil, salt, and pepper in a small bowl.

In a salad bowl, mix the grilled bread, tomatoes, onion, zucchini, basil, parsley, and garlic. Gently add the arugula, and toss all in the dressing. Serve on a chilled serving plate.

*PANZANELLA [pahn-zah-NEHL-lah]—An Italian bread salad made with onions, tomatoes, basil, olive oil, vinegar, seasonings, and chunks of bread. Some versions also include cucumbers, anchovies, and/or peppers.

**CHIFFONADE [shihf-uh-NAHD, shihf-uh-NAYD]—Literally translated, this French phrase means "made of rags." Culinarily, it refers to thin strips or shreds of vegetables (classically, sorrel and lettuce), either lightly sautéed or used raw to garnish soups.

Nutrition Facts

Serving Size 308 g

Amount Per Serving

Calories 240 — Calories from Fat 116

	% Daily Value*
Total Fat 12.9g	20%
Saturated Fat 1.6g	8%
Trans Fat 0.0g	
Cholesterol 0mg	0%
Sodium 170mg	7%
Total Carbohydrates 26.1g	9%
Dietary Fiber 4.3g	17%
Sugars 5.9g	
Protein 6.2g	

Vitamin A 54% • Vitamin C 73%
Calcium 7% • Iron 18%

Nutrition Grade B+
* Based on a 2000 calorie diet

Yield: 4 to 6 servings
Peter Gruenfelder

Brock's Best

Quinoa Salad

3 cups quinoa*
3 cups cooked black beans
3 tablespoons red wine vinegar
3 cups cooked corn kernels
1 ½ cup diced, mixed, red and green peppers
2 jalapeño peppers, diced in small cubes
¼ cup chopped cilantro
½ cup freshly squeezed lime juice
1 tablespoon ground cumin
⅔ cup olive oil
Salt and freshly ground black pepper

Rinse the quinoa well, and cook in a large pot in about 6 cups of water. Drain. Also cook the beans in a saucepot, and drain.

Combine the quinoa and beans with all the rest of the ingredients in a salad or mixing bowl. Season with salt and pepper.

Serve as a side dish for an entrée, a base for a salad with protein, or on a salad bar.

Yield: 12 servings
Jen Foy

*QUINOA [KEEN-wah]—Tiny and bead-shaped, the ivory-colored quinoa cooks like rice (taking half the time of regular rice) and expands to four times its original volume. Its flavor is delicate, almost bland, and has been compared to that of couscous.

Nutrition Facts

Serving Size 149 g

Amount Per Serving

Calories 476 — Calories from Fat 146

% Daily Value*

Total Fat 16.2g — 25%
Saturated Fat 2.6g — 13%
Trans Fat 0.0g
Cholesterol 0mg — 0%
Sodium 77mg — 3%
Total Carbohydrates 66.4g — 22%
Dietary Fiber 13.0g — 52%
Sugars 2.7g
Protein 17.9g

Vitamin A 3% • Vitamin C 18%
Calcium 9% • Iron 26%

Nutrition Grade A-
* Based on a 2000 calorie diet

Salads

Red Bliss Potato Salad

5 pounds (8 to 10) red bliss potatoes
10 (3 eggs) hard-boiled eggs
3 cups (1 cup) mayonnaise
1 cup (⅓ cup) sour cream
4 tablespoons (4 teaspoons) yellow mustard
2 tablespoons (3 teaspoons) chopped fresh parsley
Salt and freshly ground black pepper
1 ½ cup (½ cup) diced celery

Boil the potatoes until a fork can be easily inserted. Drain and chill them.

Leaving the skin on, cut the potatoes into small cubes. Transfer the potato cubes to a salad bowl. Criss-cross cut the eggs and add them to the potatoes.

In a separate bowl, mix the mayonnaise, sour cream, mustard, and parsley. Season with salt and pepper. Add this mayonnaise dressing and the diced celery to the potatoes. Fold together completely, chill, and serve.

Nutrition Facts

Serving Size 195 g

Amount Per Serving

Calories 328	Calories from Fat 210
	% Daily Value*
Total Fat 23.3g	36%
Saturated Fat 5.6g	28%
Trans Fat 0.0g	
Cholesterol 98mg	33%
Sodium 645mg	27%
Total Carbohydrates 26.0g	9%
Dietary Fiber 1.7g	7%
Sugars 4.1g	
Protein 5.6g	
Vitamin A 8% •	Vitamin C 11%
Calcium 6% •	Iron 5%

Nutrition Grade D+

* Based on a 2000 calorie diet

Yield: 20 servings-food service version
(6 to 7 servings-home version)
Tim McCarty

Brock's Best

Sesame Snow Pea Salad

2 pounds fresh snow peas
2 red onion, sliced rough against grain
2 carrots, shredded on box grater
2 red peppers, julienned
Salt and freshly ground black pepper

Sesame Dressing
¾ cup toasted sesame oil
¼ cup rice vinegar
2 tablespoons soy sauce
3 tablespoons fresh grated ginger root
1 tablespoon fresh chopped garlic

Nutrition Facts
Serving Size 104 g

Amount Per Serving	
Calories 149	Calories from Fat 83
	% Daily Value*
Total Fat 9.2g	14%
Saturated Fat 1.3g	7%
Trans Fat 0.0g	
Cholesterol 0mg	0%
Sodium 314mg	13%
Total Carbohydrates 12.6g	4%
Dietary Fiber 4.1g	17%
Sugars 3.4g	
Protein 4.8g	
Vitamin A 8%	Vitamin C 51%
Calcium 19%	Iron 20%
Nutrition Grade A	

* Based on a 2000 calorie diet

Preheat your oven to 400° F. Bring a large pot of water to a boil. Drop in the snow peas for 20 seconds, drain or fish them out, and plunge them into a large pot of ice water. Skim the snow peas out of the ice water, dry, and reserve.

Lightly toss the chopped red onions in sesame oil. Place them on a sheet pan and roast in the oven for 9 to 12 minutes, until they wilt and turn a bit brown. Remove them from the oven and cool.

In a salad bowl, combine the snow peas, red onions, carrots, and red peppers. Toss liberally in the sesame dressing (recipe follows). Season with salt and pepper, and serve.

Sesame Dressing
In small bowl whisk together the sesame oil, rice vinegar, and soy sauce. Add the ginger and garlic, and whisk again.

Yield: 8 to 10 side servings
Chris Gearin

Salads

Seven-Layer Salad

1 head of iceberg lettuce, chopped
2 stalks of celery, chopped
1 red bell pepper, chopped
10 ounce frozen peas, thawed
¾ cup ranch dressing
8 slices turkey bacon, cooked, crumbled
½ cup grated cheddar cheese

Place the lettuce in a clear glass salad bowl (the transparency enhances the appeal of the layers). Top with a layer of celery, then bell pepper, and then the peas. Spread ranch dressing over the peas. Top with a layer each of bacon and cheddar cheese, and serve.

Yield: 8 servings
Elena Zenchenko

Spinach Pasta Salad

1 cup pine nuts
⅓ cup white wine vinegar
2 teaspoons dried basil
2 large cloves garlic
1 teaspoon salt
1 tsp pepper
¾ cup olive oil
1 lb (6 cups) bow-tie pasta
1 bag baby spinach
8 oz feta cheese

Toast the pine nuts in a 350° F oven for about 12 minutes, or until golden brown, stirring midway. Be careful not to burn them, as this can happen easily.

To make the dressing, mix the wine vinegar, basil, garlic, salt, and pepper together. Whisk in the olive oil. Set aside.

Cook the bow tie pasta. Combine pasta, baby spinach, pine nuts and feta cheese. Toss all in a salad bowl at least 1 hour before serving.

Yield: 10 servings
Lori Testa

Brock's Best

Turkey Barley Mandarin Salad

Pearl Barley
¾ cup of pearl barley
2 ¼ cup water
½ teaspoon of salt

Salad
4 to 5 tablespoons sesame oil salad dressing
1 (11 ounce) can mandarin oranges, undrained
1 ½ cup cooked cubed turkey or chicken
½ cup sliced celery
¼ cup sliced green onions
3 ½ cup fresh salad greens, torn
Crunchy oriental noodles, for garnish

Place the barley, water, and salt in a saucepan. Bring to boil. Reduce heat to low, cover, and cook 45 minutes, or until barley is tender and liquid is absorbed.

Salad

Drizzle the salad dressing over the hot cooked barley (cooking instructions above). Toss gently to coat. Cover the barley and refrigerate until cool.

To assemble the rest of the salad, drain the mandarin oranges, reserving 2 tablespoons of liquid. Next combine the mandarin oranges, reserved mandarin oranges liquid, cooled barley, turkey (or chicken), celery, and green onions. Toss gently.

Arrange the salad greens on four dinner plates. Mound the barley salad over the greens. Sprinkle each serving with crunchy noodles if desired.

Yield: 4 servings
Gerrard Zolezi

Nutrition Facts

Serving Size 321 g

Amount Per Serving	
Calories 696	Calories from Fat 188
	% Daily Value*
Total Fat 20.9g	32%
Saturated Fat 4.9g	24%
Trans Fat 0.0g	
Cholesterol 40mg	13%
Sodium 651mg	27%
Total Carbohydrates 101.1g	34%
Dietary Fiber 17.8g	71%
Sugars 9.2g	
Protein 29.1g	
Vitamin A 27%	Vitamin C 50%
Calcium 10%	Iron 21%
Nutrition Grade B+	

* Based on a 2000 calorie diet

Salads

Vegetarian Pasta Salad

1 box pasta (rotini, bows, macaroni)
1 cucumber, peeled and chopped
1 cup grape tomatoes
1 cup Italian dressing
1 can black olives
1 can artichoke hearts
McCormick Perfect Pinch Salad Supreme Seasoning

Cook the pasta according to its box directions. Rinse and cool. In a salad bowl, combine the pasta, cucumber, tomatoes, Italian dressing, olives, and artichokes. Season with the mentioned McCormick's seasoning (or salt and freshly ground pepper). Serve cold.

Yield: 6 to 8 servings
Larry Stelitano

Nutrition Facts
Serving Size 128 g

Amount Per Serving	
Calories 142	Calories from Fat 114
	% Daily Value*
Total Fat 12.6g	19%
Saturated Fat 1.9g	10%
Trans Fat 0.0g	
Cholesterol 26mg	9%
Sodium 130mg	5%
Total Carbohydrates 7.7g	3%
Dietary Fiber 1.0g	4%
Sugars 3.9g	
Protein 0.8g	
Vitamin A 2%	Vitamin C 11%
Calcium 2%	Iron 7%

Nutrition Grade C+
* Based on a 2000 calorie diet

Warm Potato Salad With Honey Mustard Dressing

⅓ cup cider vinegar
2 tablespoons vegetable oil
¼ cup honey
1 tablespoon Dijon mustard
Dash of hot sauce
1 ½ pound cooked red bliss potatoes, cut into wedges
5 slices Applewood bacon, crisp, crumbled
2 tablespoons chopped parsley
2 tablespoons green chopped onions
½ teaspoon salt

Combine the vinegar, oil, honey, mustard, and hot sauce. Mix well. Add the potatoes and mix to coat all surfaces. Heat in a large saucepot on medium heat, until the potatoes are thoroughly heated. Add the bacon, parsley, green onions, and salt. Toss to mix well. Serve immediately.

Yield: 6 servings
Essie Brown

Nutrition Facts
Serving Size 235 g

Amount Per Serving	
Calories 270	Calories from Fat 131
	% Daily Value*
Total Fat 14.6g	22%
Saturated Fat 3.3g	17%
Trans Fat 0.0g	
Cholesterol 14mg	5%
Sodium 698mg	29%
Total Carbohydrates 30.8g	10%
Dietary Fiber 1.8g	7%
Sugars 17.2g	
Protein 3.5g	
Vitamin A 3%	Vitamin C 31%
Calcium 1%	Iron 4%

Nutrition Grade D+
* Based on a 2000 calorie diet

Brock's Best

Notes

Seafood

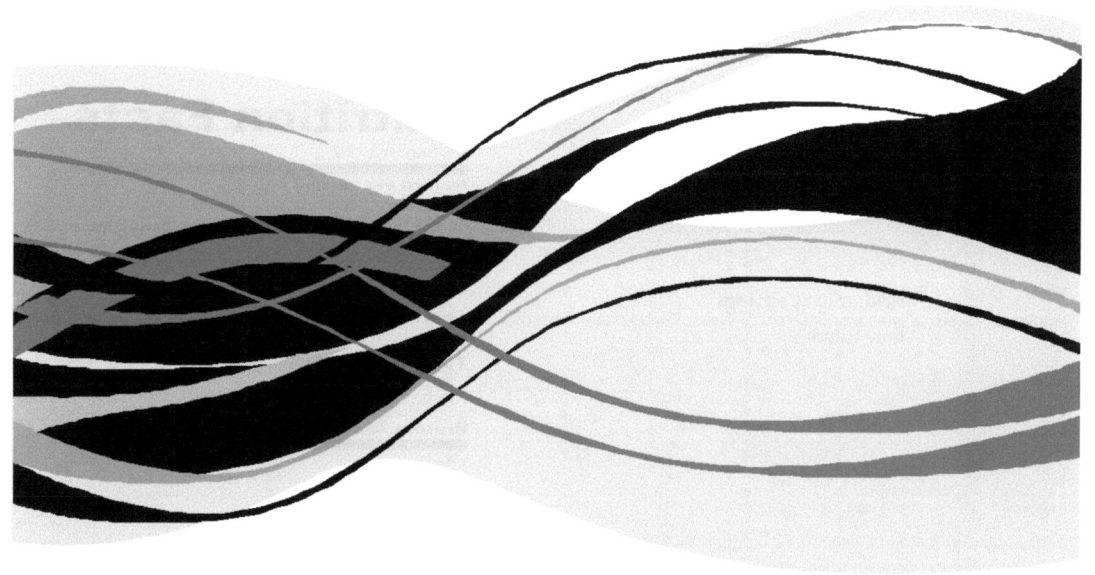

Brock's Best

Brock's Best

Bay Scallops and Bulgur Wheat with Fresh Mint

2 pounds bay scallops
1 pound bulgur wheat
2 cucumbers, peeled, seeded, and diced
2 tomatoes, peeled, seeded, and diced
½ bunch mint, chopped
½ bunch parsley, chopped
4 limes freshly squeezed for juice
1 teaspoon kosher salt
3 ounces olive oil

Steam or poach the bay scallops until tender. Drain and chill.

In a large stockpot, boil bulgur wheat in about 6 quarts of water until cooked (approximately 20 to 30 minutes). Drain in a colander and rinse with cold water to chill.

Mix the chilled bulgur wheat and scallops with the remaining ingredients. Chill and serve.

Yield: 12 to 14 servings
Tony Paterno

Nutrition Facts

Serving Size 592 g

Amount Per Serving	
Calories 126	Calories from Fat 61
	% Daily Value*
Total Fat 6.8g	10%
Saturated Fat 0.9g	5%
Trans Fat 0.0g	
Cholesterol 23mg	8%
Sodium 306mg	13%
Total Carbohydrates 4.5g	1%
Dietary Fiber 0.6g	2%
Sugars 0.6g	
Protein 12.2g	
Vitamin A 6%	Vitamin C 14%
Calcium 3%	Iron 9%

Nutrition Grade B+
* Based on a 2000 calorie diet

Seafood

Braised Sea Bass and Fennel With Saffron and Harissa

Yield: 4 servings
Tony Powell

6 tablespoons extra virgin olive oil
2 onions, thinly sliced
6 large fennel bulbs, quartered and thinly sliced
4 cups fresh fish stock
Pinch of saffron threads
Coarse sea salt and freshly ground black pepper
4 small sea bass fillets
1 pound red potato, boiled and peeled
3 teaspoons harissa paste*

Heat the oil in a large sauté pan. Add the onions and fennel, and cook for about 5 minutes, or until lightly golden brown. Add the fish stock and saffron. Cover and simmer for 15 minutes. Season with sea salt and pepper.

Also season the inside and outside of the sea bass fillets with sea salt and freshly ground pepper. Put the fish on top of the fennel, cover, and simmer about 10 minutes, or until the fish is cooked through.

While the fish is cooking, crush the potatoes with a fork and set aside.

Remove the sea bass fillets from the fennel mixture and set them on a large dinner plate. Keep them warm in a low temperature oven.

Raise the heat to high and cook the remaining fennel mixture for another 5 minutes. Add the crushed potatoes and harissa paste, and continue cooking about 5 more minutes, or until warmed throughout. Again, adjust the seasoning with salt and pepper, if needed.

On a serving platter, spoon the fennel and the potato mixture beside the sea bass fillets and serve.

Nutrition Facts

Serving Size 658 g

Amount Per Serving

Calories 470 — Calories from Fat 221

	% Daily Value*
Total Fat 24.5g	38%
Saturated Fat 3.5g	18%
Trans Fat 0.0g	
Cholesterol 2mg	1%
Sodium 748mg	31%
Total Carbohydrates 33.3g	11%
Dietary Fiber 7.2g	29%
Sugars 3.5g	
Protein 32.6g	

| Vitamin A 4% | • | Vitamin C 56% |
| Calcium 8% | • | Iron 10% |

Nutrition Grade B
* Based on a 2000 calorie diet

---

*HARISSA PASTE [hah-REE-suh]—From Tunisia, this fiery-hot sauce is usually made with hot chilies, garlic, cumin, coriander, caraway, and olive oil. It's the traditional accompaniment for couscous but is also used to flavor soups, stews, and other dishes. Harissa can be found in cans and jars.

Brock's Best

Brock's Best

Caramelized Salmon with Citrus Salsa

Citrus Salsa
6 oranges, peeled and sectioned—
save zest before peeling
1 fresh pineapple, small dice
1 tablespoon cilantro
2 jalapeño peppers, seeded and
chopped fine
1 green onion, sliced
1 lime

Caramelized Salmon
2 tablespoons grated orange zest
6 tablespoons sugar
6 (5 ounce) salmon fillets, skinned and cut
2 tablespoons salt and pepper mix

Citrus Salsa
Mix together all the ingredients and let stand overnight for best flavor.

Caramelized Salmon
In a small bowl, mix the orange zest and the sugar together. Sprinkle on top of the salmon and broil at the low setting first, and then move to a higher setting to finish. Cook for a total 4 to 8 minutes, until firm to the touch.

Top the Caramelized Salmon with the Citrus Salsa, and serve on a serving platter.

Yield: 6 servings
Michael Hamilton

Nutrition Facts

Serving Size 420 g

Amount Per Serving	
Calories 374	Calories from Fat 90
	% Daily Value*
Total Fat 10.0g	15%
Saturated Fat 1.4g	7%
Trans Fat 0.0g	
Cholesterol 63mg	21%
Sodium 186mg	8%
Total Carbohydrates 45.6g	15%
Dietary Fiber 6.0g	24%
Sugars 35.1g	
Protein 29.9g	

Vitamin A 15%	•	Vitamin C 219%
Calcium 14%	•	Iron 8%

Nutrition Grade A
* Based on a 2000 calorie diet

? Did you know that salmon contains high omega-3 fatty acids and can help reverse stress symptoms by boosting serotonin levels, and that an omega-3-rich diet can also help suppress the production of the anxiety hormones cortisol and adrenaline?

Seafood

Crab Cakes with Peach Salsa

Peach Salsa
1 pound peaches, frozen
½ red bell pepper, diced
½ cup sliced green onions
1 jalapeño pepper, seeded and diced
4 tomatoes, seeded and diced
2 limes, freshly squeezed juiced
3 teaspoons cilantro
Salt

Crab Cakes
3 tablespoons heavy cream
1 egg
2 tablespoons mayonnaise
½ cup dry mustard
¼ teaspoon freshly ground black pepper
½ teaspoon salt
2 teaspoons Worcestershire sauce
¼ teaspoon Tabasco sauce
¼ teaspoon Old Bay seasoning
½ teaspoon parsley flakes
1 pound lump crabmeat
3 ounces breadcrumbs

Yield: 4 servings
Michael Hamilton

Peach Salsa
Mix all the ingredients and let stand overnight.

Crab Cakes
In a bowl, blend all the ingredients except the crabmeat and breadcrumbs. Fold in the crabmeat and breadcrumbs. Form the batter into cakes.

Either bread the crab cakes with more breadcrumbs and fry, or fry without breading, for 4 to 8 minutes, until golden brown. Serve the crab cakes with the Peach Salsa (recipe above).

Nutrition Facts
Serving Size 472 g

Amount Per Serving
Calories 460 — Calories from Fat 155

	% Daily Value*
Total Fat 17.2g	26%
Saturated Fat 4.2g	21%
Trans Fat 0.0g	
Cholesterol 172mg	57%
Sodium 953mg	40%
Total Carbohydrates 44.4g	15%
Dietary Fiber 8.3g	33%
Sugars 17.7g	
Protein 35.1g	

Vitamin A 46% • Vitamin C 95%
Calcium 30% • Iron 39%

Nutrition Grade A
* Based on a 2000 calorie diet

Brock's Best

Fresh Tuna Tacos

⅓ cup sour cream
¼ cup chopped red onions
3 tablespoons chopped cilantro
1 teaspoon minced canned chipotle chilies
1 (8 ounce) tuna steak, cut in ¾-inch pieces
1 tablespoon taco seasoning mix
1 tablespoon vegetable oil
Taco shells

Garnish
Lettuce, shredded
Avocado, sliced
Black olives
Salsa

Mix the sour cream, red onions, cilantro, and chilies in a small bowl.

Sprinkle the tuna steak pieces with taco seasoning. Heat the oil in a heavy skillet over medium high heat. Add the tuna and sauté to desired doneness (3 minutes for medium). Reduce heat to medium low.

Stir in the sour cream mixture. Cook about 2 minutes (do not boil), just until heated throughout, stirring frequently.

Fill the taco shells with the tuna mixture. Garnish with salsa, shredded lettuce, sliced avocado, and black olives.

Nutrition Facts

Serving Size 411 g

Amount Per Serving
Calories 455 — Calories from Fat 247

	% Daily Value*
Total Fat 27.4g	42%
Saturated Fat 7.7g	39%
Trans Fat 1.3g	
Cholesterol 39mg	13%
Sodium 745mg	31%
Total Carbohydrates 30.5g	10%
Dietary Fiber 5.9g	23%
Sugars 5.7g	
Protein 21.7g	

Vitamin A 38% • Vitamin C 12%
Calcium 7% • Iron 13%

Nutrition Grade B
* Based on a 2000 calorie diet

Yield: 4 servings
Mark Gazo

Seafood

Lemon Shrimp Bean Thread Vermicelli

Yield: 2 servings
Jie Astri

1 tablespoon fish sauce
1 teaspoon freshly squeezed lemon juice
1 teaspoon chopped garlic
½ teaspoon sugar
Pinch of crushed red peppers or Szechwan* pepper
4 ounces bean thread noodles or vermicelli
10 shrimp, 16/20 count
1 tomato, diced
1 lemon
Salt and white pepper

In a saucepan, combine the fish sauce, lemon juice, garlic, sugar, and red pepper. Bring to a boil, decrease to simmer, and hold until needed.

In a pot, cook the bean thread noodles or vermicelli until al dente.

Cook the shrimp in a wok with the diced tomato. Squeeze in lemon juice. Add the cooked noodles to the shrimp.

Add the held fish sauce mixture to the wok and the noodles. Adjust the seasoning with salt and white pepper. Plate and serve.

*SZECHWAN PEPPER; SZECHWAN [SEHCH-wahn, SEHCH-oo-ahn]—Native to the Szechwan province of China, this mildly hot spice comes from the prickly ash tree. Though not related to the peppercorn family, Szechwan berries resemble black peppercorns but contain a tiny seed.

Nutrition Facts

Serving Size 241 g

Amount Per Serving

Calories 353 — Calories from Fat 19

	% Daily Value*
Total Fat 2.1g	3%
Saturated Fat 0.6g	3%
Cholesterol 232mg	77%
Sodium 1049mg	44%
Total Carbohydrates 56.3g	19%
Dietary Fiber 1.5g	6%
Sugars 2.9g	
Protein 26.3g	

Vitamin A 12% • Vitamin C 35%
Calcium 13% • Iron 13%

Nutrition Grade B+

* Based on a 2000 calorie diet

Brock's Best

Maryland Crab Cake Salad

4 cups mixed salad greens

Crabmeat Salad
⅓ cup mayonnaise
1 ½ teaspoon Old Bay seasoning
1 tablespoon drained capers
½ teaspoon Worcestershire sauce
1 teaspoon Dijon mustard
1 pound fresh lump crabmeat, drained
½ cup finely diced red bell pepper
½ cup finely diced cucumber
½ cup minced green onions

Toasted Breadcrumbs
1 tablespoon butter
¼ cup Japanese breadcrumbs (panko)

Serve crabmeat salad (recipe follows) over mixed greens, and top each serving with toasted breadcrumbs (recipe follows).

Crabmeat Salad
Combine the mayonnaise, Old Bay seasoning, capers, Worcestershire sauce, and Dijon mustard in a large bowl and mix well. Gently fold in the crabmeat. Fold in the bell peppers, cucumbers, and green onions.

Toasted Breadcrumbs
Melt the butter in a skillet. Add the breadcrumbs and cook, stirring frequently, over high heat for 4 minutes, or until golden brown and toasted.

Nutrition Facts
Serving Size 321 g

Amount Per Serving	
Calories 264	Calories from Fat 105
	% Daily Value*
Total Fat 11.7g	18%
Saturated Fat 3.1g	15%
Trans Fat 0.0g	
Cholesterol 126mg	42%
Sodium 926mg	39%
Potassium 689mg	20%
Total Carbohydrates 13.9g	5%
Dietary Fiber 0.8g	3%
Sugars 2.5g	
Protein 25.8g	
Vitamin A 44% • Vitamin C 89%	
Calcium 15% • Iron 13%	

Nutrition Grade A-
* Based on a 2000 calorie diet

Yield: 2 to 3 servings
Paul Pruitt [via Coastal Living]

Seafood

Maryland Jumbo Lump Crab Imperial

1 large egg lightly beaten
½ cup mayonnaise
1 teaspoon sugar
1 teaspoon Old Bay seasoning
Freshly squeezed juice from one squeeze of a lemon
1 teaspoon finely chopped Italian parsley
1 pound jumbo lump crabmeat (or lump)

Preheat your oven to 350° F. In a bowl, mix the egg, mayonnaise, sugar, Old Bay seasoning, lemon juice, and parsley together and blend well. Gently fold the crabmeat into the other ingredients, being careful not to break up the meat.

Place equal portions in small baking dishes such as ramekins or small casseroles. Bake for about 20 minutes, until the tops turn golden brown.

Allow to cool just a few minutes before serving; it will set and be more flavorful as it cools slightly.

Yield: 2 to 3 servings
Paul Pruitt [via Dennis Littley]

Nutrition Facts
Serving Size 253 g

Amount Per Serving	
Calories 398	Calories from Fat 316
	% Daily Value*
Total Fat 35.1g	54%
Saturated Fat 7.0g	35%
Trans Fat 0.0g	
Cholesterol 197mg	66%
Sodium 1426mg	59%
Potassium 30mg	1%
Total Carbohydrates 4.0g	1%
Sugars 3.9g	
Protein 17.4g	
Vitamin A 3%	Vitamin C 1%
Calcium 5%	Iron 6%

Nutrition Grade D-
* Based on a 2000 calorie diet

Brock's Best

Salmon Reuben

Yield: 1 serving
Samuel Cole

4 ounce salmon filet, halved
½ ounce (1 tablespoon) margarine or butter
2 tablespoons Cajun tartar sauce
2 slices marble rye bread
2 slices Swiss cheese
3 ounces dry, juice squeezed out, coleslaw (about ½ cup)
3 slices tomato

Fully cook salmon in the oven for 35 minutes on 350° F.

When the salmon is finished cooking, place the margarine/butter on a flat top grill or in a preheated sauté pan. Spread the Cajun tartar sauce on each slice of bread. Place the bread on the grill or in the sauté pan with the tartar sauce side up. Layer one slice of Swiss cheese on top of each piece of bread on top of the tartar sauce.

Place the salmon on an open spot on the grill or in the sauté pan. Also place the coleslaw on the grill or pan to heat it up.

Place three slices of cold tomatoes on top of the cheese on one of the slices of bread. Place the salmon on top of the tomatoes. Squeeze excess juice from coleslaw and place it on top of the salmon, and then turn and place the other slice of bread with cheese, face down on the coleslaw.

Keep flipping the entire sandwich on the grill or pan until the bread is golden brown. Remove, cut diagonally and enjoy.

Nutrition Facts

Serving Size 429 g

Amount Per Serving

Calories 872	Calories from Fat 493
	% Daily Value*
Total Fat 54.8g	84%
Saturated Fat 15.5g	78%
Trans Fat 0.0g	
Cholesterol 119mg	40%
Sodium 1556mg	65%
Total Carbohydrates 55.8g	19%
Dietary Fiber 2.5g	10%
Sugars 4.6g	
Protein 44.8g	
Vitamin A 35%	Vitamin C 22%
Calcium 56%	Iron 24%

Nutrition Grade B
* Based on a 2000 calorie diet

Scallops and Shrimp Sambuca

Seafood

¼ cup julienned fennel bulb
¼ cup julienned carrots
3 large shrimp
3 large sea scallops
2 tablespoons butter
2 tablespoons Sambuca
¼ cup heavy cream
Salt and freshly ground black pepper
1 bouchée* of puff pastry
Fresh dill for garnish

Blanch the fennel and carrots by boiling them in water in a saucepan for 2 to 5 minutes. Chill them with ice cold water, and pat them dry.

In a frying pan, sauté the shrimp in butter for 1 minute. Add scallops and sauté another minute. Deglaze the pan with Sambuca and heavy cream. Add the chilled blanched vegetables and reduce until it thickens. Season with salt and pepper.

Place in a bouchée and top with dill.

*BOUCHEE [boo-SHAY]—a small pastry shell, usually filled with a savory mixture and served hot with cocktails or as an hors d'oeuvre

Nutrition Facts
Serving Size 377 g

Amount Per Serving
Calories 729 — Calories from Fat 473

	% Daily Value*
Total Fat 52.6g	**81%**
Saturated Fat 32.3g	**161%**
Trans Fat 0.0g	
Cholesterol 221mg	**74%**
Sodium 770mg	**32%**
Total Carbohydrates 25.9g	**9%**
Dietary Fiber 2.2g	**9%**
Sugars 1.9g	
Protein 22.9g	

Vitamin A 43%	•	Vitamin C 16%
Calcium 10%	•	Iron 8%

Nutrition Grade C
* Based on a 2000 calorie diet

Yield: 1 serving
Michael Hamilton

Brock's Best

Seafood Gumbo

½ cup (1 stick) butter
1 cup chopped onions
½ cup chopped celery
½ cup chopped green pepper
4 cloves garlic, chopped
2 cups sliced okra
12 cups water
1 tablespoon Worcestershire sauce
Salt and freshly ground black pepper
Tony Chachere's Creole seasoning
4 crabs, cleaned
2 pounds shrimp, peeled and deveined
½ pound fish fillets, cut in bite size pieces
½ pint oysters
1 can whole tomatoes
½ cup green onion tops, for sprinkling/garnish
½ cup chopped parsley, for sprinkling/garnish

Roux
1 cup oil
1 cup flour

First start the roux* (recipe follows).

Next, in a large aluminum pot, (do not use a black iron pot), sauté the onions, celery, green peppers, garlic, and okra for 10 minutes in butter.

Add the roux, water and Worcestershire sauce. Adjust the seasoning with salt, pepper and/or Tony Chachere's Creole seasoning. Cook for 1 hour.

Add the rest of the ingredients except the green onions and parsley. Cook for another hour. Further adjust the seasoning. Serve over rice. Sprinkle with finely chopped green onion tops and parsley.

Roux
Add the flour to the oil in a saucepan and cook over low heat.

*ROUX [roo]—A mixture of flour and fat which, after being slowly cooked over low heat, is used to thicken mixtures such as soups and sauces.

Yield: 10 servings
Samuel Cole

Nutrition Facts

Serving Size 563 g

Amount Per Serving	
Calories 512	Calories from Fat 307
	% Daily Value*
Total Fat 34.1g	**52%**
Saturated Fat 9.4g	**47%**
Trans Fat 0.1g	
Cholesterol 269mg	**90%**
Sodium 784mg	**33%**
Total Carbohydrates 16.6g	**6%**
Dietary Fiber 1.8g	**7%**
Sugars 2.0g	
Protein 34.0g	

| Vitamin A 25% | • | Vitamin C 27% |
| Calcium 17% | • | Iron 19% |

Nutrition Grade B-
* Based on a 2000 calorie diet

Seafood

Seared Scallops With Parmesan Risotto

5 cups chicken stock
2 tablespoons butter
½ cup diced onion
1 ½ cup Arborio rice
1 cup dry white wine
1 cup green peas
1 cup Parmesan cheese
Salt and freshly ground black pepper
2 to 3 tablespoons olive oil
12 sea scallops, thoroughly dried, salted, and peppered

In a saucepot, bring the chicken stock to a boil, then lower the heat to a simmer.

In a frying pan, heat the butter over medium heat. Add the onions and sauté for 4 to 5 minutes, until translucent. Add the rice and sauté for another minute. Increase the heat to medium high and add white wine. Cook for 4 minutes until the alcohol cooks off and the wine is reduced by half. Reduce the heat back down to medium.

Add 1 cup of the chicken stock to the rice, stir slowly, and simmer until most of the stock is absorbed. Repeat periodically, adding the stock and cooking for the next 20 to 30 minutes, until the risotto is al dente, or still has a little bit of a firm taste in the mouth. You may not need all 5 cups of chicken stock.

Add the peas and Parmesan, and stir to incorporate. Season with salt and pepper. Turn heat off. Hold covered until ready to serve.

Heat a sauté pan over high heat. Add olive oil and when the oil is hot add the scallops. Allow the scallops to caramelize and do not attempt to turn them over until they release easily from the pan. It should take 1 to 2 minutes. Turn scallops over and caramelize the second side. Remove the scallops from the pan and serve over the rice.

Nutrition Facts

Serving Size 818 g

Amount Per Serving

Calories 832 — Calories from Fat 240

% Daily Value*

Total Fat 26.7g	41%
Saturated Fat 11.4g	57%
Trans Fat 0.0g	
Cholesterol 84mg	28%
Sodium 1863mg	78%
Total Carbohydrates 91.7g	31%
Dietary Fiber 5.5g	22%
Sugars 5.4g	
Protein 41.2g	

Vitamin A 18% • Vitamin C 43%
Calcium 38% • Iron 16%

Nutrition Grade C-
* Based on a 2000 calorie diet

Yield: 3 to 4 servings
Michael Varacalle

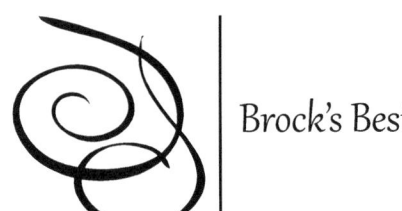

Brock's Best
Shrimp and Grits

Yield: 4 to 6 servings
Kristopher Schweitzer-Pfaff

2 teaspoons Cajun seasoning
1 teaspoon paprika
1 teaspoon dried Italian seasoning
Salt and freshly ground black pepper
1 ½ pound peeled deveined wild Georgia shrimp (26 to 30 count)
2 tablespoons butter or margarine
1 teaspoon minced garlic
3 tablespoons all-purpose flour
1 cup chicken stock
½ cup heavy whipping cream
1 teaspoon Worcestershire sauce
½ teaspoon hot sauce
1 slice sugar-cured country ham

Cheese Grits
2 cups water
2 chicken bouillon cubes
2 tablespoons butter or margarine
1 cup quick grits
1 teaspoon tomato paste
¾ cup heavy whipping cream
3 ½ ounces extra sharp cheddar cheese

In a bowl, combine the Cajun seasoning, paprika, and Italian seasoning. Adjust the seasoning more with salt and pepper. Sprinkle the spice mixture over the shrimp and coat well.

In a large sauté pan, melt 2 tablespoons of butter. Add the minced garlic and stir for 30 seconds. Add in the spice-coated shrimp, and cook only until they are just done and tender. Remove the shrimp from the sauté pan and set them aside in a bowl.

Add the flour to the drippings from the shrimp sauté pan and stir with a wooden spatula to make a roux. Cook for 10 to 15 minutes until the roux reaches a medium-tan color, and then slowly add the chicken stock and heavy whipping cream. Whisk together and cook for 2 minutes, then whisk in the Worcestershire and hot sauces. Set aside. Cook one center slice of cured country ham in another sauté pan, and cut into cubes.

To serve, place a few heaping spoonfuls of steaming cheese grits (recipe follows) onto a plate, and top with several sizzling shrimp. Drizzle the roux sauce over top of the shrimp and sprinkle with a few cubes of country ham.

Cheese Grits
In a saucepan, bring water, chicken bouillon cubes and 2 tablespoons of butter to a boil. Slowly add the grits, whisking often with wire whisk for 5 minutes. Add the tomato paste, cream and cheese. Keep whisking for another 2 or 3 minutes until the grits become creamy.

Nutrition Facts

Serving Size 235 g

Amount Per Serving

Calories 270	Calories from Fat 131
	% Daily Value*
Total Fat 14.6g	22%
Saturated Fat 3.3g	17%
Trans Fat 0.0g	
Cholesterol 14mg	5%
Sodium 698mg	29%
Total Carbohydrates 30.8g	10%
Dietary Fiber 1.8g	7%
Sugars 17.2g	
Protein 3.5g	
Vitamin A 3%	Vitamin C 31%
Calcium 1%	Iron 4%

Nutrition Grade D+
* Based on a 2000 calorie diet

Seafood

Shrimp and Feta Cheese Pasta

2 tablespoons olive oil for cooking the shrimp plus 1 tablespoon for the tomatoes
1 pound shrimp, peeled and deveined
5 cloves garlic, minced
1 tablespoon white wine
1 pound linguine pasta
2 tomatoes, chopped
1 teaspoon dried oregano
½ teaspoon dried basil
1 (6 ounce) package crumbled feta cheese

In a skillet over medium heat, heat the olive oil. Add and cook the shrimp, garlic, and white wine for about 5 minutes, until the shrimp is pink. Remove the shrimp with a slotted spoon and set aside. Do not discard the contents of the skillet.

Bring a large pot of lightly salted water to a boil. Add the pasta and cook for 8 to 10 minutes, until al dente. Drain.

While the pasta is cooking, add the tomatoes, remaining oil, oregano, and basil to the wine mixture used previously for the shrimp. Cook over medium heat for about 10 minutes, or until the tomatoes are tender.

Toss the hot pasta with the shrimp, tomato sauce, and feta. The feta will melt slightly. Serve.

Yield: 6 to 8 servings
Paul Pruitt [via J. Weary]

Nutrition Facts

Serving Size 1400 g

Amount Per Serving

Calories 2,712	Calories from Fat 828
	% Daily Value*
Total Fat 92.0g	141%
Saturated Fat 35.5g	177%
Cholesterol 1240mg	413%
Sodium 3042mg	127%
Potassium 1558mg	45%
Total Carbohydrates 280.6g	94%
Dietary Fiber 14.6g	59%
Sugars 19.0g	
Protein 184.2g	

Vitamin A 85%	•	Vitamin C 65%
Calcium 141%	•	Iron 95%

Nutrition Grade C
* Based on a 2000 calorie diet

Brock's Best

Teriyaki Grilled Salmon

4 cups teriyaki sauce
1 teaspoon fresh chopped garlic
4 to 6 ounce salmon fillet
2 tablespoons sesame oil
1 teaspoon freshly ground black pepper
1 stalk fresh leeks
1 tablespoon of butter

Teriyaki Glaze
Pour the teriyaki sauce and garlic into a 2 quart saucepan and bring to a boil. Adjust the heat to a simmer and reduce by half. Set aside.

Salmon
Rub the salmon with sesame oil on both sides and sprinkle with black pepper. Place the fillet belly side down on a grill. Cook for 2 minutes. Rotate 90 degrees clockwise and continue cooking for 2 more minutes.

Flip the salmon so that the grill marks are showing. Take the teriyaki glaze (recipe above) and brush with a basting brush, then continue cooking for 4 to 5 minutes longer.

Remove the salmon from the grill and let rest for a few minutes. Brush once before serving to guests with the Leeks on top (cooking instructions follow). You can also serve with additional or other sides such as white or brown basmati or fried rice, buckwheat noodles, steamed asparagus, broccoli, etc.

Leeks
Keeping and using only the white part of the leaf, julienne the leeks. Place them in cold water and rinse off the dirt. Remove and dry on a towel.

In a sauté pan, melt the butter and sauté the leeks until they are caramelized.

Nutrition Facts

Serving Size 347 g

Amount Per Serving

Calories 370 — Calories from Fat 78

	% Daily Value*
Total Fat 8.7g	13%
Saturated Fat 1.2g	6%
Trans Fat 0.0g	
Cholesterol 13mg	4%
Sodium 11056mg	461%
Total Carbohydrates 48.5g	16%
Dietary Fiber 0.8g	3%
Sugars 41.5g	
Protein 23.0g	

| Vitamin A 8% | • | Vitamin C 5% |
| Calcium 10% | • | Iron 32% |

Nutrition Grade C
* Based on a 2000 calorie diet

Yield: 4 servings
Michael Demar

Soups And Stews

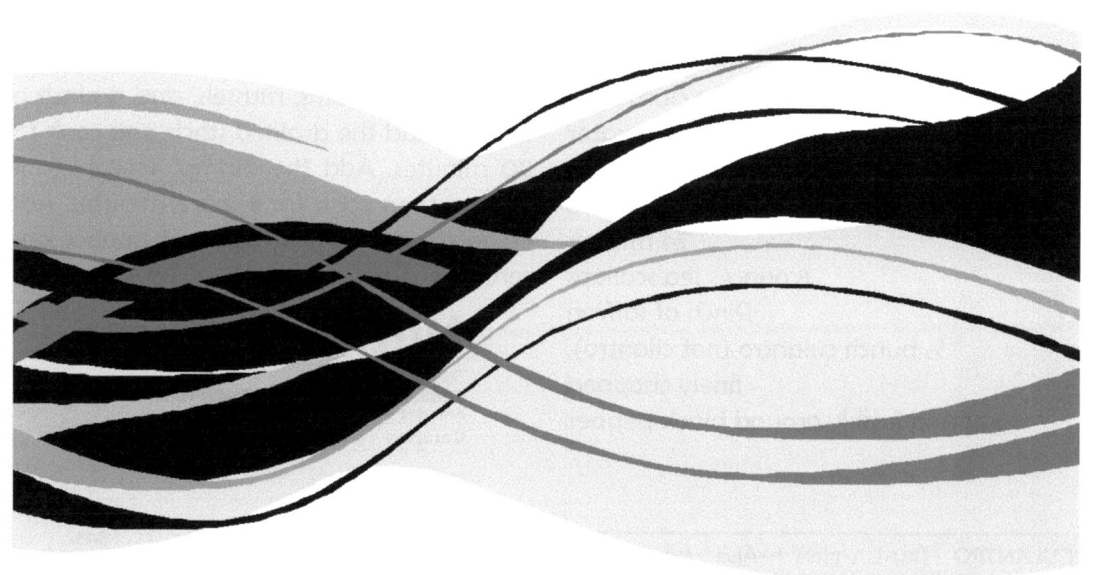

Brock's Best

Brock's Best

Asopao De Marisco (Seafood Stew)

Yield: 10 servings
Jerry Vazquez

Olive oil, as needed
2 large onions—1 coarsely chopped, 1 finely diced
2 green peppers—1 coarsely chopped, 1 finely diced
2 (1 ½ pound) headless lobsters for stock, with quartered tails and cracked claws
8 ounces large shrimp peeled and cleaned, save shells for stock
1 cup crushed tomato
1 cup fine white wine
1 bay leaf
4 cups clam juice
4 cups water
2 cups long grain rice
24 little neck clams
24 mussels
8 ounces sea scallops
Pinch of saffron
½ bunch culantro (not cilantro), finely chopped
Salt and freshly ground black pepper

In a large soup pot, add enough olive oil to coat the bottom and sauté the coarsely chopped onion and green pepper until caramelized. Add the lobster heads and shrimp shells. Sauté until they get nice and pink. Add the tomato, white wine, bay leaf, clam juice, and water. Cook for two hours, then drain. Saved the drained stock, discard the solids.

In a large soup pot sauté in oil, the finely diced onion and pepper until caramelized. Add the rice, clams, mussels, and a pinch of saffron. Add the drained stock and cook for 20 minutes. Add the shrimp, scallops, and lobster, then cook for 8 more minutes. Add culantro, season with salt and pepper and serve.

*CULANTRO [ku-LA-ntrow]—Also known as Mexican coriander or long coriander, is related to ordinary cilantro but has a stronger taste. It is not well known in the U.S. outside of Latino and Caribbean communities.

Nutrition Facts

Serving Size 756 g

Amount Per Serving

Calories 548	Calories from Fat 28
	% Daily Value*
Total Fat 3.1g	5%
Cholesterol 66mg	22%
Sodium 2013mg	84%
Total Carbohydrates 92.9g	31%
Dietary Fiber 3.7g	15%
Sugars 19.7g	
Protein 30.4g	

Vitamin A 22%	•	Vitamin C 71%
Calcium 9%	•	Iron 26%

Nutrition Grade C+
* Based on a 2000 calorie diet

Soups & Stews

Black Bean Chili

1 tablespoon canola oil
¼ pound chorizo sausage chopped
⅓ pound cooked ham
1 pound onion (about 3 ½ cups), chopped
2 cloves garlic, minced
2 pounds sweet potatoes, peeled and diced
1 large red bell pepper
1 (#10 can) diced or stewed tomatoes
1 hot green chile pepper
4 cups water
1 (#10 can) black beans, rinsed and drained
2 mangoes, peeled, seeded, and diced
¼ cup chopped fresh cilantro
¼ teaspoon salt

Heat the oil in a large soup pot over medium heat, and cook the sausage and ham for 2 to 3 minutes. Add the onions and cook until tender. Stir in the garlic, and cook until tender, then mix in the sweet potatoes, bell pepper, tomatoes with juice, chile pepper, and water. Bring to a boil, decrease heat to low, cover, and simmer for 15 minutes, until sweet potatoes are tender.

Stir the beans into the pot, and cook uncovered until heated throughout. Mix in the mango and cilantro, and season with salt.

Nutrition Facts

Serving Size 264 g

Amount Per Serving

Calories 523	Calories from Fat 32
	% Daily Value*
Total Fat 3.5g	5%
Saturated Fat 0.9g	4%
Trans Fat 0.0g	
Cholesterol 8mg	3%
Sodium 206mg	9%
Potassium 2255mg	64%
Total Carbohydrates 94.7g	32%
Dietary Fiber 21.4g	86%
Sugars 7.1g	
Protein 30.4g	
Vitamin A 5% • Vitamin C 33%	
Calcium 17% • Iron 37%	

Nutrition Grade A
* Based on a 2000 calorie diet

Yield: 24 servings
Samuel Cole

 Did you know that sweet potatoes are rich in vitamin A?

Brock's Best

Butternut Squash Soup

2 pounds (4 to 5 cups) onions, chopped
4 tablespoons (½ stick) unsalted butter
6 cloves garlic
6 pounds butternut squash, cooked and cubed
9 cups chicken stock
1 tablespoon ground cumin
2 teaspoons salt
Pinch of cayenne pepper
2 cups heavy cream
1 ½ cup honey
¾ cup sour cream, for garnish

In a large soup pot, sauté the onions in butter for about 10 minutes, or until soft. Stir in the garlic and squash. Stir in the chicken stock, cumin, salt, and cayenne pepper. Simmer until the squash is very soft. Puree the results, then stir in the cream and honey. Garnish each serving with sour cream.

Yield: 10 to 12 servings

Sharon Houck

Nutrition Facts

Serving Size 407 g

Amount Per Serving	
Calories 334	Calories from Fat 133
	% Daily Value*
Total Fat 14.8g	23%
Saturated Fat 9.0g	45%
Cholesterol 44mg	15%
Sodium 519mg	22%
Total Carbohydrates 51.3g	17%
Dietary Fiber 4.2g	17%
Sugars 41.9g	
Protein 4.8g	

| Vitamin A 19% | • | Vitamin C 79% |
| Calcium 8% | • | Iron 8% |

Nutrition Grade C+

* Based on a 2000 calorie diet

Cheddar Asparagus And Crab Chowder

18 spears (6 spears) of fresh asparagus
1 cup (⅓ cup) vegetable oil
2 cups (⅔ cup) diced yellow onions
1 cup (⅓ cup) flour
8 cups (2 ⅔ cup) half and half cream
12 cups (4 cups) chicken stock
2 pounds (3 to 4)—9 to 12—red potatoes, diced
1 teaspoon (⅓ teaspoon) salt
½ teaspoon (1 pinch) ground red peppers
4 cups (1 ⅓ cup) shredded sharp cheddar cheese
1 cup (⅓ cup) sour cream
2 pounds (⅔ pound or 1 ⅔ cup) crabmeat
2 cups (⅔ cup) tomato concassee*
2 teaspoons (⅔ teaspoon) chopped parsley
Garlic croutons, for garnish

Cut the asparagus into 1-inch pieces, and then blanch by boiling them in water for 2 to 5 minutes, and then dunking them in cold water. Set the blanched asparagus aside.

In a large soup pot, cook the onions in hot oil until tender. Sprinkle the flour over the onions and stir to coat. Add the half and half, chicken stock, potatoes, salt, and red pepper. Cook and stir until thickened. Decrease heat, and simmer.

When the potatoes are tender, add the cheddar cheese and sour cream. Next, add the asparagus, crabmeat, and tomato concassee. Heat until hot. Garnish with chopped parsley and garlic croutons.

Nutrition Facts

Serving Size 584 g

Amount Per Serving

Calories 577 — Calories from Fat 375

	% Daily Value*
Total Fat 41.7g	**64%**
Saturated Fat 18.3g	**92%**
Cholesterol 107mg	**36%**
Sodium 1728mg	**72%**
Total Carbohydrates 30.1g	**10%**
Dietary Fiber 3.4g	**14%**
Sugars 5.2g	
Protein 21.4g	
Vitamin A 76% • Vitamin C 20%	
Calcium 60% • Iron 17%	

Nutrition Grade C
* Based on a 2000 calorie diet

Yield: 16 servings-food service version
(5 to 6 servings-home version)
Michael Hamilton

*CONCASSEE [kon-kah-SAY]—Tomato that has been peeled, seeded, and chopped.

Brock's Best

Chilled Cucumber Soup with Lobster, Mint, and Lobster Brioche Sandwich

4 large cucumbers, peeled, seeded, and sliced
2 tablespoons butter
1 tablespoon salad oil
4 scallions, sliced, white parts only
2 tablespoons flour
2 ½ cup chicken stock
½ cup milk
1 ½ teaspoon freshly squeezed lemon juice
2 tablespoons mint
2 cups sour cream
Salt and freshly ground black pepper
Brioche, toasted
Lobster
Arugula (a type of lettuce)

In a heavy soup pot, melt the butter and add the oil. Sauté the cucumbers and the scallions for 10 minutes. Stir in the flour to form a roux.

In a separate pot, heat the chicken stock and the milk. Slowly add the stock-milk mixture to the cucumbers and scallions.

Also add the lemon juice and mint to the cucumbers and scallions. Season with salt and pepper. Simmer the developing soup until thick and then blend in a blender or with a hand mixer until smooth.

Cool the soup. Mix in the sour cream. Season with salt and pepper.

Make a mini sandwich with lobster meat, arugula, and brioche. Serve with the soup.

Yield: 6 to 8 servings
Michael Bongiorno

Nutrition Facts

Serving Size 362 g

Amount Per Serving

Calories 237	Calories from Fat 180
	% Daily Value*
Total Fat 19.9g	**31%**
Saturated Fat 11.2g	**56%**
Trans Fat 0.0g	
Cholesterol 39mg	**13%**
Sodium 345mg	**14%**
Total Carbohydrates 12.7g	**4%**
Dietary Fiber 1.4g	**6%**
Sugars 1.4g	
Protein 4.4g	
Vitamin A 14% • Vitamin C 16%	
Calcium 12% • Iron 21%	

Nutrition Grade C+

* Based on a 2000 calorie diet

Soups & Stews

Cold Strawberry Soup

4 cups (2 pints) strawberries
1 ½ cup water
½ cup sugar
¾ cup Bordeaux wine
Dash of freshly squeezed lemon juice
Pinch of cinnamon
½ cup heavy cream
3 tablespoons sour cream

Slice the tops of strawberries off and wash, reserving six of them for garnish. Place the rest into a soup pot with water, sugar, and Bordeaux wine.

Place the pot on a stove on low heat. When the mix begins to cook, add the lemon juice and cinnamon. Bring to a simmer and cook for 15 minutes. Cool overnight.

Beat the heavy cream to a peak. Add the sour cream and blend. Prior to service, combine the strawberry mixture with this cream-sour cream blend. Mix well, portion into soup cups, and garnish with strawberries.

Yield: 6 servings
Michael Hamilton

Nutrition Facts

Serving Size 163 g

Amount Per Serving

Calories 171	Calories from Fat 45
	% Daily Value*
Total Fat 5.0g	8%
Saturated Fat 3.1g	16%
Trans Fat 0.0g	
Cholesterol 16mg	5%
Sodium 9mg	0%
Total Carbohydrates 25.3g	8%
Dietary Fiber 1.4g	5%
Sugars 22.2g	
Protein 1.1g	

Vitamin A 4%	•	Vitamin C 109%
Calcium 3%	•	Iron 2%

Nutrition Grade D+
* Based on a 2000 calorie diet

Brock's Best

Crab and Corn Chowder

8 ounces bacon, diced in small cubes
1 cup (2 sticks) of butter
1 large onion, small dice
8 stalks celery, small dice
1 tablespoon minced garlic
2 cups flour, all-purpose
12 cups crab stock
1 pound corn
1 ⅔ cups (12 ounces) potatoes, diced in small cubes
1 pound crabmeat
1 tablespoon Old Bay seasoning
Salt and freshly ground black pepper
2 cups half and half

Place the bacon and butter into a soup pot. Cook until the fat is rendered from the bacon and it is browned. Add the onion, celery, and garlic. Cook until the onions are translucent. Add the flour and mix well. Continue cooking on low for about 5 minutes, stirring continuously.

Whisk the stock into the mixture. Decrease the heat on the soup to a simmer. Add the corn and the potatoes. Continue to simmer until the potatoes are tender. Add the crabmeat and Old Bay seasoning. Season with salt and pepper. Slowly add the half and half while whisking. Serve warm.

Nutrition Facts

Serving Size 800 g

Amount Per Serving

Calories 608	Calories from Fat 329
	% Daily Value*
Total Fat 36.6g	56%
Saturated Fat 18.6g	93%
Trans Fat 0.0g	
Cholesterol 123mg	41%
Sodium 2165mg	90%
Total Carbohydrates 47.1g	16%
Dietary Fiber 3.9g	15%
Sugars 3.4g	
Protein 23.6g	

Vitamin A 16%	•	Vitamin C 23%
Calcium 23%	•	Iron 28%

Nutrition Grade B-

* Based on a 2000 calorie diet

Yield: 8 servings
Jerry Goard

Soups & Stews

Cream of Crab Soup

4 gallons (4 cups) whole milk
6 quarts (1 ½ cup) heavy cream
1 ¼ cup (2 tablespoons) crab base
¾ cup (3 ½ teaspoon) chicken base
7 tablespoons (1 ¼ teaspoon) Old Bay seasoning
4 tablespoons (¾ teaspoon) ground dry mustard
1 tablespoon (¼ teaspoon) ground white pepper
3 tablespoons (½ teaspoon) dried parsley flakes
2 pounds (4 tablespoons) butter
8 cups (½ cup) all-purpose flour
2 cups (2 tablespoons) cooking sherry or dry sherry
4 pounds (¼ pound) claw or special crabmeat

To prepare, use a double boiler system. Combine the milk, heavy cream, crab base, chicken base, and dry spices.

While the ingredients are getting hot, in a separate saucepot, melt the butter – do not scorch. Whisk in the flour slowly to make a smooth roux.

When the ingredients in the double boiler reach a temperature of 180° F to 200° F, start gradually adding in the roux. Reduce the heat under the double boiler to a simmer. Simmer for 45 to 60 minutes, until the floury taste is gone.

Add 2 cups (2 tablespoons for home cooking version) of dry cooking sherry. Drain the excess liquid from the crabmeat. Mix the crabmeat into the soup and serve.

Nutrition Facts

Serving Size 270 g

Amount Per Serving	
Calories 438	Calories from Fat 323
	% Daily Value*
Total Fat 35.9g	55%
Saturated Fat 21.7g	108%
Trans Fat 0.0g	
Cholesterol 130mg	43%
Sodium 994mg	41%
Total Carbohydrates 17.6g	6%
Sugars 8.6g	
Protein 10.0g	
Vitamin A 26% •	Vitamin C 1%
Calcium 29% •	Iron 5%
Nutrition Grade D	

* Based on a 2000 calorie diet

Yield: 96 servings-food service version
(6 cups-home version)
Joe Mathis

Brock's Best

Dovga

½ cup white rice
1 egg
4 cups plain yogurt
2 cups water
3 tablespoons flour
½ bunch Italian parsley, chopped
½ bunch cilantro, chopped
½ bunch spinach, chopped
1 small bunch dill, chopped

In a small bowl, mix the rice and egg. In a large bowl mix the yogurt, water, and flour. Add the rice mixture to the yogurt mixture and transfer to a large soup pot. Put on the stove and bring to a boil, stirring constantly.

When the rice is soft, add the chopped greens and keep stirring. When the greens are soft, serve in small bowls or glasses, with or without spoons.

Yield: 4 servings
Sofia Tsitrinbaum

Nutrition Facts

Serving Size 305 g

Amount Per Serving

Calories 308	Calories from Fat 41
	% Daily Value*
Total Fat 4.5g	7%
Saturated Fat 2.9g	14%
Cholesterol 56mg	19%
Sodium 205mg	9%
Total Carbohydrates 42.8g	14%
Dietary Fiber 1.3g	5%
Sugars 17.5g	
Protein 18.7g	
Vitamin A 36% •	Vitamin C 27%
Calcium 53% •	Iron 21%

Nutrition Grade A
* Based on a 2000 calorie diet

Soups & Stews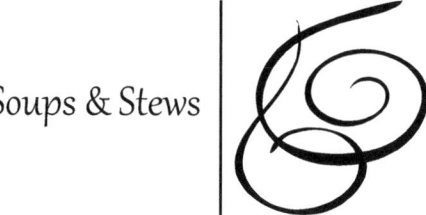

Green Borscht

Yield: 6 to 8 servings
Suren Sarkisov

3 bunches green onion
10 cups chicken stock
3 potatoes
Salt and freshly ground black pepper
1 pound sorrel or spinach
2 tablespoons cilantro
2 tablespoons dill
3 eggs, hardboiled
Sour cream

Sauté the green onions in oil for about 15 minutes, until they reach a deep golden color.

In a large soup pot, bring the stock to a simmer and add the potatoes. Simmer covered for about 20 minutes, until the potatoes are cooked through.

Remove the potatoes with a slotted spoon and mash them coarsely. They should not be puréed, but still be in tiny lumps. Return them to the pot.

Also add the onions to the developing soup. Adjust the seasoning with salt and pepper. Bring the stock to a simmer again and add the sorrel. Let simmer for 3 additional minutes, and then remove from the heat. Stir in the cilantro and dill, and serve immediately. Keep in mind that sorrel overcooks very quickly.

Before pouring the soup, place hardboiled egg slices in each bowl. Serve with sour cream on the side.

Nutrition Facts

Serving Size 513 g

Amount Per Serving

Calories 71	Calories from Fat 31
	% Daily Value*
Total Fat 3.5g	5%
Saturated Fat 1.0g	5%
Cholesterol 82mg	27%
Sodium 1367mg	57%
Total Carbohydrates 5.3g	2%
Dietary Fiber 2.0g	8%
Sugars 1.8g	
Protein 6.4g	
Vitamin A 147% •	Vitamin C 39%
Calcium 14% •	Iron 18%

Nutrition Grade A
* Based on a 2000 calorie diet

Brock's Best

Brock's Best
Italian Wedding Soup

1 onion, diced into ¼-inch cubes
8 stalks celery, diced into ¼-inch cubes
1 large carrot, diced into ¼-inch cubes
1 teaspoon chopped garlic
2 tablespoons olive oil
8 cups chicken stock
1 pound spinach, chopped
½ cup pasta (acini di pepe)*
¾ cup cornstarch
1 pound mini meatballs, cooked
1 pound chicken, cooked, diced
Basil
Kosher salt and freshly ground black pepper

Heat the olive oil in a large soup pot until nearly smoking hot. Add the onions, celery, carrots, and garlic. Sauté until the onions are translucent. Add the chicken stock and the spinach. Bring to a boil. Reduce to a simmer, add the pasta, and cook for 5 minutes.

In a small bowl, mix the cornstarch with cold water to a smooth consistency. Add the cornstarch mixture to the developing soup.

Add the meatballs and chicken and continue to cook for 5 minutes. Season with basil, kosher salt, and pepper.

Nutrition Facts
Serving Size 386 g

Amount Per Serving
Calories 287 — Calories from Fat 125

	% Daily Value*
Total Fat 13.9g	21%
Saturated Fat 4.7g	24%
Trans Fat 0.0g	
Cholesterol 67mg	22%
Sodium 1093mg	46%
Total Carbohydrates 18.3g	6%
Dietary Fiber 1.9g	7%
Sugars 2.6g	
Protein 22.5g	

Vitamin A 111% • Vitamin C 25%
Calcium 9% • Iron 18%

Nutrition Grade B-
* Based on a 2000 calorie diet

Yield: 10 servings
Staff of Blue Cross Blue Shield

*ACINI DE PEPE [ah-CHEE-nee dee PAY-pay]—tiny peppercorn-shaped pasta.

Soups & Stews

Jambalaya

4 shrimp
2 ounces chicken, diced
2 teaspoons Creole seasoning
2 tablespoons olive oil
1 ounce ham or smoked sausage
1 tablespoon diced onions
3 tablespoons seeded and diced bell pepper
2 tablespoons diced celery
¼ cup—2 ounces—white wine
¼ cup chopped tomatoes
¼ cup—2 ounces—chicken stock
1 teaspoon chopped garlic
2 tablespoons sliced scallions
1 tablespoon fresh parsley
Salt and freshly ground black pepper
1 cup cooked saffron rice

In a bowl combine the shrimp, chicken, and Creole seasoning, ensuring the seasoning is distributed evenly throughout.

In a large saucepan heat the oil over high heat. Sauté the ham or sausage, onions, peppers, and celery for about 3 minutes.

Add the shrimp and chicken. Add the white wine and continue cooking until the proteins are completely cooked. Add the garlic, tomatoes, and chicken broth. Let reduce slightly. Finally, add the scallions and parsley.

Season with salt and pepper and serve over saffron rice.

Nutrition Facts
Serving Size 461 g

Amount Per Serving
Calories 562   Calories from Fat 308
                              % Daily Value*
Total Fat 34.3g   53%
  Saturated Fat 5.9g   30%
  Trans Fat 0.0g
Cholesterol 245mg   82%
Sodium 3608mg   150%
Total Carbohydrates 11.4g   4%
  Dietary Fiber 2.4g   9%
  Sugars 4.1g
Protein 42.7g

Vitamin A 65%   •   Vitamin C 90%
Calcium 13%   •   Iron 14%
Nutrition Grade C
* Based on a 2000 calorie diet

Yield: 1 serving
Alena Khvesiukovich

Brock's Best

Lemongrass-Scented Noodle Soup with Shrimp

¼ pound Asian rice noodles (or pad Thai noodles)
4 cups chicken stock or broth
2 stalks lemongrass, inner bulbs— very thinly sliced, tops crushed
1 garlic clove, thinly sliced
Salt and freshly ground black pepper
¾ pound shrimp, peeled and deveined
1 cup halved crosswise snow peas
½ bunch watercress, stemmed
¼ finely chopped cup cilantro
2 scallions, thinly sliced
2 tablespoons freshly squeezed lime juice

Soak the noodles in a bowl of hot water for about 15 minutes, or until pliable.

Meanwhile, in a large soup pot combine the stock with the lemongrass and garlic. Cover and simmer over low heat for 20 minutes. Season with salt and pepper and discard the large lemongrass stalks.

Put a saucepan of water on high heat. When the water reaches a boil, drain the noodles and cook them in the water for about 2 minutes, or until tender. Drain well and rinse under cool water.

Add the shrimp, snow peas, and watercress to the lemongrass broth and cook about 2 minutes, until the shrimp are pink and the vegetables are crisp but tender. Stir in the cilantro, scallions, lime juice, and noodles and cook until just heated through.

Yield: 4 servings
Carl J. Scharle

Nutrition Facts

Serving Size 438 g

Amount Per Serving

Calories 181	Calories from Fat 20
	% Daily Value*
Total Fat 2.2g	3%
Saturated Fat 0.6g	3%
Cholesterol 179mg	60%
Sodium 984mg	41%
Total Carbohydrates 17.2g	6%
Dietary Fiber 1.7g	7%
Sugars 2.9g	
Protein 22.6g	

Vitamin A 24%	•	Vitamin C 46%
Calcium 14%	•	Iron 14%

Nutrition Grade A
* Based on a 2000 calorie diet

Soups & Stews

Maryland Crab Soup

2 tablespoons butter
1 small yellow onion, diced
2 stalks celery, diced
1 cup diced carrots
2 (14 ½ ounce) cans stewed tomatoes
1 cup fresh lima beans
1 cup fresh corn
3 tablespoons Old Bay seasoning
3 cups beef broth
1 can clam juice
3 cups light chicken stock
1 pound back-fin lump crabmeat—picked for shells
Crab claws—we save them whenever we pick crabs and freeze them until it's time to make soup

Yield: 10 servings
Russell Brannon

Melt the butter in a 4-quart soup pot. Add the onion, celery, and carrots and sauté until tender. Add everything else except the crabmeat and claws, and bring to a quick boil.

Reduce the heat to a simmer, add the crabmeat, and stir lightly. Add the claws to the top and cover. Simmer for 10 to 15 minutes. Serve hot.

Nutrition Facts
Serving Size 246 g

Amount Per Serving
Calories 130 — Calories from Fat 35

% Daily Value*
Total Fat 3.8g — 6%
 Saturated Fat 1.7g — 9%
 Trans Fat 0.0g
Cholesterol 51mg — 17%
Sodium 1192mg — 50%
Total Carbohydrates 11.0g — 4%
 Dietary Fiber 2.0g — 8%
 Sugars 3.0g
Protein 12.9g

Vitamin A 40% • Vitamin C 22%
Calcium 6% • Iron 11%

Nutrition Grade A
* Based on a 2000 calorie diet

Brock's Best

Peanut and Chestnut Soup

¼ cup margarine or butter
1 ½ tablespoon all-purpose flour
4 cups chicken broth
4 cups water
1 cup smooth peanut butter
1 tablespoon Worcestershire sauce
½ cup chopped unsalted peanuts, for garnish
½ cup chopped water chestnuts, for garnish

Melt the margarine/butter in a large saucepan. Stir in the flour to make a roux. Cook on medium heat while frequently stirring until the roux is light tan in color.

Once the roux is ready, add chicken broth and water and bring to a boil. Then add peanut butter and Worcestershire sauce and stir. Hold on the stove at a low heat until ready to serve. The longer it heats, the thicker it gets.

Garnish with chopped peanuts and water chestnuts.

Nutrition Facts
Serving Size 115 g

Amount Per Serving	
Calories 212	Calories from Fat 163
	% Daily Value*
Total Fat 18.1g	28%
Saturated Fat 3.4g	17%
Trans Fat 0.0g	
Cholesterol 0mg	0%
Sodium 317mg	13%
Total Carbohydrates 6.5g	2%
Dietary Fiber 1.8g	7%
Sugars 2.7g	
Protein 8.7g	

Vitamin A 3%	•	Vitamin C 0%
Calcium 2%	•	Iron 5%

Nutrition Grade B-
* Based on a 2000 calorie diet

Yield: 10 to 12 servings
Barry Pinkowicz

Soups & Stews

Pulled Pork Green Chili

Yield: 25 servings-food service version
(6 to 7 servings-home version)
Samuel Stern

2 tablespoons (1 ½ teaspoon) seasoned salt
1 tablespoon (¾ teaspoon) chili powder
1 teaspoon (¼ teaspoon) thyme
1 tablespoon (¾ teaspoon) freshly ground black pepper plus 1 teaspoon (¼ teaspoon) for the chili steps
1 tablespoon (¾ teaspoon) garlic pepper
2 tablespoons (1 ½ teaspoon) brown sugar
5 to 6 pounds (1 ¼ to 1 ½ pound) pork picnic shoulder
¾ (3 tablespoons) cup butter or lard
1 cup (¼ cup) flour
2 tablespoons (1 ½ teaspoon) fresh chopped garlic
⅔ cup chopped onions (2 ½ tablespoon)
4 quarts (4 cups) chicken broth
4 cups (1 cup) diced roasted green chilies
1 cup (¼ cup) diced tomatillos*
¼ teaspoon (pinch) cayenne pepper
1 tablespoon (¾ teaspoon) oregano

Pork Shoulder

In a small bowl mix the seasoned salt, chili powder, thyme, black pepper, garlic pepper, and brown sugar. Rub this spice mixture onto the pork picnic shoulder. Cook in a gas, electric, or charcoal smoker with hickory wood chips. Maintain a temperature of 250° to 275° F for 6 to 7 hours. The pork should reach an internal temperature of 190° F. Cover with aluminum foil and let rest for 30 minutes.

Chili

In a thick-bottomed soup pot, melt the butter or lard over medium heat. Whisk in the flour and cook for 3 minutes. Add the fresh garlic and onion. Slowly whisk in the chicken stock. Simmer for 10 minutes. Add the green chilies and tomatillos.

Heat a small sauté pan over medium heat. Add 1 tablespoon more of black pepper, the cayenne pepper, and the oregano. Toast the spice mixture for 2 minutes. Sprinkle on the pork shoulder. Chop or pull the pork shoulder (recipe above) into bite size pieces. Add to the soup pot with the other ingredients and simmer for 30 minutes. Adjust the seasoning.

Note: This version of green chili is good in the summer and is excellent as a soup or to smother on burritos.

Nutrition Facts

Serving Size 286 g

Amount Per Serving

Calories 298 — Calories from Fat 184

% Daily Value*

Total Fat 20.4g — 31%
Saturated Fat 10.2g — 51%
Trans Fat 0.0g
Cholesterol 63mg — 21%
Sodium 1710mg — 71%
Total Carbohydrates 11.1g — 4%
Dietary Fiber 0.9g — 4%
Sugars 4.6g
Protein 16.6g

Vitamin A 6% • Vitamin C 2%
Calcium 2% • Iron 9%

Nutrition Grade C-
* Based on a 2000 calorie diet

*TOMATILLO [toh-mah-TEE-yoh]—This fruit, which is also called Mexican green tomato, belongs to the same nightshade family as the tomato.

Brock's Best

Russian Okhroshka Soup

5 red potatoes
5 eggs
6 green onions, finely diced
10 radishes, finely diced
½ bunch dill, finely diced
4 cups buttermilk
1 tablespoon sour cream
Salt

In a large soup pot, boil the potatoes and eggs. Let them chill. When potatoes and eggs cool down, peel and finely dice them.

Combine the onions, radishes, and dill in a large bowl with the buttermilk. Add the eggs and potatoes. Add the sour cream and mix.

Season the soup with salt, and chill. Serve cold.

Nutrition Facts

Serving Size 248 g

Amount Per Serving

Calories 154 — Calories from Fat 32

	% Daily Value*
Total Fat 3.5g	5%
Saturated Fat 1.4g	7%
Cholesterol 87mg	29%
Sodium 382mg	16%
Total Carbohydrates 22.9g	8%
Dietary Fiber 2.1g	8%
Sugars 6.5g	
Protein 8.4g	

Vitamin A 5% • Vitamin C 21%
Calcium 15% • Iron 8%

Nutrition Grade A

* Based on a 2000 calorie diet

Yield: 10 servings
Veta Mesh

Soups & Stews

Sopa De Caracol (Conch Soup)

Yield: 8 servings
Marlon Paz

- ¼ pound butter
- 2 large onion, yellow or white, coarsely, chopped
- 3 cloves garlic, coarsely, chopped
- 2 green peppers, coarsely, chopped
- 2 carrots, peeled and coarsely chop
- 2 pounds yucca, peeled and coarsely chop
- 2 fish or chicken bouillon cubes
- 1 small bunch of coriander, chopped
- 1 scotch bonnet peppers
- 4 cups coconut milk
- 3 green bananas, cut in large chunks
- 1 pound fresh conch

Melt the butter in a large soup pot on low heat. Add the onions, garlic, and green peppers. Sauté in the butter for 5 to 10 minutes. Add the carrots and yucca to the pan. Turn up the heat and fast fry for 5 minutes. Add the bouillon cubes and chopped coriander to the mix.

Burst the scotch bonnet pepper between your fingers (watch that it doesn't get in your eyes) and add it to the pot. Add the coconut milk and let simmer for another 20 minutes. Add the bananas and simmer for an additional 7 minutes, or until the bananas are soft.

Wash, peel, and cut the conch into small pieces and add to the pot. Let simmer for 5 more minutes, then serve the soup.

Nutrition Facts

Serving Size 447 g

Amount Per Serving

Calories 594	Calories from Fat 380
	% Daily Value*
Total Fat 42.2g	65%
Saturated Fat 34.2g	171%
Trans Fat 0.0g	
Cholesterol 61mg	20%
Sodium 401mg	17%
Total Carbohydrates 48.7g	16%
Dietary Fiber 9.6g	38%
Sugars 20.5g	
Protein 11.8g	

Vitamin A 451%	•	Vitamin C 120%
Calcium 10%	•	Iron 26%

Nutrition Grade B-

* Based on a 2000 calorie diet

Brock's Best

Thai Sweet Corn Soup

3 teaspoons sesame or sunflower oil
3 spring onions, sliced thin
1 garlic clove, crushed
2 cups chicken stock
1 large can cream style sweet corn
2 cups cooked and peeled shrimp
2 teaspoons green chili paste or chili sauce
Salt and freshly ground black pepper
Fresh coriander leaves, for garnish

Heat the oil in a soup pot and sauté the onions and garlic. Stir in the chicken stock, cream style sweet corn, shrimp, and chili and bring to a boil. Season with salt and pepper. Sprinkle with fresh coriander leaves and serve.

*Make the soup a day before, letting it sit in the refrigerator overnight so the flavors stand out.

Nutrition Facts

Serving Size 207 g

Amount Per Serving

Calories 112	Calories from Fat 35
	% Daily Value*
Total Fat 3.9g	6%
Trans Fat 0.0g	
Cholesterol 24mg	8%
Sodium 622mg	26%
Total Carbohydrates 14.7g	5%
Dietary Fiber 0.9g	4%
Sugars 5.7g	
Protein 4.4g	

Vitamin A 6%	•	Vitamin C 5%
Calcium 3%	•	Iron 1%

Nutrition Grade C+

* Based on a 2000 calorie diet

Yield: 5 servings

Soups & Stews

Vegetarian Chili

12 (2) carrots, peeled and coarsely chopped
4 (⅓ cup) celery stalks, coarsely chopped
1 pound (1 cup chopped) fresh mushrooms coarsely chopped
3 (1 cup) onions, diced
¼ cup (2 teaspoons) minced garlic
½ cup (4 teaspoons) blended oil
1 can (½ cup) tomatoes, diced
1 cup (3 tablespoons) bulgur wheat
4 cups (⅔ cup) vegetable broth
1 dried chipotle pepper
1 dried ancho chili pepper
(¼ teaspoon chipotle or ancho chili)
1 cup (3 tablespoons) brewed coffee
¼ cup (2 teaspoons) chili powder
2 tablespoons (1 teaspoon) ground cumin
1 (¼ teaspoon) cinnamon stick
3 cups (½ cup) cooked pinto or kidney beans

Yield: 20 servings-food service version
(4 cups-home version)
Jen Foy

In a soup pot, sauté the carrots, celery, mushrooms, onions, and garlic in the oil. Add the tomatoes, bulgur, vegetable stock, peppers, coffee, and spices (chili powder, cumin, and cinnamon). Cook until the liquid is almost gone.

Remove the peppers and adjust the seasoning if necessary with salt and pepper. Add the cooked beans, mix well, and serve.

Nutrition Facts
Serving Size 198 g

Amount Per Serving
Calories 222 — Calories from Fat 61
% Daily Value*
Total Fat 6.8g — 10%
Saturated Fat 0.9g — 5%
Trans Fat 0.0g
Cholesterol 0mg — 0%
Sodium 206mg — 9%
Total Carbohydrates 32.4g — 11%
Dietary Fiber 7.1g — 28%
Sugars 4.2g
Protein 10.0g

Vitamin A 19% • Vitamin C 18%
Calcium 5% • Iron 26%
Nutrition Grade A
* Based on a 2000 calorie diet

Notes

Veggies And Sides

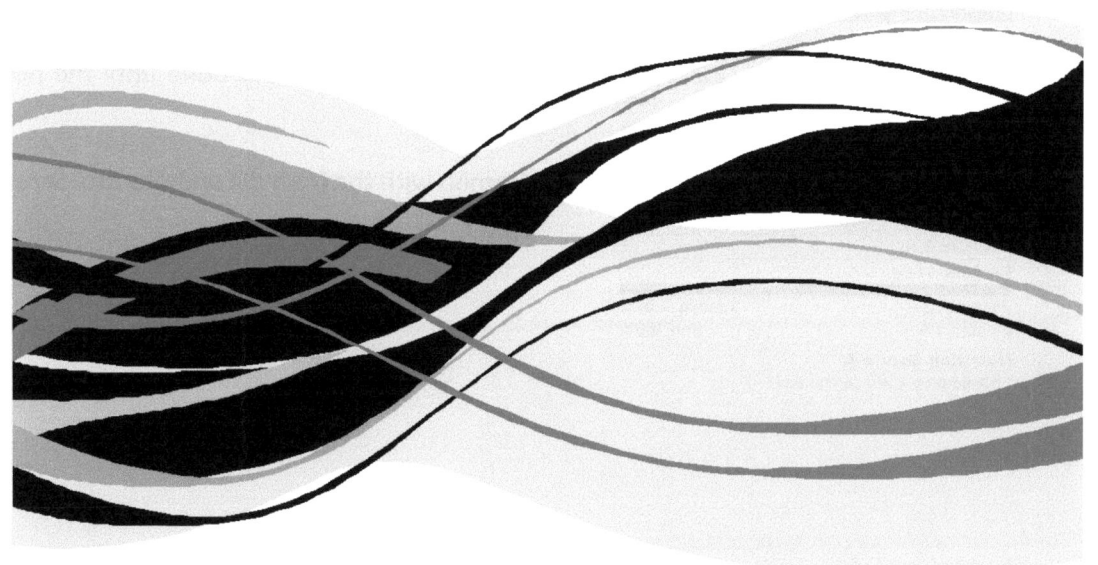

Brock's Best

Brock's Best

Armenian "Musaca"

1 ½ pound beef, sliced
Salt and freshly ground black pepper
1 tablespoon vegetable oil
3 eggplants, sliced into rounds
¾ cup uncooked rice
5 tomatoes, sliced
3 tablespoons dill, for garnish
3 tablespoons cilantro, for garnish

Preheat your oven to 350° F. Slice the beef and season with salt and pepper. Fry the meat in a sauté pan until brown. Remove the beef and set aside on a plate (on top of a paper towel if you want to sop up the grease). Fry the eggplant rounds in the pan that you used for the beef.

Place the half the eggplant slices in the bottom of a 9 by 13-inch baking dish. Add a layer with all the beef. Next, make a layer with the rice. Make another layer with the sliced tomatoes. Top with the remaining eggplant. Add enough water to cover the rice. Cover the dish and bake until the rice is cooked.

Garnish with the fresh dill and cilantro. Serve and enjoy.

Yield: 10 servings
Liudmila Sarkisova

Nutrition Facts

Serving Size 532 g

Amount Per Serving

Calories 458	Calories from Fat 95
	% Daily Value*
Total Fat 10.5g	16%
Saturated Fat 3.2g	16%
Cholesterol 101mg	34%
Sodium 92mg	4%
Total Carbohydrates 50.8g	17%
Dietary Fiber 11.3g	45%
Sugars 9.1g	
Protein 41.0g	
Vitamin A 3%	Vitamin C 54%
Calcium 4%	Iron 160%

Nutrition Grade A
* Based on a 2000 calorie diet

Veggies & Sides

Asparagus and Hollandaise Sauce

⅓ cup almonds
2 pounds asparagus, fresh

<u>Hollandaise sauce</u>
4 egg yolks
1 cup (2 sticks) butter, in chunks
½ teaspoon sea salt
Pinch of white pepper (optional)
Pinch of cayenne pepper
2 tablespoons freshly squeezed lemon juice, or water

Blanch the almonds by boiling for 1 minute, then running cold water over them in a colander and drying them with paper towels.

Snap the tough ends off the asparagus. The ends may be discarded, or reserved for flavoring a vegetable stock. Steam the asparagus until tender (not mushy) and drain. Asparagus should be bright green when done; not an olive color. The length of cooking time depends on how young and what size the shoots were when harvested.

Pour Hollandaise sauce (recipe follows) over the asparagus and sprinkle with the blanched almonds.

<u>Hollandaise sauce</u>
In a saucepan, beat the egg yolks over low heat for about 5 minutes. If the temperature nears a boil, the eggs will scramble, which is not wanted. If the mixture is not hot enough, the sauce may be too thin, and is more likely to separate. The sauce is ready when, with a stroke of the whisk, you see the clean bottom of the pan.

On the lowest heat setting, add the chunks of butter, one at a time, and beat after each addition. Stir in the salt, white pepper, cayenne pepper, and lemon juice. Adjust the seasoning.

This Hollandaise sauce is also good as a substitute for the cream sauce of the Quick and Easy Eggs Benedict recipe (page 40).

Nutrition Facts

Serving Size 158 g

Amount Per Serving

Calories 277	Calories from Fat 246
	% Daily Value*
Total Fat 27.4g	42%
Saturated Fat 15.6g	78%
Trans Fat 0.0g	
Cholesterol 166mg	55%
Sodium 287mg	12%
Total Carbohydrates 5.7g	2%
Dietary Fiber 2.9g	12%
Sugars 2.4g	
Protein 5.0g	
Vitamin A 34% •	Vitamin C 14%
Calcium 6% •	Iron 16%

Nutrition Grade C+
* Based on a 2000 calorie diet

Yield: 6 to 8 servings
Mark Snyder

Brock's Best

Baked Beans

1 pound dry northern beans
½ pound bacon, cut in 1-inch pieces
1 teaspoon salt
1 sweet onion
1 bottle chili sauce
½ cup brown sugar
⅔ cup molasses
3 teaspoons dry mustard
2 teaspoons freshly squeezed lemon juice
1 to 2 tablespoons of bacon fat
Freshly ground black pepper

Soak the navy beans overnight. Drain the beans, place in a stockpot, and cover again with water. Boil for about 1 hour, until tender. Mix in the salt. Drain the beans again, but reserve the liquid this time.

While the beans cook, in a small frying pan, fry the bacon until crisp. Reserve 1 to 2 tablespoons of bacon fat.

In the bean pot, combine all of the ingredients including drained beans and the bacon fat but not the reserved liquid. Once combined, add a bit of the liquid to create some sauce for the beans.

Transfer the bean mixture to a crock pot. Cook for 4 to 6 hours. Occasionally stir and add additional amounts of the reserved liquid to maintain the bean sauce. Season with pepper.

Nutrition Facts
Serving Size 144 g

Amount Per Serving
Calories 375 | Calories from Fat 184
| | % Daily Value* |
Total Fat 20.5g | 32%
Saturated Fat 6.6g | 33%
Trans Fat 0.0g |
Cholesterol 53mg | 18%
Sodium 1568mg | 65%
Total Carbohydrates 28.9g | 10%
Dietary Fiber 1.9g | 8%
Sugars 20.4g |
Protein 19.1g |

Vitamin A 7% • Vitamin C 25%
Calcium 8% • Iron 13%

Nutrition Grade B-
* Based on a 2000 calorie diet

Yield: 8 to 10 servings
Tracey Woomer

Veggies & Sides

Basil Roasted Vegetable Couscous Salad

2 tablespoons fresh minced basil
2 tablespoons balsamic vinegar
1 tablespoon extra-virgin olive oil
¼ teaspoon salt
2 cloves garlic, crushed
2 zucchini, cut into 1-inch slices
2 squash, cut into 1-inch slices
2 eggplant, cut into 1-inch slices
2 red bell peppers, cut into 1-inch slices
2 yellow peppers, cut into 1-inch slices
1 yellow onions, cut into 8 wedges
1 (8 ounce) package baby bella mushrooms
3 cups cooked couscous

Dressing
2 tablespoons freshly squeezed lemon juice
5 tablespoons olive oil
Salt and freshly ground black pepper

Preheat your oven to 425° F. In a large bowl, combine the basil, balsamic vinegar, olive oil, salt, and garlic. Stir well. Add the zucchini, squash, eggplant, red bell peppers, yellow peppers, yellow onions and mushrooms. Toss well to coat.

Arrange the vegetables on a single layer in a shallow roasting pan. Bake for 35 minutes, or until tender and browned, stirring occasionally.

Combine the roasted vegetables with the couscous. Add the dressing (recipe follows), and stir well to combine. Can be served warm or chilled.

Dressing
Combine the lemon juice and olive oil. Season with salt and pepper.

Nutrition Facts
Serving Size 272 g

Amount Per Serving	
Calories 315	Calories from Fat 82
	% Daily Value*
Total Fat 9.2g	14%
Saturated Fat 1.3g	7%
Trans Fat 0.0g	
Cholesterol 0mg	0%
Sodium 76mg	3%
Total Carbohydrates 50.5g	17%
Dietary Fiber 7.2g	29%
Sugars 4.4g	
Protein 9.2g	
Vitamin A 4% •	Vitamin C 32%
Calcium 3% •	Iron 12%
Nutrition Grade A	

* Based on a 2000 calorie diet

Yield: 8 to 10 servings
Tracey Woomer

Brock's Best

Black Bean Cakes With Tomato and Jack Cheese

Yield: 20 servings-food service version (5 servings-home version)

Tony Paterno

6 cups (1 ½ cups) presoaked black beans
4 tablespoon (1 tbsp) oil plus more for frying the cakes
2 onions (1 cup), finely diced
10 cloves (1 ⅔ tsp) fresh chopped garlic
¼ teaspoon (1 pinch) cayenne pepper
2 tablespoons (1 ½ tsp) ground cumin
1 ½ tablespoon (1 tsp) ground chili powder
½ cup (2 tbsp) white wine for sautéing
½ cup (2 tbsp) flour, all-purpose
¾ cup (3 tbsp) corn meal
6 scallions (2 tbsp + 1 ½ tsp), chopped
2 tablespoons (1 ½ tsp) kosher salt
½ bunch (4 ½ tsp) cilantro, chopped
1 cup (¼ cup) eggs, pasteurized
2 ½ pounds—about 11 cups—(2 ¾ cup) Jack cheese, shredded
6 cups (1 ½ cup) tomato salsa

Preheat your oven to 350° F. In a saucepan cook the beans in boiling water for about 45 minutes, until tender.

Heat up the oil in a sauté pan. Add the onions and garlic and sauté until translucent. Add the cumin, cayenne pepper, and chili powder. Deglaze with white wine, remove from heat, and chill.

Combine the beans and the onion mixture in an electric mixer bowl and mix with a paddle at low speed. (This can also be done in a food processor or by hand. The texture of hand mixed bean cakes will be rougher.) Add the flour, cornmeal, scallions, salt, cilantro, and eggs. Mix until well blended.

Scoop the bean mix into ¾ cup portions and form into cakes. Cook on a skillet in oil and sear on both sides. Place on a baking pan and finish in the oven for 5 to 15 minutes, until the minimum internal temperatures reach 165° F.

Top with shredded jack cheese. Return the cakes to the oven to melt. Remove from the oven and top with 4 tablespoons of tomato salsa.

Nutrition Facts

Serving Size 219 g

Amount Per Serving

Calories 465 — Calories from Fat 192

	% Daily Value*
Total Fat 21.3g	33%
Saturated Fat 11.1g	55%
Trans Fat 0.0g	
Cholesterol 96mg	32%
Sodium 1089mg	45%
Total Carbohydrates 40.2g	13%
Dietary Fiber 8.8g	35%
Sugars 1.7g	
Protein 29.5g	

Vitamin A 23% • Vitamin C 5%
Calcium 48% • Iron 19%

Nutrition Grade D+

* Based on a 2000 calorie diet

Veggies & Sides

Bulgur Risotto With Spring Peas and Asparagus

4 tablespoons butter plus 1 more tablespoon for the end of the recipe
1 large onion, chopped
3 cloves garlic, minced
1 ½ cup bulgur
4 cups chicken stock
1 pound asparagus, trimmed and cut into ¾-inch pieces
1 ½ cup unthawed frozen peas
¾ cup freshly grated Parmesan cheese
¼ cup whipping cream
2 tablespoons chopped fresh tarragon
Freshly grated Parmesan cheese (optional)

Melt 4 tablespoons of butter in a heavy large saucepan over medium heat. Add the onion and garlic. Sauté until light golden, about 5 minutes.

Mix in bulgur. Add ½ cup of stock and cook about 5 minutes, until the liquid is absorbed, stirring often. Add another ½ cup of stock two more times, simmer after each addition, and stir often until the liquid is absorbed.

Mix in the asparagus. Add more stock ½ cup at a time until the bulgur is just tender and the mixture is creamy after about 20 more minutes.

Add the peas and cook 3 minutes longer. Stir in the Parmesan cheese, cream, tarragon, and remaining 1 tablespoon of butter.

Serve, sprinkling on additional grated Parmesan, if desired.

Yield: 6 servings
Gerrard Zolezi

Nutrition Facts

Serving Size 391 g

Amount Per Serving

Calories 357	Calories from Fat 135
	% Daily Value*
Total Fat 15.0g	23%
Saturated Fat 10.0g	50%
Trans Fat 0.0g	
Cholesterol 40mg	13%
Sodium 726mg	30%
Total Carbohydrates 45.4g	15%
Dietary Fiber 5.1g	21%
Sugars 4.9g	
Protein 13.8g	
Vitamin A 37%	Vitamin C 21%
Calcium 18%	Iron 29%

Nutrition Grade B+
* Based on a 2000 calorie diet

? Did you know that legumes are low in fat? Foods like those from the peas and beans family are excellent sources of proteins, fiber, and flavor. They are great to serve as a side dish.

Brock's Best
Bulgur Stuffed Tomato Au Gratin

5 ½ cups (1 ¾ cup) uncooked bulgur wheat
½ cups (3 tablespoons) olive oil
3 carrots (1 carrot), finely diced
3 red peppers (1 red pepper), finely diced
2 red sweet onions (1 cup), finely diced
½ bunch (⅓ cup) celery, finely diced
2 tablespoons (2 teaspoons) fresh garlic
½ teaspoon (1 pinch) salt
1 teaspoon (⅓ teaspoon) freshly ground black pepper
2 to 3 cups (⅔ to 1 cup) cream sauce or alfredo sauce, made in advance (page 40)
24 tomatoes (8 tomatoes)
Parmesan cheese

Preheat your oven to 300° F. In a stockpot, cook the bulgur wheat following the box directions. When done, drain and refrigerate.

In another saucepan heat the oil. Start sautéing the carrots first and let them cook for 4 minutes before adding the rest of the diced vegetables and garlic. Continue cooking until the vegetables soften. Season with the salt and pepper.

Add the cooked vegetables to the bulgur wheat and return the mixture to the refrigerator.

Core out the twenty-four tomatoes (eight tomatoes for the home version), leaving some of the tomato at the bottom. Also, carefully slice the bottoms off, so the tomatoes have a flat spot, but are not completely hollowed out.

Make 24 equal balls (8 balls for the home version) of the bulgur-vegetable mixture, and then stuff them into the tomatoes.

Grease a baking pan, then pour the previously prepared Alfredo or cream sauce into the pan. Transfer the stuffed tomatoes to the pan. Sprinkle shaved Parmesan cheese on top. Be generous. Tightly cover with aluminum foil. Bake for 45 minutes. Uncover and cook another 5 to 10 minutes to lightly brown.

Nutrition Facts

Serving Size 20 g

Amount Per Serving

Calories 21	Calories from Fat 6
	% Daily Value*
Total Fat 0.7g	1%
Trans Fat 0.0g	
Cholesterol 0mg	0%
Sodium 54mg	2%
Total Carbohydrates 3.3g	1%
Protein 0.6g	
Vitamin A 3%	Vitamin C 6%
Calcium 0%	Iron 2%

Nutrition Grade B-
* Based on a 2000 calorie diet

Yield: 24 servings-food service version
(8 servings-home version)
Chuck Wilde

Veggies & Sides

Creamed Cabbage

1 small head of cabbage (4 pounds)

<u>Dressing</u>
½ cup heavy cream
1 teaspoon salt
½ cup sugar
½ cup chilled white vinegar

Discard the outer leaves and the core of the cabbage head. Chop the rest of the head to a medium consistency. Combine with the dressing (recipe follows) just before serving.

<u>Dressing</u>
With an electric mixer, thoroughly beat the heavy cream, salt, sugar, and vinegar, until the consistency resembles whipped cream.

Yield: 8 to 10 servings
Evelyn Bitner

Brock's Best

Dinsztelt Wilted Greens

¼ cup butter
¼ cup olive oil
6 cloves garlic, minced
1 tin anchovies
½ teaspoon crushed red pepper
1 bunch Swiss chard, discard stems, tear leaves
1 bunch mustard greens, stems trimmed—tear leaves into smaller pieces
1 head escarole, stems trimmed, tear leaves
10 ounces fresh spinach leaves, torn—about 6 cups of leaves
1 can black olives, chopped
2 tablespoons red wine vinegar
¼ cup chicken stock
Salt and freshly ground black pepper

Melt the butter and heat the olive oil in a heavy large pot over medium-high heat. Add the garlic, anchovies, and crushed red pepper. Cook until the anchovies begin to fall apart.

Add the chard, mustard greens, escarole, spinach, olives, vinegar, and stock. Cover and cook for about 3 minutes, until the greens wilt, stirring occasionally. Uncover. Cook until juices thicken slightly, about 4 more minutes. Season with salt and pepper, and serve.

Yield: 4 to 6 servings
Eric Rappaport

Nutrition Facts

Serving Size 114 g

Amount Per Serving	
Calories 178	Calories from Fat 160
	% Daily Value*
Total Fat 17.8g	27%
Saturated Fat 6.3g	31%
Trans Fat 0.0g	
Cholesterol 20mg	7%
Sodium 256mg	11%
Total Carbohydrates 4.4g	1%
Dietary Fiber 2.0g	8%
Sugars 0.5g	
Protein 2.4g	
Vitamin A 123%	Vitamin C 38%
Calcium 8%	Iron 11%

Nutrition Grade B-
* Based on a 2000 calorie diet

Veggies & Sides

Dolma* (Stuffed Grape Leaves)

1 pound ground beef
¾ cup (5 ounces) uncooked rice
4 onions, quartered
1 bunch cilantro
1 tablespoon dried mint
Salt and freshly ground black pepper
1 large jar of grape leaves, drained

Sauce
32 ounces sour cream, plain yogurt, or whipped yogurt
5 cloves garlic, large, minced

In a large bowl, mix the ground beef, rice, onions, cilantro, and mint. Season with salt and pepper. Using a meat grinder, grind the meat mixture using a large die.

Drain the grape leaves and place in boiling water for 5 minutes. Remove and separate the leaves, laying them flat on a cutting board or other clean surface.

Divide the ground meat mixture among the grape leaves. Roll the leaves, folding in the sides to contain the mixture. Place in boiling water for about 2 hours, or until the leaves are tender. Serve with the sauce (recipe follows).

Sauce
You can use plain sour cream, whipped yogurt, or whipped yogurt. Mix one of the three with the minced garlic.

*DOLMA [dOl-'mä]—Means "stuffed."

Nutrition Facts
Serving Size 199 g

Amount Per Serving	
Calories 221	Calories from Fat 36
	% Daily Value*
Total Fat 4.0g	6%
Saturated Fat 2.0g	10%
Cholesterol 46mg	15%
Sodium 101mg	4%
Total Carbohydrates 22.4g	7%
Dietary Fiber 1.2g	5%
Sugars 8.2g	
Protein 20.5g	
Vitamin A 4%	Vitamin C 10%
Calcium 18%	Iron 52%
Nutrition Grade A	

* Based on a 2000 calorie diet

Yield: 10 servings
Veta Mesh

Brock's Best

Home-Style Baked Beans

16 ounces baked beans
15 ½ ounces kidney beans, rinsed and drained
15 ounces butter beans, rinsed and drained
¼ cup tomato sauce
⅓ cup catsup
1 onion, finely chopped
1 teaspoon dry mustard
2 cloves garlic, minced
¾ cup packed brown sugar
1 tablespoon Worcestershire sauce

Preheat your oven to 350° F. Combine all the ingredients together in a bowl. Pour into a greased 13 by 9-inch baking dish. Bake, uncovered for 30 minutes, or until the beans are a desired consistency.

Yield: 12 servings

Donna Dunn

Nutrition Facts

Serving Size 142 g

Amount Per Serving

Calories 270	Calories from Fat 25
	% Daily Value*
Total Fat 2.7g	4%
Saturated Fat 0.9g	4%
Trans Fat 0.0g	
Cholesterol 2mg	1%
Sodium 284mg	12%
Total Carbohydrates 49.9g	17%
Dietary Fiber 9.7g	39%
Sugars 12.5g	
Protein 13.1g	

| Vitamin A 3% | • | Vitamin C 21% |
| Calcium 8% | • | Iron 25% |

Nutrition Grade A

* Based on a 2000 calorie diet

Veggies & Sides

Hummus

Yield: 70 servings
Jeffrey Chamberlain

½ cup chopped garlic
1 ¾ cup tahini*
1 ½ cup freshly squeezed lemon juice
¾ cup olive oil
1 ½ tablespoon salt
2 tablespoons Sriracha sauce**
1 #10 can garbanzo beans, drained liquid reserved

Add the garlic, tahini, lemon juice, olive oil, salt, and Sriracha sauce into a food processor and blend well. Transfer the mixture to a mixing bowl, but don't clean the food processor.

Drain garbanzo beans and reserve the liquid. Blend the garbanzo beans in the food processor in small batches. Blend well, thinning as needed with the reserved liquid to the consistency of runny peanut butter.

Add each batch of garbanzo beans into the mixing bowl with the other ingredients. After all the garbanzo bean batches have been transferred, mix well and serve.

Nutrition Facts

Serving Size 19 g

Amount Per Serving	
Calories 72	Calories from Fat 51
	% Daily Value*
Total Fat 5.7g	9%
Saturated Fat 0.8g	4%
Cholesterol 0mg	0%
Sodium 163mg	7%
Total Carbohydrates 4.2g	1%
Dietary Fiber 1.3g	5%
Sugars 0.6g	
Protein 1.9g	
Vitamin A 0%	Vitamin C 5%
Calcium 3%	Iron 5%

Nutrition Grade B-

* Based on a 2000 calorie diet

*TAHINI [tuh-HEE-nee]—a thick paste made of ground sesame seed.

**SRIRACHA [SEE-rah-chah]—Hot sauce made from sun-ripened chilies, which are ground into a smooth paste with garlic.

Brock's Best

Olive Balls

1 cup (4 ounces) shredded cheddar cheese
¼ cup butter or margarine, softened
¼ teaspoon Worcestershire sauce
1 cup Bisquick Original Pancake and Baking Mix
1 (5 ounce) jar pimiento-stuffed olives

Preheat your oven to 400° F. Stir together the cheese, butter, and the Worcestershire sauce. Stir in Bisquick mix until a dough forms (work with your hands if necessary).

Pat the olives completely dry on a paper towel. Shape 1 teaspoon dough around each olive. Place the balls about 1 inch apart on an ungreased cookie sheet. Bake for about 10 minutes, or until light golden brown.

Nutrition Facts

Serving Size 11 g

Amount Per Serving	
Calories 40	Calories from Fat 28
	% Daily Value*
Total Fat 3.1g	**5%**
Saturated Fat 1.6g	**8%**
Trans Fat 0.0g	
Cholesterol 6mg	**2%**
Sodium 146mg	**6%**
Total Carbohydrates 1.9g	**1%**
Protein 0.9g	

Vitamin A 2%	•	Vitamin C 0%
Calcium 3%	•	Iron 1%

Nutrition Grade D
* Based on a 2000 calorie diet

Yield: 40 balls
Teresa Flebbe

Veggies & Sides

Veggies & Sides

Potato Salad

10 pounds (2 ½ pound) potatoes, cut in ¾-inch cubes
2 large onions/2 ounces onion powder (½ cup diced onions or 2 tablespoons onion powder)
2 cups—1 pound—(½ cup) diced celery
2 cups (½ cup) sweet relish
1 cup (¼ cup) yellow mustard
4 cups (1 cup) mayonnaise
Salt and freshly ground black pepper

Cook the potatoes in boiling water until tender but firm. Drain them and transfer to a salad bowl. Add all the other ingredients to the bowl and mix thoroughly. Adjust the seasoning with salt and pepper.

Allow to sit refrigerated until the flavors blend well.

Yield: 64 servings-food service version (16 servings-home version)
Antoine Lee

Nutrition Facts
Serving Size 105 g

Amount Per Serving	
Calories 116	Calories from Fat 44
	% Daily Value*
Total Fat 4.8g	7%
Saturated Fat 0.7g	4%
Trans Fat 0.0g	
Cholesterol 4mg	1%
Sodium 240mg	10%
Total Carbohydrates 17.5g	6%
Dietary Fiber 2.1g	8%
Sugars 4.2g	
Protein 1.5g	
Vitamin A 3% •	Vitamin C 24%
Calcium 1% •	Iron 3%
Nutrition Grade B+	

* Based on a 2000 calorie diet

Brock's Best

Red Quinoa

4 cups (1 cup) red quinoa
8 cups (2 cups) vegetable stock
1 ½ cup (⅓ cup) dried cranberries
1 ½ cup (⅓ cup) raisins
1 ½ cup (⅓ cup) almonds, toasted, slivered
1 ½ cup (⅓ cup) salted sunflower seeds
2 tablespoons (1 ½ teaspoon) fresh thyme leaves

Place quinoa on a sheet pan. Toast the grains in a 350° F convection oven for 15 minutes (or 375° F for 18 minutes in a conventional oven). Remove and let cool.

Bring 8 cups (2 cups for the home version) of vegetable broth to boil. Add the quinoa. Cook for 15 to 20 minutes, until a white "tail" shows on the grains. Test for doneness. (Some people like crunchier, others softer quinoa.) When satisfied with the texture, drain and cool on the sheet pan again.

In a large mixing bowl combine the quinoa, cranberries, raisins, almonds, sunflower seeds, and thyme. Mix thoroughly and serve.

Nutrition Facts
Serving Size 83 g

Amount Per Serving

Calories 171	Calories from Fat 77
	% Daily Value*
Total Fat 8.5g	13%
Saturated Fat 0.9g	4%
Trans Fat 0.0g	
Cholesterol 0mg	0%
Sodium 122mg	5%
Total Carbohydrates 19.5g	6%
Dietary Fiber 3.5g	14%
Sugars 8.0g	
Protein 5.6g	
Vitamin A 0%	Vitamin C 2%
Calcium 4%	Iron 9%

Nutrition Grade B
* Based on a 2000 calorie diet

QUINOA [KEEN-wah]—This ancient seed was a staple of the Incas. It cooks quickly and has a mild flavor and a delightful, slightly crunchy, texture. It has a lot of the amino acid lysine, so it provides a more complete protein than many other cereal grains. It comes in different colors, ranging from a pale yellow to red to black. Rinse quinoa before using to remove its bitter natural coating.

Yield: 15 to 20 servings-food service version
(4 to 5 servings-home version)
Chris Gearin

Veggies & Sides

Roasted Parsnips

2 pounds parsnips, peeled—cut on diagonal into ½-inch slices
2 tablespoons extra virgin olive oil
1 teaspoon coarse kosher salt
2 tablespoons butter
Freshly ground black pepper

Preheat your oven to 450° F. Toss the parsnips, olive oil, and kosher salt in a bowl. Transfer to a rimmed baking sheet and spread in a single layer. Dot with butter.

Roast the parsnips for about 35 minutes in total, until browned on both sides and soft. Use tongs to turn the slices over midway through the roasting. Season further with pepper and more salt, and serve.

Nutrition Facts

Serving Size 266 g

Amount Per Serving	
Calories 221	Calories from Fat 58
	% Daily Value*
Total Fat 6.4g	10%
Saturated Fat 3.8g	19%
Cholesterol 15mg	5%
Sodium 2944mg	123%
Total Carbohydrates 40.8g	14%
Dietary Fiber 11.1g	44%
Sugars 10.9g	
Protein 2.8g	

Vitamin A 4%	•	Vitamin C 64%	
Calcium 8%	•	Iron 7%	

Nutrition Grade A-
* Based on a 2000 calorie diet

Yield: 4 servings
Tracey Woomer

Brock's Best

Russian Golubtsi– Stuffed Cabbage Rolls

Yield: about 5 servings
Bella Raykin

1 head of green cabbage
¾ cup uncooked rice
Salt
¾ cup finely diced peeled onions
Oil or butter for sautéing
1 ¾ cup seeded, skinned, and finely chopped tomatoes
1 ¾ cup peeled and shredded carrots
14 ounces ground beef
2 tablespoons tomato paste
Salt and freshly ground black pepper
2 cups water
Sour cream

Preheat your oven to 145° F. Wash the cabbage and remove the outer leaves, discarding them. Place the cabbage head in a large pot with boiling water, cover, and simmer for about 15 minutes. Remove and cool the cabbage head with cold water, then drain. Separate the cabbage leaves.

In another pot, cook the rice in salted water until half cooked (10 minutes).

In a large sauté pan, sauté the onions in oil or butter until translucent. Add the tomatoes and carrots. Add the half-cooked rice and ground beef. Season with salt and pepper, and mix well.

Put 1 tablespoon of filling on the inner side of each separated cabbage leaf. Carefully fold the leaves, like envelopes, seam side down. Heat oil or butter in a skillet and fry the golubtsi on both sides until golden brown.

In a soup pot or large saucepan, bring the 2 cups of water to a boil and add the tomato paste. Place the golubtsi in the pot and simmer for about 1 hour, or slow cook in the pre-heated oven for 1 hour.

Remove from the pot or oven and serve with sour cream.

Nutrition Facts

Serving Size 446 g

Amount Per Serving

Calories 396 — Calories from Fat 91

	% Daily Value*
Total Fat 10.2g	16%
Saturated Fat 4.9g	25%
Trans Fat 0.0g	
Cholesterol 81mg	27%
Sodium 155mg	6%
Total Carbohydrates 43.8g	15%
Dietary Fiber 7.5g	30%
Sugars 11.9g	
Protein 30.5g	

Vitamin A 134%	•	Vitamin C 196%
Calcium 15%	•	Iron 101%

Nutrition Grade A
* Based on a 2000 calorie diet

Veggies & Sides

Russian Mushrooms

2 tablespoons butter
2 onions, finely chopped
1 pound mushrooms, thinly sliced
1 ¼ cups (10 ounces) fresh beef stock
1 cup (8 ounces) sour cream
Salt and freshly ground black pepper

Heat the butter in a saucepan. Add the onions and sauté gently for 3 to 5 minutes until softened. Add the mushrooms and continue sautéing for about 5 minutes, or until just tender.

Add the beef stock and heat to a simmer, and then stir in the sour cream. Season with salt and pepper. Serve hot.

Nutrition Facts

Serving Size 303 g

Amount Per Serving	
Calories 224	Calories from Fat 163
	% Daily Value*
Total Fat 18.1g	28%
Saturated Fat 11.1g	56%
Cholesterol 40mg	13%
Sodium 308mg	13%
Total Carbohydrates 11.1g	4%
Dietary Fiber 2.2g	9%
Sugars 4.2g	
Protein 6.8g	

Vitamin A 11%	•	Vitamin C 15%	
Calcium 7%	•	Iron 19%	

Nutrition Grade B+
* Based on a 2000 calorie diet

Yield: 4 servings
Boris Reznik

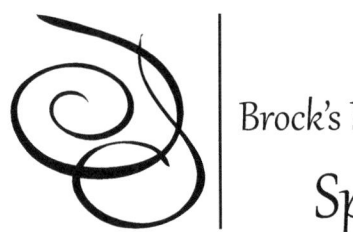

Brock's Best

Spaetzle* Noodles Bergkase

Yield: 4 servings
Eric Rappaport

4 eggs
½ cup milk
2 cups all-purpose flour
1 teaspoon salt
½ teaspoon ground nutmeg
¼ teaspoon white pepper
¼ cup butter
1 cup sliced thin onions
1 cup grated Bergkase cheese—
or other hard German cheese
Salt and freshly ground black pepper

Combine the eggs and milk, and mix well. Add the flour, salt, nutmeg, and pepper. Combine to form a sticky dough. Bring a large pot of salted water to a boil. Form the Spaetzle by using a special Spaetzle maker or use a rubber spatula to push the batter through the holes of a large bore colander. Cook the Spaetzle in boiling water for approximately 5 minutes, or until the noodles rise to the surface. Drain well.

Heat a heavy-bottomed sauté pan over medium high heat, melt the butter, and add the onions. Cook the onions until lightly browned. Add the drained Spaetzle and sauté for about 2 minutes. Add the grated Bergkase cheese, and toss well to coat.

Season with salt and pepper and serve immediately.

*SPAETZLE [SHPATES-luh]—Spaetzle is a dish of tiny noodles or dumplings made with flour, eggs, water (or milk), salt, and sometimes nutmeg.

Nutrition Facts

Serving Size 210 g

Amount Per Serving

Calories 535	Calories from Fat 239
	% Daily Value*
Total Fat 26.5g	41%
Saturated Fat 15.2g	76%
Cholesterol 226mg	75%
Sodium 914mg	38%
Total Carbohydrates 52.6g	18%
Dietary Fiber 2.4g	9%
Sugars 3.4g	
Protein 20.5g	
Vitamin A 17% •	Vitamin C 5%
Calcium 24% •	Iron 22%

Nutrition Grade B-
* Based on a 2000 calorie diet

Veggies & Sides

Veggies & Sides

Spicy Asian Lettuce Wraps

Yield: 4 servings
Eric Smith

1 package cellophane noodles
1 flank steak
4 boneless skinless chicken breasts
16 lettuce leaves (such as bibb, butter, or iceberg lettuce)
1 red pepper, seeded and julienne
1 carrot, julienne
3 to 4 green onions, sliced bias cut
½ cup sliced shiitake mushrooms
1 halved cucumber, deseeded and cut in strips
4 tablespoons canola oil
2 tablespoons chopped ginger
2 tablespoons chopped garlic
2 tablespoons rice wine vinegar
3 tablespoons hoisin sauce
1 tablespoon Japanese ponzu
½ teaspoon Sriracha sauce
1 tablespoon warm water
4 tablespoons soy sauce
½ teaspoon chili flakes
1 teaspoon chopped cilantro
2 teaspoons sliced green onions
1 teaspoon freshly squeezed lime juice
½ tsp sesame oil

Cook the cellophane noodles in boiling water until tender.

Marinate the flank steak in half the marinade mixture (recipe follows) and the chicken in the other half. Grill the flank steak and chicken separately on a charcoal grill until done. Julienne the meat into strips.

Take one lettuce leaf and put a small amount of cellophane noodles on top. Add the chicken or beef strips (both if you would like), the peppers, carrots, green onion, shiitake mushroom, and cucumber. Top with the hot hoisin sauce (recipe follows) or the chili cilantro sauce (recipe follows). Also serve the sauces on the side for dipping.

Marinate
Mix the canola oil, ginger, garlic, and rice wine vinegar.

Hot Hoisin Sauce
Mix together the hoisin sauce, ponzu, Sriracha, and warm water. Make sure the sauce is not too thick or too thin. Allow to sit so the flavors will gel.

Chili Cilantro Sauce
Combine the soy sauce, chili flakes, cilantro, green onions, lime juice, and sesame oil, and allow to sit.

Nutrition Facts
Serving Size 481 g

Amount Per Serving	
Calories 756	Calories from Fat 283
	% Daily Value*
Total Fat 31.4g	48%
Saturated Fat 6.6g	33%
Trans Fat 0.1g	
Cholesterol 156mg	52%
Sodium 1322mg	55%
Total Carbohydrates 53.0g	18%
Dietary Fiber 3.3g	13%
Sugars 10.0g	
Protein 62.1g	

Vitamin A 76%	•	Vitamin C 76%	
Calcium 9%	•	Iron 29%	

Nutrition Grade B+
* Based on a 2000 calorie diet

Brock's Best

Sweet Potato Salad

2 pounds sweet potatoes
½ pound bacon
1 cup mayonnaise
½ cup Dijon mustard
¼ cup maple syrup
2 tablespoons cider vinegar
¼ cup chopped parsley
½ cup diced red onion
½ cup diced celery
Salt and freshly ground black pepper

Peel, cube, steam, and cool the sweet potatoes. Cook, cool, and crumble the bacon.

In a bowl, mix the mayonnaise, Dijon mustard, maple syrup, vinegar, and parsley.

Combine the sweet potatoes, bacon, mayonnaise mix, onions and celery all together in a salad bowl and mix well.

Season with salt and pepper. Chill and serve.

Nutrition Facts
Serving Size 87 g

Amount Per Serving
Calories 177 — Calories from Fat 81

	% Daily Value*
Total Fat 9.0g	14%
Saturated Fat 2.2g	11%
Trans Fat 0.0g	
Cholesterol 16mg	5%
Sodium 424mg	18%
Total Carbohydrates 19.0g	6%
Dietary Fiber 2.2g	9%
Sugars 3.6g	
Protein 5.3g	

Vitamin A 3%	•	Vitamin C	15%
Calcium 2%	•	Iron	3%

Nutrition Grade B-
* Based on a 2000 calorie diet

Yield: 10 four ounce servings
Michael Hamilton

Veggies & Sides

Unstuffed Cabbage

Yield: 4 servings
Debbie O'Donovam

1 to 2 pounds head of green cabbage—quartered lengthwise and cored
½ cup reduced-sodium chicken broth
1 clove garlic, thinly sliced and 2 cloves more for cooking the meats
¼ teaspoon salt and ½ teaspoon more for cooking the meats
1 large onion, thinly sliced
1 tablespoon olive oil
½ pound ground beef chuck
½ pound ground pork
½ teaspoon freshly ground black pepper
2 (14 ounce) cans diced tomatoes with juice
⅓ cup dried cranberries
3 tablespoons red wine vinegar
1 tablespoon dark brown sugar
2 tablespoons flat leaf chopped parsley
Serve with steamed white rice

Place the cabbage in a deep 12-inch heavy skillet with broth, 1 clove of garlic (sliced), and a rounded ¼ teaspoon of salt. Bring to a simmer over medium heat, then cook, covered turning cabbage occasionally for about 45 minutes, or until very tender. (Add more broth or water if necessary – do not let the pan go dry).

Meanwhile, cook the onion and remaining garlic in oil in a heavy pot over medium heat, stirring occasionally, until golden (about 8 minutes). Increase the heat to medium-high and stir in the ground beef and pork along with ½ teaspoon each of salt and pepper. Cook for about 3 minutes, stirring and breaking up the lumps with a wooden spoon, until the meat is no longer pink.

Stir in the tomatoes with their juices, the cranberries, vinegar, and brown sugar. Simmer uncovered, stirring occasionally, and breaking up the tomatoes with a spoon, until slightly thickened after about 20 minutes. Season with additional salt, if needed.

Pour the meat sauce into the skillet with the cabbage and simmer, uncovered for 5 minutes. Serve sprinkled with parsley and accompanied by steamed rice, if desired.

Nutrition Facts

Serving Size 637 g

Amount Per Serving

Calories 385	Calories from Fat 159
	% Daily Value*
Total Fat 17.6g	27%
Saturated Fat 5.8g	29%
Trans Fat 0.0g	
Cholesterol 82mg	27%
Sodium 632mg	26%
Total Carbohydrates 28.8g	10%
Dietary Fiber 9.3g	37%
Sugars 14.5g	
Protein 30.0g	
Vitamin A 8%	Vitamin C 222%
Calcium 11%	Iron 34%
Nutrition Grade A	

* Based on a 2000 calorie diet

Brock's Best

Notes

Index

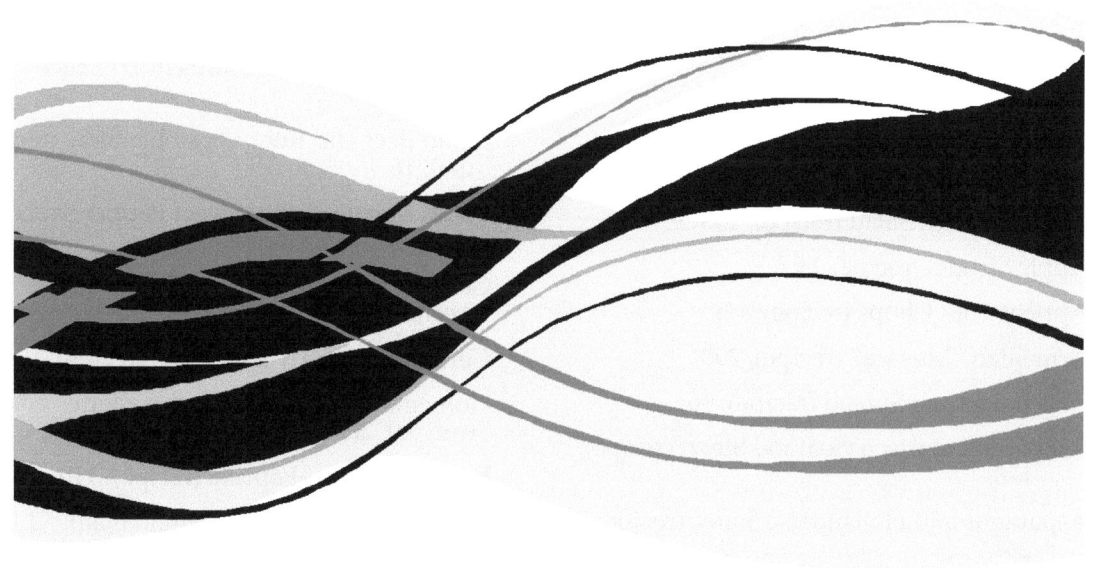

Brock's Best

 Brock's Best

Index

20-Minute Tuna Casserole, 118

A

Adobo Seasoned Baked Chicken Wings (recipe), 48

Anjyab Sandale (recipe), 49

Apple Butter Pork Loin (recipe), 128

Apple Cream Pie (recipe), 64

Apple Crumb Cake (recipe), 65

Apple Fritters (recipe), 66

Apple Oat Bars (recipe), 67

Apple Pie Bars Home Version (recipe), 68

Apple Spinach Salad (recipe), 138

Apple Strudel (recipe), 69

Apricot Pork Chops (recipe), 129

Armenian "Musaca" (recipe), 200

Artichoke Crab Spread (recipe), 96

Asopao De Marisco (Seafood Stew) (recipe), 178

Asparagus and Hollandaise Sauce (recipe), 201

B

Baby Blue Salad, 90 (recipe), 139

Baltimore Chicken (recipe), 50

Banana Granola Cookies (recipe), 70

Barley and Mushroom Salad (recipe), 141

Basil Roasted Vegetable Couscous Salad (recipe), 203

Bavarian Apple Torte (recipe), 71

Bay Scallops and Bulgur Wheat with Fresh Mint (recipe), 162

beef

    Braised Short Ribs (recipe), 14

    Broiled Flank Steak Chimichurri Sauce (recipe), 15

    Cajun Beef and Root Vegetable Stew (recipe), 16

    Cajun Meatloaf with Sweet Pepper Sauce (recipe), 17

    German Beef Roulades over Spaetzle (recipe), 18

    German Braised Veal Shanks (recipe), 19

    Homemade Meatballs for Spaghetti (recipe), 20

    Hungarian Beef Paprika (recipe), 110

    Marinated and Grilled Buffalo Flank Steak with Lime Chipotle Sauce (recipe), 21

    Meatloaf (recipe), 22

    Mom's Meatloaf (recipe), 113

    New Mexican Burger (recipe), 22

Index

beef (cont.)

    Russian Cutlets (recipe), 23

    Spare Ribs in Wine Sauce (recipe), 24

    Stuffed Flank Steak (recipe), 25

    Teriyaki Burger (recipe), 26

    Texas Style BBQ Brisket (recipe), 26

    Wiener-Bean Casserole (recipe), 27

Bisquick mix, 32, 212

Black Bean Cakes with Tomato and Jack Cheese (recipe), 204

Black Bean Chili (recipe), 179

Braised Sea Bass and Fennel with Saffron and Harissa (recipe), 163

Braised Short Ribs (recipe), 14

bread

    Bread Pudding (recipe), 30

    Bread Salad, (recipe for Panzanella) 153

    Breakfast and Breads (section), 29–46

    Butternut Squash Bread Pudding with Leeks and Parmesan (recipe), 31

    Cheese-Garlic Biscuits (recipe), 32

    Chocolate Brioche Bread Pudding (recipe), 32

    Crème Brûlée French Toast (recipe), 33

    Crunchy French Toast with Banana and Strawberry (recipe), 34

    Currant Scones (recipe), 35

    Golden Baked French Toast (recipe), 36

    Guatemalan Banana Bread (recipe), 36

    Open Faced Broiled Egg, Spinach, and Tomato Sandwich (recipe), 37

    Pizza Dough (recipe), 38

    Puffy Maine Pancakes (recipe), 39

    Quick and Easy Eggs Benedict (recipe), 40

    Roasted Vegetable Pizza (recipe), 41

    Scones (recipe), 42

    Scrambled Egg Beggar's Purses (recipe), 43

    Sweet Milk Griddle Cakes (recipe), 44

    Syrniki Cottage Cheese Pancakes (recipe), 45

Broccoli Slaw Salad (recipe), 142

Broiled Flank Steak Chimichurri Sauce (recipe), 15

Brown Rice Salad (recipe), 143

Buffalo Shrimp Dip (recipe), 96

Bulgur Risotto with Spring Peas and Asparagus (recipe), 205

Bulgur Stuffed Tomato Au Gratin (recipe), 206

Butternut Squash Bread Pudding with Leeks and Parmesan (recipe), 31

Butternut Squash Soup (recipe), 180

C

Carolina Cabbage (recipe), 145

Brock's Best

Cajun Beef and Root Vegetable Stew (recipe), 16

Cajun Meatloaf with Sweet Pepper Sauce (recipe), 17

California Mango Chicken Salad (recipe), 144

Caramelized Salmon with Citrus Salsa (recipe), 164

Carrot Cake (recipe), 106

casseroles, 27, 30, 49, 52, 58, 101, 118, 120, 129, 169

Cedar Planked Apples with Walnut Praline Stuffing (recipe), 72

Celeste's Best BBQ Sauce (recipe), 97

Celyodka pod Shuboy—Herring Under a "Fur Coat" (recipe), 146

Cheaty Ziti (recipe), 119

Cheddar Asparagus and Crab Chowder (recipe), 181

Cheese Encrusted Chicken (recipe), 51

Cheese-Garlic Biscuits

Cheesecake, 83

Cheesecake Supreme (recipe), 73

Cherry-O Cream Cheese Pie (recipe), 74

Cherry or Cranberry Pie (recipe), 74

chicken

    Adobo Seasoned Baked Chicken Wings (recipe), 48

    Anjyab Sandale (recipe), 49

    Baltimore (recipe), 50

    California Mango Chicken Salad (recipe), 144

    Cheese Encrusted (recipe), 51

    Chicken (section), 47–62

    Chicken and Broccoli Casserole (recipe), 52

    Chicken and Stuffing (recipe), 53

    Chicken Mole Verde (recipe), 54

    Chicken Sicilian (recipe), 55

    Chicken Tingas (recipe), 56

    Chinamerica Chicken Pineapple Feast (recipe), 57

    Deconstructed Chicken Ratatouille Salad (recipe), 149

    Grilled Chicken Kabobs with Greek Style Barley Salad (recipe), 58

    Grilled Chicken Penne Alfredo (recipe), 59

    Latin Combo—Sky, Sea, and Land (recipe), 60

    Rotisserie Style Chicken (recipe), 61

    Tortellini with Chicken, Basil, and Tomato (recipe), 61

    wings, 48

Chilled Cucumber Soup with Lobster, Mint, and Lobster Brioche Sandwich (recipe), 182

Chinamerica Chicken Pineapple Feast (recipe), 57

chocolate

    Brioche Bread Pudding (recipe), 32

Index

chocolate (cont.)

    Chocolate Chip Cheeseball (recipe), 75

Citrus-Basil Vinaigrette (recipe), 143

Citrus Salsa (recipe), 164

Coconut Mango Rice Pudding (recipe), 75

Cold Strawberry Soup (recipe), 183

cook, slow, 96, 110, 172, 216

cookies

    Banana Granola Cookies (recipe), 70

    Gluten Free Banana-Oatmeal Chocolate Chip Cookies (recipe), 80

    Oatmeal Raisin Spice Cookies (recipe), 84

    Tookies (recipe), 93

corn

    Crab and Corn Chowder (recipe), 184

    Thai Sweet Corn Soup (recipe), 196

Couscous Salad (recipe), 147

crab(s)

    Crab Cakes with Peach Salsa (recipe), 165

    Crabmeat Salad (recipe), 147

    Cream of Crab Soup (recipe), 185

Cream Cheese Flan (recipe), 76

Cream of Crab Soup (recipe), 185

Creamed Cabbage (recipe), 207

Crème Brûlée French Toast (recipe), 33

Currant Scones (recipe), 35

D

Dan's Country Style Coleslaw (recipe), 148

Deconstructed Chicken Ratatouille Salad (recipe), 149

desserts

    Apple Cream Pie (recipe), 64

    Apple Crumb Cake (recipe), 65

    Apple Fritters (recipe), 66

    Apple Oat Bars (recipe), 67

    Apple Pie Bars Home Version (recipe), 68

    Apple Strudel (recipe), 69

    Banana Granola Cookies (recipe), 70

    Bavarian Apple Torte (recipe), 71

    Bread Pudding (recipe), 30

    Carrot Cake (recipe), 106

    Cedar Planked Apples with Walnut Praline Stuffing (recipe), 72

    Cheesecake Supreme (recipe), 73

    Cherry or Cranberry Pie (recipe), 74

    Cherry-O Cream Cheese Pie (recipe), 74

    Chocolate Brioche Bread Pudding (recipe), 33

    Chocolate Chip Cheeseball (recipe), 75

    Coconut Mango Rice Pudding (recipe), 75

    Cream Cheese Flan (recipe), 76

    Cream Cheese Pie (recipe), 107

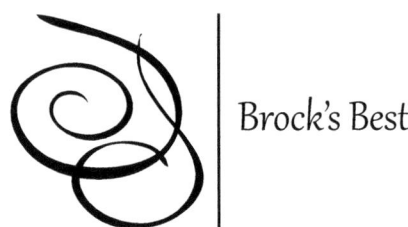

Brock's Best

desserts (cont.)
- Crème Brûlée French Toast (recipe), 33
- Crunchy French Toast with Banana and Strawberry (recipe), 34
- Desserts and Sweets (section), 63–94
- Dirt (recipe), 77
- Donut Bread Pudding with Chocolate (recipe), 78
- Fresh Berry Trifle (recipe), 79
- Gluten Free Banana-Oatmeal Chocolate Chip Cookies (recipe), 80
- Golden Baked French Toast (recipe), 36
- Granny Sullivan's Pineapple Upside Down Cake (recipe), 108
- Guatemalan Banana Bread (recipe), 36
- Jell-O Pie (recipe), 81
- Lemon Basil Smoothie (recipe), 81
- Mary's Zucchini Bread (recipe), 112
- Mexican Flan (recipe), 82
- Mini Peanut Butter Cup Cheese Cakes (recipe), 83
- Mom's Peach Cobbler (recipe), 114
- Oatmeal Raisin Spice Cookies (recipe), 84
- Peanut Butter Bars (recipe), 85
- Poppy Seed Cake (recipe), 86
- Pound Cake (recipe), 86
- Puffy Maine Pancakes (recipe), 39
- Russian Cheese Wheels (recipe), 87
- Sand Dessert (recipe), 88
- Shoo-Fly Pie (recipe), 89
- Strawberry Topping (recipe), 90
- Sweet and Spicy Pecans (recipe), 90
- Sweet Milk Griddle Cakes (recipe), 44
- Swiss Apple Pie (recipe), 91
- Tiramisu (recipe), 92
- Warm Nutty Caramel Brownies (recipe), 94

Dinsztelt Wilted Greens, 19 (recipe), 208

dips and sauces
- Artichoke Crab Spread (recipe), 96
- Buffalo Shrimp Dip (recipe), 96
- Celeste's Best BBQ Sauce (recipe), 97
- Cranberry Salsa (recipe), 97
- Hot Artichoke Heart Dip (recipe), 98
- Maple Chipotle BBQ Sauce (recipe), 99
- Nacho Bake (recipe), 100
- Peach Salsa (recipe), 100
- Pepperoni Dip (recipe), 101
- Pizza Dip (recipe), 101
- Pizza Sauce (recipe), 102
- Southwest American Indian Salsa Salad (recipe), 102
- Spinach Dip (recipe), 103
- Spring Pea Dip (recipe), 103
- Vidalia Onion Relish (recipe), 104

Dirt, (a dessert recipe) 77

Dolma (Stuffed Grape Leaves) (recipe), 209

Index

Donut Bread Pudding with Chocolate, 78

Dovga (recipe), 186

E

Easy Add-In Macaroni and Cheese, 120

egg(s)

    Open Faced Broiled Egg, Spinach, and Tomato Sandwich (recipe), 37

    Quick and Easy Eggs Benedict (recipe), 40, 201

    Scrambled Egg Beggar's Purses (recipe), 43

F

Family Heirlooms (section)

    Carrot Cake (recipe), 106

    Cream Cheese Pie (recipe), 107

    Granny Sullivan's Pineapple Upside Down Cake (recipe), 108

    Green and Red Peppers with Crab Meat (recipe), 109

    Hungarian Beef Paprika (recipe), 110

    Mary's Easter Bread (recipe), 111

    Mary's Zucchini Bread (recipe), 112

    Mom's Meatloaf (recipe), 113

    Mom's Peach Cobbler (recipe), 114

    Pork Adobo (recipe), 115

    Ratatouille (recipe), 116

Fettuccine Carbonara (recipe), 121

fish

    20-Minute Tuna Casserole (recipe), 118

    Braised Sea Bass and Fennel with Saffron and Harissa (recipe), 163

    Caramelized Salmon with Citrus Salsa (recipe), 164

    Celyodka pod Shuboy—Herring Under a "Fur Coat" (recipe), 146

    Fresh Tuna Tacos (recipe), 166

    Salmon Reuben (recipe), 170

    Seafood Gumbo (recipe), 172

    Teriyaki Grilled Salmon (recipe), 176

French bread, 30

    baguette, 96

French Green Lentil Salad (recipe), 150

French Vanilla Pudding, Jell-O Instant, 88

Fresh Berry Trifle (recipe), 79

Fresh Tuna Tacos (recipe), 166

G

Georgian Style Bean Salad (recipe), 151

German Beef Roulades over Spaetzle (recipe), 18

German Braised Veal Shanks (recipe), 19

Gluten Free Banana-Oatmeal Chocolate Chip Cookies (recipe), 80

Brock's Best

Golden Baked French Toast (recipe), 36

Granny Sullivan's Pineapple Upside Down Cake (recipe), 108

Green and Red Peppers with Crab Meat (recipe), 109

Green Borscht (recipe), 187

greens

    Baby Mixed Greens with Apple Pear, Pecans, and Feta (recipe), 140

    Dinsztelt Wilted Greens, 19 (recipe), 208

    Orecchiette with Mixed Greens and Goat Cheese (recipe), 122

Grilled Chicken Kabobs with Greek Style Barley Salad (recipe), 58

Grilled Chicken Penne Alfredo (recipe), 59

Guatemalan Banana Bread (recipe), 36

H

health(y), iv, vi, 2–10, 12, 90, 112, 151

    Living, 2–6, 8–10, 12

    Snacks, 5, 90

heart disease, 4

High-Protein Snack, 5–6

Homemade Meatballs for Spaghetti (recipe), 20

Home-Style Asian Burger (recipe), 130

Home-Style Baked Beans (recipe), 210

Honey Mustard Dressing (recipe), 159

Hot Artichoke Heart Dip (recipe), 98

Hummus (recipe), 211

Hungarian Beef Paprika (recipe), 110

I

Italian Wedding Soup (recipe), 188

J

Jambalaya (recipe), 189

K

Kielbasa and Lentil Salad with Warm Mustard Fennel Dressing (recipe), 152

L

Latin Combo–Sky, Sea, and Land (recipe), 60

Lemon Basil Smoothie (recipe), 81

Lemon Shrimp Bean Thread Vermicelli (recipe), 167

Lemongrass-Scented Noodle Soup with Shrimp (recipe), 190

liqueur

    Grand Marnier, 79

Index

liqueur (cont.)

Kahlúa, 92

orange, 33

M

Maple Chipotle BBQ Sauce (recipe), 99

Marinated and Grilled Buffalo Flank Steak with Lime Chipotle Sauce (recipe), 21

Maryland Crab Cake Salad (recipe), 168

Maryland Crab Soup (recipe), 191

Maryland Jumbo Lump Crab Imperial (recipe), 169

Mary's Easter Bread (recipe), 111

Mary's Zucchini Bread (recipe), 112

Mexican Flan (recipe), 82

Mini Peanut Butter Cup Cheese Cakes (recipe), 83

mixed greens

Baby Mixed Greens with Apple Pear, Pecans, and Feta (recipe), 140

Orecchiette with Mixed Greens and Goat Cheese (recipe), 122

Mom's Meatloaf (recipe), 113

Mom's Peach Cobbler (recipe), 114

mushrooms

Barley and Mushroom Salad (recipe), 141

Russian Mushrooms (recipe), 217

N

New Mexican Burger (recipe), 22

nuts

almonds, 5–6, 71, 80, 93, 142, 201, 214

cashews, 36, 142

peanuts, 6, 192

roasted pine, 102

walnuts, 71, 112

O

Oatmeal Raisin Spice Cookies (recipe), 84

Open Faced Broiled Egg, Spinach, and Tomato Sandwich (recipe), 37

Orecchiette with Mixed Greens and Goat Cheese (recipe), 122

P

Panzanella (Bread Salad) (recipe), 153

pasta (noodles)

20-Minute Tuna Casserole (recipe), 118

Cheaty Ziti (recipe), 119

Easy Add-In Macaroni and Cheese (recipe), 120

Fettuccine Carbonara (recipe), 121

Brock's Best

pasta (noodles) (cont.)
- Lemon Shrimp Bean Thread Vermicelli (recipe), 167
- Lemongrass-Scented Noodle Soup with Shrimp (recipe), 190
- Orecchiette with Mixed Greens and Goat Cheese (recipe), 122
- Pasta Primavera (recipe), 123
- Philly Mac and Cheese Steak (recipe), 124
- Shrimp and Feta Cheese Pasta (recipe), 175
- Skillet Lasagna (recipe), 125
- Spaetzle Noodles Bergkase, 19, 218 (recipe)
- Spinach Pasta Salad (recipe), 157
- Vegetarian Pasta Salad (recipe), 159

peach(es)
- Crab Cakes with Peach Salsa (recipe), 165
- Mom's Peach Cobbler (recipe), 114
- Peach Salsa (recipe), 100, 165
- Pork Roast with Ginger Peach Glaze (recipe), 131

peanut(s)
- Mini Peanut Butter Cup Cheese Cakes (recipe), 83
- Peanut and Chestnut Soup (recipe), 192
- Peanut Butter Bars (recipe), 85

Pear, Apple, 140

pea(s)
- Bulgur Risotto with Spring Peas and Asparagus (recipe), 205
- Sesame Snow Pea Salad (recipe), 156
- Spring Pea Dip (recipe), 103

pepper(s)
- Cajun Meatloaf with Sweet Pepper Sauce (recipe), 17
- Green and Red Peppers with Crabmeat (recipe), 109

Philly Mac and Cheese Steak (recipe), 124

physical exercises, 8

pies
- Apple Cream Pie (recipe), 64
- Bars Home Version, Apple (recipe), 68
- cherry, 74
- Cream Cheese Pie (recipe), 107
- Cherry-O Cream Cheese Pie (recipe), 74
- Cherry or Cranberry Pie (recipe), 74
- Jell-O Pie (recipe), 81
- Shoo-Fly Pie (recipe), 89
- Swiss Apple Pie (recipe), 91

pineapple
- Chinamerica Chicken Pineapple Feast (recipe), 57
- Granny Sullivan's Pineapple Upside Down Cake (recipe), 108

pizza
- Pepperoni Dip (recipe), 101
- Pizza Dough (recipe), 38

Index

pizza (cont.)
- Pizza Sauce (recipe), 102
- Roasted Vegetable Pizza (recipe), 41

Poppy Seed Cake (recipe), 86

pork (and ham)
- Apple Butter Pork Loin (recipe), 128
- Apricot Pork Chops (recipe), 129
- Heaven on a Bun (recipe), 129
- Home-Style Asian Burger (recipe), 130
- Pork Adobo (recipe), 115
- Pork Roast with Ginger Peach Glaze (recipe), 131
- Pork Stew (recipe), 132
- Pulled Pork Green Chili (recipe), 193
- Roast Pork Tenderloin with Balsamic Reduction, Fall Fruit Compote (recipe), 133
- Root Beer-Glazed Ham (recipe), 134
- South Carolina Style Pulled Pork Sandwich (recipe), 135
- Southwest Roasted Pork Loin (recipe), 136

potatoes
- Red Bliss Potato Salad (recipe), 155
- Sweet Potato Salad (recipe), 220
- Warm Potato Salad with Honey Dressing (recipe), 159

Puffy Maine Pancakes (recipe), 39

Pulled Pork Green Chili (recipe), 193

Q

Quick and Easy Eggs Benedict (recipe), 40

R

Ratatouille (recipe), 116
- Deconstructed Chicken Ratatouille Salad (recipe), 149

Recommended Dietary Allowance (RDA)
- iron, 50, 142
- vitamin C, 50

Red Bliss Potato Salad (recipe), 155

ribs
- Braised Short Ribs (recipe), 14
- Spare Ribs in Wine Sauce (recipe), 24

rice
- Brown Rice Salad with Citrus-Basil Vinaigrette (recipe), 143
- Coconut Mango Rice Pudding (recipe), 75

Root Beer–Glazed Ham (recipe), 134

Rotisserie Style Chicken (recipe), 61

Russian Cheese Wheels (recipe), 87

Russian Cutlets (recipe), 23

Russian Golubtsi—Stuffed Cabbage Rolls (recipe), 216

Russian Mushrooms (recipe), 217

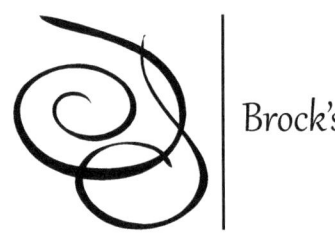

Brock's Best

Russian Okroshka Soup (recipe), 194

S

salad(s)

Apple Spinach Salad (recipe), 138

Arugula (a type of salad green), 182

Baby Blue Salad, 90 (recipe), 139

Baby Mixed Greens with Apple Pear, Pecans, and Feta (recipe), 140

Barley and Mushroom Salad (recipe), 141

Basil Roasted Vegetable Couscous (recipe), 203

Broccoli Slaw Salad, 142

Brown Rice Salad with Citrus-Basil Vinaigrette (recipe), 143

California Mango Chicken Salad (recipe), 144

Carolina Cabbage (recipe), 145

Celyodka pod—Herring Under a "Fur Coat" (recipe), 146

Couscous Salad (recipe), 147

Crabmeat Salad (recipe), 147

Cucumber Salad (recipe), 148

Dan's Country Style Coleslaw (recipe), 148

Deconstructed Chicken Ratatouille Salad (recipe), 149

French Green Lentil Salad (recipe), 150

Georgian Style Bean Salad (recipe), 151

Grilled Kabobs with Greek Style Barley Salad (recipe), 58

Kielbasa and Lentil Salad with Warm Mustard Fennel Dressing (recipe), 152

Maryland Crab Cake Salad, 168

Panzanella (a Bread Salad recipe), 153

Potato Salad, 155, 159 (recipe), 213

Quinoa Salad (recipe), 154

Red Bliss Potato Salad (recipe), 155

Romaine lettuce, 54

Salads (section), 137–160

Sesame Snow Pea Salad (recipe), 156

Seven-Layer Salad (recipe), 157

Southwest American Indian Salsa Salad (recipe), 102

Spinach Pasta Salad (recipe), 157

Sweet Potato Salad (recipe), 220

Turkey Barley Mandarin Salad (recipe), 158

Vegetarian Pasta Salad (recipe), 159

Warm Potato Salad with Honey Dressing (recipe), 159

salmon

Caramelized Salmon with Citrus Salsa (recipe), 164

Teriyaki Grilled Salmon (recipe), 176

salsa

Caramelized Salmon with Citrus Salsa (recipe), 164

Crab Cakes with Peach Salsa (recipe), 165

Index

salsa (cont.)

    Cranberry Salsa (recipe), 97

    Peach Salsa (recipe), 100

    Southwest American Indian Salsa Salad (recipe), 102

    tomato, 204

Sand Dessert (recipe), 88

sandwiches

    California Mango Chicken Salad (recipe), 144

    Chilled Cucumber Soup with Lobster, Mint, and Lobster Brioche (recipe), 182

    Open Faced Broiled Egg, Spinach, and Tomato (recipe), 37

    South Carolina Style Pulled Pork (recipe), 135

sauces (see also Dips and Sauces)

    Asparagus and Hollandaise Sauce (recipe), 201

    Broiled Flank Steak Chimichurri Sauce (recipe), 15

    Cajun Meatloaf with Sweet Pepper Sauce (recipe), 17

    Celeste's Best BBQ (recipe), 97

    Maple Chipotle BBQ Sauce (recipe), 99

    Marinated and Grilled Buffalo Flank Steak with Lime Chipotle Sauce (recipe), 21

    Pizza Sauce (recipe), 102

    Spare Ribs in Wine Sauce (recipe), 24

scallops

    Bay Scallops and Bulgur Wheat with Fresh Mint (recipe), 162

    Scallops and Shrimp Sambuca (recipe), 171

    Seared Scallops with Parmesan Risotto (recipe), 173

Scones (recipe)

    Currant Scones (recipe), 35

Scrambled Egg Beggar's, 43

seafood

    20-Minute Tuna Casserole (recipe), 118

    Bay Scallops and Bulgur Wheat with Fresh Mint (recipe), 162

    Braised Sea Bass and Fennel with Saffron and Harissa (recipe), 163

    Buffalo Shrimp Dip (recipe), 96

    Caramelized Salmon with Citrus Salsa (recipe), 164

    Celyodka pod Shuboy—Herring Under a "Fur Coat" (recipe), 146

    Crab Cakes with Peach Salsa (recipe), 165

    Fresh Tuna Tacos (recipe), 166

    Lemon Shrimp Bean Thread Vermicelli (recipe), 167

    Lemongrass-Scented Noodle Soup with Shrimp (recipe), 190

    Maryland Crab Cake Salad (recipe), 168

    Maryland Jumbo Lump Crab Imperial (recipe), 169

    Salmon Reuben (recipe), 170

Brock's Best

seafood (cont.)

    Scallops and Shrimp Sambuca (recipe), 171

    Seafood (section), 161–176

    Seared Scallops with Parmesan Risotto (recipe), 173

    shrimp, 96, 103, 167, 171-72, 174, 175, 190

    Shrimp and Feta Cheese Pasta (recipe), 175

    Shrimp and Grits (recipe), 174

    Sopa De Caracol (Conch Soup) (recipe), 195

    Spinach Dip (recipe), 103

    Teriyaki Grilled Salmon (recipe), 176

Sesame Snow Pea Salad (recipe), 156

Seven-Layer Salad (recipe), 157

Shoo-Fly Pie (recipe), 89

Shrimp and Feta Cheese Pasta (recipe), 175

Shrimp and Grits (recipe), 174

Skillet Lasagna (recipe), 125

smoked kielbasa, 152

smoker, 72

    charcoal, 193

Sopa De Caracol (Conch Soup) (recipe), 195

soups

    Asopao De Marisco (Seafood Stew) (recipe), 178

    Black Bean Chili (recipe), 179

    Butternut Squash Soup (recipe), 180

    Cheddar Asparagus and Crab Chowder (recipe), 181

    Chilled Cucumber Soup with Lobster, Mint, and Lobster Brioche Sandwich (recipe), 182

    Cold Strawberry Soup (recipe), 183

    condensed tomato, (can of) 20

    Crab and Corn Chowder (recipe), 184

    Cream of Crab Soup (recipe), 185

    Dovga (recipe), 186

    Green Borscht (recipe), 187

    Italian Wedding Soup (recipe), 188

    Jambalaya (recipe), 189

    Lemongrass-Scented Noodle Soup with Shrimp (recipe), 190

    Maryland Crab Soup (recipe), 191

    mix, dry onion, 27, 129

    Peanut and Chestnut Soup (recipe), 192

    Pulled Pork Green Chili (recipe), 193

    Russian Okroshka Soup (recipe), 194

    Sopa De Caracol (Conch Soup) (recipe), 195

    Soups and Stews (section), 177–98

    Thai Sweet Corn Soup (recipe), 196

    Vegetarian Chili] (recipe), 197

South Carolina Style Pulled Pork Sandwich (recipe), 135

Southwest American Indian Salsa Salad (recipe), 102

Southwest Roasted Pork Loin (recipe), 136

Index

Spaetzle Noodles Bergkase (recipe), 218

Spare Ribs in Wine Sauce (recipe), 24

spinach

    Apple Spinach Salad (recipe), 138

    Open Faced Broiled Egg, Spinach, and Tomato Sandwich (recipe), 37

    Spinach Dip (recipe), 103

    Spinach Pasta Salad (recipe), 157

Spring Pea Dip (recipe), 103

steak

    Philly Mac and Cheese Steak (recipe), 124

    Stuffed Flank Steak (recipe), 25

Strawberry Topping (recipe), 90

Stuffed Flank Steak (recipe), 25

Sweet and Spicy Pecans (recipe), 90, 139

Sweet Milk Griddle Cakes (recipe), 44

Sweet Potato Salad (recipe), 220

Swiss Apple Pie (recipe), 91

Syrniki Cottage Cheese Pancakes (recipe), 45

T

Teriyaki Burger (recipe), 26

Teriyaki Grilled Salmon (recipe), 176

Texas Style BBQ Brisket (recipe), 26

Thai Sweet Corn Soup (recipe), 196

tomato(es)

    Black Bean Cakes with Tomato and Jack Cheese (recipe), 204

    Bulgur Stuffed Tomato Au Gratin (recipe), 206

    Open Faced Broiled Egg, Spinach, and Tomato Sandwich (recipe), 37

    Tortellini with Chicken, Basil, and Tomato (recipe), 61

Tookies (recipe), 93

Tortellini with Chicken, Basil, and Tomato (recipe), 61

Turkey Barley Mandarin Salad (recipe), 158

U

Unstuffed Cabbage (recipe), 221

V

vegetables

    Armenian "Musaca" (recipe), 200

    Asparagus and Hollandaise Sauce (recipe), 201

    Baked Beans (recipe), 202

    Basil Roasted Vegetable Couscous Salad (recipe), 203

    Black Bean Cakes with Tomato and Jack Cheese (recipe), 204

    Bulgur Risotto with Spring Peas and Asparagus (recipe), 205

    Bulgur Stuffed Tomato Au Gratin (recipe), 206

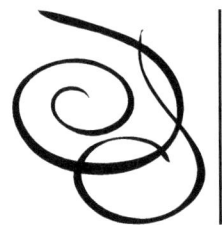

Brock's Best

vegetables (cont.)
- Cajun Beef and Root Vegetable Stew (recipe), 16
- Creamed Cabbage (recipe), 207
- Dinsztelt Wilted Greens (recipe), 208
- Dolma (Stuffed Grape Leaves) (recipe), 209
- Home-Style Baked Beans (recipe), 210
- Hummus (recipe), 211
- Olive Balls (recipe), 212
- Potato Salad (recipe), 213
- Recipe Mix, Knorr, 103
- Red Quinoa (recipe), 214
- Roasted Parsnips (recipe), 215
- Roasted Vegetable Pizza (recipe), 41
- Russian Golubtsi - Stuffed Cabbage Rolls (recipe), 216
- Russian Mushrooms (recipe), 217
- Spaetzle Noodles Bergkase (recipe), 218
- Spicy Asian Lettuce Wraps (recipe), 219
- Sweet Potato Salad (recipe), 220
- Unstuffed Cabbage (recipe), 221
- Vegetarian Chili (recipe), 197
- Vegetarian Pasta Salad (recipe), 159
- Veggies and Sides (section), 200–221

Vidalia Onion Relish (recipe), 104

W

walnuts
- Cedar Planked Apples with Walnut Praline Stuffing (recipe), 72
- Warm Nutty Caramel Brownies (recipe), 94
- Warm Potato Salad with Honey Mustard Dressing (recipe), 159

wheat
- Bay Scallops and Bulgur Wheat with Fresh Mint (recipe), 162
- Bulgur Risotto with Spring Peas and Asparagus (recipe), 205
- Bulgur Stuffed Tomato Au Gratin (recipe), 206

Wiener–Bean Casserole (recipe), 27

Z

zucchini
- Mary's Zucchini Bread (recipe), 112

Printed by Libri Plureos GmbH in Hamburg, Germany